THE LAST GOOD DAY ON THE INTERNET

Mark Little is an entrepreneur and journalist working to understand the impact of technology on media and democracy. Mark is the co-founder of Kinzen, which used AI and human analysis to detect online harms, and the founder of Storyful, the world's first social news agency. Mark has worked on trust and safety issues at Spotify, and developed media partnerships for Twitter. He is a former TV presenter and foreign correspondent for RTÉ, and was a member of the Future of Media Commission, tasked with mapping the future of public media in Ireland.

The Last Good Day on the Internet

Mark Little

HACHETTE
BOOKS
IRELAND

First published in Ireland in 2026 by HACHETTE BOOKS IRELAND

1

Cataloguing in Publication Data is available from the British Library.

ISBN 9781399755825

Typeset in Bembo Book Std by Bookends Publishing Services, Dublin
Printed and bound in Great Britain by Clays Ltd, Elcograf S.p.A.

Hachette Books Ireland policy is to use papers that are natural, renewable and recyclable products and made from wood grown in sustainable forests. The logging and manufacturing processes are expected to conform to the environmental regulations of the country of origin.

MIX
Paper | Supporting responsible forestry
FSC www.fsc.org FSC® C104740

Hachette Books Ireland
8 Castlecourt Centre
Castleknock
Dublin 15, Ireland
(info@hbgi.ie)

Authorised representative in the EEA

A division of Hachette UK Ltd
Carmelite House, 50 Victoria Embankment, London EC4Y 0DZ

www.hachettebooksireland.ie

To the people who give me hope in humanity:
Tara, Daisy, Tommy, Sorcha and Naoise

Contents

Introduction

When was your last good day on the internet? When was the last time you found yourself feeling elevated by an online experience? It doesn't have to be life-changing. Let's settle for life-affirming. When was the last time you went on the internet and felt more human?

If something doesn't immediately come to mind, don't worry. We have time. And countless stories to jog your internet memory. For now, let's ask the internet what its last good day was.

I happen to know the answer: 26 February 2015.

It was a busy Thursday, filled with a bumper crop of eye-catching headlines. Hopes were rising for a fragile ceasefire in Ukraine, said the BBC. Donald Trump was serious about a bid for the White House, the *Washington Post* reported, while *Nature* magazine was reporting on a young black hole 'having a monstrous growth spurt'.

The day didn't come good until early afternoon Arizona time, when two llamas being taken on a visit to a retirement home in

Sun City broke free of their handlers and made a run for it. News helicopters were dispatched to follow the two animals – Kahneeta and Laney – and a global audience tuned into the live feed on the internet and lost their collective minds on Twitter and Facebook. 'Everyone's trapped at work,' one viewer reflected later. 'Hell, I'd love to go run around the streets right now if I could.'[1]

The llama chase turned into a 90-minute keystone cops caper, generating 220,000 tweets and taking up four of Twitter's top ten trending topics that day. 'I've covered presidents, earthquakes, all that stuff,' said the helicopter cameraman dispatched to the scene, 'but nothing touched the world like two llamas in Sun City.'

Until the dress. Three hours later.

As the llamas were still gallivanting, a reporter for BuzzFeed was tipped off to a fierce debate on Tumblr, the trusty foundry of internet culture, about the colour of a dress bought for a wedding in Scotland. Some saw blue and black. Others saw white and gold. Both sides disagreed with uncommon ferocity.

BuzzFeed published a post about the dress shortly after 6 p.m. New York time, and within a couple of hours it was driving 11,000 tweets a minute, equally divided by colour. This simple optical illusion became a global phenomenon, generating record-breaking traffic for BuzzFeed and any online publication which joined the gleeful pile-on.

Together, the llamas and the dress were stars of the 'internet's greatest day', the phrase coined by BuzzFeed's Charlie Warzel. 'We lost our shit, and we lost it together twice in the same day,' he wrote. 'And we had fun doing it. And we haven't seen anything like it since.'

So, when I ask you about your last good day on the internet, I'm asking about a time you metaphorically lost your shit with others and felt better for it, not worse. Think of an internet moment that had the feel of an epic night out with new friends.

The important quality of your last good day is serendipity – a human connection that was unplanned but wonderful. This could also apply to the day on the internet where you stumbled across a new idea that took your breath away, or met someone who offered you a transformative perspective on the world.

Here's a personal example. In February 2013, I found myself floating weightlessly inside the International Space Station with Commander Chris Hadfield, a charismatic Canadian astronaut who once performed David Bowie's 'Space Oddity' while actually 'sitting in a tin can'. On this good day, Hadfield sent a tweet to me and his half a million other followers on Twitter with a photo of an apple and a little haiku attached:

'Eating my fresh green apple, a rare and tasty treat in space. I wonder who picked it, where, and if they know?'

If they know? The words floated out of my phone with the glow of a cosmic inside joke. I thought of astronaut Bill Anders, credited with taking the first colour photo of Earth from moon orbit on Christmas Eve 1968. We had to go to the moon, he later said, to discover the Earth. Thanks to the internet, a mere mortal like me could travel into space and find the human soul. What a great day.

Savvy people insist the internet was never real life. They miss the point. The internet is real life without hierarchy or physical limits, a space of infinite possibility and experimentation. Besides raucous joy or orbital humour, the internet is a rocket-engine of collaboration, participation and innovation. On the best days, you find your cause, your people, and your power to make a mark on the world.

Back in 2009, I left my job as a television journalist to start a business solely on the strength of connections I had made on the internet. I recruited the real-life team which built the company online. Our team fanned out on social media platforms to discover and elevate the most authentic observers of world events, to verify and validate the testimony of ordinary people bearing witness to history.

The internet opened a universe of information previously out of reach to all but the most affluent and educated. The more connected people became, the more literate they became and the more life-changing opportunities they had. With the internet baked into our mobile devices, our capacity to explore became infinite. With the touch of a screen, we acquired instant skills – to cook, fix, translate, to exercise our body and mind. Entire cultures lodged in our pockets. Curiosity no longer had boundaries.

Between the late 1990s and that Last Good Day in 2015, the internet shifted the balance of power from institutions to citizens. The internet offered tools to ordinary people to bear witness to injustice and oppression, to access a world of expertise, and to find an audience without the help of a publisher or broadcaster. There was always a community just for you – and your authentic weirdness.

I could offer endless examples of the transformative power of the internet, but this is not that kind of book. I'm starting our journey with your last good day on the internet because I want to remind you what it feels like to be conscious of technology in your daily life. That unexpected burst of human agency is your superpower in this superhuman age.

The book revolves around moments like these, when our humanity is reflected back onto us via our technologies. Our story begins with a moment of promise, when the internet represented the limitless potential of human collaboration. But we will also explore the moment of unravelling, when we lost control of our digital lives to giant technology corporations; when the internet became a mirror to the very worst in humanity.

This book is written through the lens of my personal experience of half a century of revolutionary change. I was an internet entrepreneur in that moment of promise. I have a tech-insider's perspective of that moment of unravelling. Now, I detect the approach of another moment of truth for humanity. Superhuman technology has stirred up something fierce and determined in human souls.

As we stumble blindly into an age of machine intelligence, we need a personal reminder that the human superpowers are collaboration, connection and intention. The Last Good Day tells us the internet was never meant to be the property of a handful of mega-corporations. It does not have to be a weapon in the hands of oligarchs and autocrats. The Last Good Day reminds us that hidden algorithms are no substitute for human intention.

In the final section of the book we'll explore new patterns in our digital lives, shaped by people leaning hard into their superpowers of agency and intention. We will meet those escaping the algorithms and rising above an artificially generated reality. We will explore the potential for our resistance to blossom into a movement. At the end of our journey we will find ourselves in an Age of Intention, where technology reflects our shared human purpose and not just our darkest instincts.

I'm writing this book for those of us who have lived through the days of promise on the internet. But I want us to look to the future through the eyes of a generation with no memories of the 'before time'. I want to show what we, the last analogue generation, can learn from them, the first digital natives in human history.

My two youngest children were born in the first decade of the twenty-first century. The internet is their ecology. Their lives are mediated through a frenetic ecosystem of humanity at its worst and best. Some days, I fear for their future. But most other days, my kids make me nostalgic for their future.

I recently asked my children to tell me about their last good day on the internet. There was an uncomfortable pause. In asking for a memorable internet moment, I realised I was asking them to recall a particularly fresh breath of air, or a change in the temperature of the ocean. I was reminded of an old joke, made famous by David Foster Wallace, about an old goldfish passing two younger fish.

'How's the water, fellas?' the old goldfish asks, before swimming on.

The young goldfish are silent for a moment, before one says to the other: 'What's water?'

When technology is your natural habitat, it's hard to imagine that you have agency. That has been true ever since hidden algorithms took control of the internet's climate. What we once called the Information Age became an age of attention, with mega-corporations using machine learning systems to direct your eyeballs towards advertising.

Algorithms don't learn in a vacuum. They magnify trends in real life. Digital natives live in an upside-down internet mirroring a collapse in a generation's economic security, social mobility and faith in democracy. For the digital native, the future is no longer a straight line, but an endless recursive loop – a transitional space where you never feel at peace.

I find it hard to communicate to my children the wondrous novelty of the internet in those good old days. I sometimes feel like a screechy old dial-up modem trying to lock in to my kids' ambient broadband. But when I explain the last good day as the moment we felt more human, I feel the handshake of connection. Then there is the transfer of something more than nostalgia. Something like an electric pulse of hope. Maybe even power.

In conversations with my kids, I feel I am travelling in a time machine to a very near future where people have been forced to take conscious control of their digital environment. In this proximate world, the centre of gravity on the internet is shifting away from vast 'town squares' flooded with menace and noise, towards private digital communities bonded by strong ties.

As the floodwaters of artificial content and connection sweep across our digital environment, younger digital citizens are moving to human settlements above the waterline. This patchwork is becoming a new human internet, rising clear of our old digital realm, now controlled by synthetic intelligence. This near future is the Age of Intention.

We'll travel to that future a little later. For now, let's sit with the anxieties that have forced digital natives to rebel and resist. Not too long ago, the average human lived in a world that was largely unchanged between birth and death. Today, you can't get from breakfast to lunch without some existential shift. The speed of change outpaces our ability to keep up, a phenomenon the futurist Azeem Azhar calls the 'exponential gap'.

The digital natives are those members of Gen Z born in the early years of the twenty-first century. They have no muscle memory of the analogue world. They grew up in an age of attention-hogging algorithms and show tell-tale signs of addiction, overload and disconnection. The World Happiness Report in 2025 found one in five young people say they have no-one they can count on for social support.

It has become conventional wisdom that this unhappiness

is caused by technology. In his book *The Anxious Generation*, the social scientist Jonathan Haidt traces the epidemic of social isolation among young people back to 2012 when smartphones became the child's primary means of mediation with the world. 'Once kids get a phone,' he argues, 'it's an experience blocker, and a relationship blocker.'[2]

Plenty of scientists have pushed back on sweeping conclusions about the cause of anxiety among young people. Digital natives are disproportionately stressed on multiple fronts. They were uniquely deprived by COVID, which erased human connection at a formative stage of their young lives. The arrival of AI is transforming their potential workplaces and further eroding their prospects of economic security. When I was leaving college I worried about finding a job. Digital natives wonder if they will have a career.

I once told my children they would never know a fear as primal as that of nuclear war. They immediately began to recite their list of existential threats. Somewhere between job-killing AI, the collapse of democracy, rising sea levels and, yes, nuclear weapons, I was chastened by the unique ferocity of the futures they fear.

Is it possible that a generation facing rising inequality, pervasive anxiety and a state of permanent acceleration might have more than phones on their brain? Is it possible that anxiety is a perfectly healthy response to an unhealthy world?

The twisted mirror of social media weaponises the harshest realities of teenage life, distilling the impact of bullying, body-shaming, social exclusion and misogyny. But the internet also offers an escape from the harsh realities of the real world.

Half of young adults wish TikTok and Twitter had never been invented, according to a 2024 survey.[3] Yet, the same young adults told researchers social media had a beneficial impact on them as individuals. They value the sanctuary the internet provides for expression and self-creation, relishing its storytelling and information-seeking functions.

This conflicted experience of the internet is driving structural changes in our digital ecology. This is evident in a cascade of subtle acts of thoughtful resistance and the dramatic flowering of a communal consciousness. In search of safe spaces to be themselves, young internet users are migrating out of the world of toxic feeds. Usage of social media across 50 countries has declined from its peak in 2022, according to the *Financial Times*,[4] and the decline is most pronounced among younger citizens.

Younger digital citizens are turning from the 'great digital everybody' to smaller, safer spaces where they no longer have to perform for the algorithm. These civic alternatives range from group chats to the comment sections of activity apps. They include new online spaces like Discord servers as well as older internet sites like Reddit. Gen Z isn't looking for a platform to build a personal brand, said one internet culture writer, 'they're looking for somewhere to be weird, sad, brilliant ...

without being surveilled by advertisers or smothered by curated perfection'.[5]

For all our anxiety about this 'anxious generation', a growing body of evidence suggests that digital natives have superior civic instincts. In a recent survey of global research, *Scientific American* found young people are more empathetic and less narcissistic than in the past.[6] They engage in less alcohol and drug abuse, and less violence. They show more self-restraint and patience than members of my cohort, Gen X. I, for one, want to be a member of any community these kids are building.

The virtual world offered Gen Z online connection without the hard work of empathy in the physical world. Now, the tide appears to have turned. Humanity's first digitally native generation is actively seeking experiences they can touch and feel. They are developing a taste for the friction of human interaction.

Across generations, we see the flowering of digital resistance. It appears in resolutions to spend less time on screens and feeds, demands to restrict teenagers' access to social media, and righteous anger at sexually abusive and manipulative applications of AI. You can feel a sense of momentum in these disparate campaigns, but not yet a coherent movement. We still haven't made the critical transition from tech backlash to a blueprint for the future.

By contrast, the oligarchs and autocrats have a coherent masterplan for tomorrow. They see god-like technology concentrating power in the hands of a god-like elite, in a world where there is no need for democracy, just the rule of the strong.

★

After a twenty-first birthday celebration, my daughter told me every photo at the party was taken with old digital or Polaroid cameras. This passion for tactile experience explains the surge of popularity of vinyl music, with almost half a million vinyl records now sold in Ireland every year. For all the complaints about their attention spans, Gen Z is buying books in bigger numbers, research suggests,[7] and drifting back to book shops. They are connecting on 'circular fashion' platforms like Depop and Vinted, sharing old clothes with new friends.

A potent form of 'sincerity nostalgia' is at work in a generation battered by the culture of cringe. A recent internet trend that caught my eye was a wave of positivity for the year 2016, which, to my memory, had few redeeming features. For the younger internet citizen , this year offered the last chill days on the internet, before the onset of the algorithm and its exhausting demands on digital life.

This got me thinking about Jonathan Haidt's insight into the evolving consciousness of young adults. 'Kids being raised on screens long for real freedom,' he wrote. 'It's like they're homesick for a world they've never known.'[8]

There is a beautiful new word which captures nostalgia for a time never experienced. 'Anemoia' was coined by video-maker and writer John Koenig in 2012, just about the time our brains were captured by screens and feeds. Koenig drew inspiration from the word anemosis, which refers to the warping of a tree by a high wind. It bends, but it doesn't break. I see this in my children and their friends. Bending but never breaking. Resilient and resistant in the face of a fearsome wind.

The internet is certain to look and feel very different in the future. As AI seeps into our lives like an invisible gas, we desperately need a conscious relationship with technology that we don't have today. We will crave human spaces to collaborate, connect and innovate. As we will discover on our journey with digital natives, people are already building for this human future – in small communities out of reach of the algorithms, in new forms of social media controlled by people, not platforms, and in public sources of shared knowledge.

I should confess one thing at the outset: I am not an optimist. I don't believe faith alone will ignite a digital civil rights movement with the power to shape the future. I think purposeful panic is a more likely trigger. Unlike previous tech backlashes, the future of AI is set to become a galvanising issue in democratic politics. It will represent the sum of our fears in every aspect of our lives, from work, inequality and energy, to creativity, truth, and our cognitive health and freedom.

Fear needs to be catalysed into a plan for the future. The challenge for the leaders of a new digital rights movement is to articulate what we want from technology just as clearly as what we fear. There is no lasting hope for humanity in a backlash without a blueprint. We need a shared vision of how we become more human in an age of superhuman intelligence.

So let's avoid empty optimism. The arc of technology does not naturally bend towards justice. Instead, let's embrace the active, intentional form of hope, described beautifully by Rebecca Solnit: 'Hope is not a lottery ticket you can sit on the sofa and clutch, feeling lucky. It is an axe you break down doors with in an emergency.'[9]

I fear the hand that history has dealt my kids, but I am inspired by the story they are telling us about a future in which human connection is our most precious resource. There is something more to their resistance to manipulative technology than a passing backlash. There is the solid foundation of a movement, and a blueprint for that Age of Intention. Where they lead, we will follow.

Part One

The Right Kind of Crazy

The internet was coming.

The internet was coming.

The internet was coming.

When was it coming?

Soon.

How soon?

Not today, and maybe not tomorrow. But definitely soon.

It was always never quite there. And then, one day, there it was – impossible to avoid and impossible to recognize until the update was complete and all alternatives had been eliminated.

There's no date for when the transfer of power occurred.

Chuck Klosterman, *The Nineties*

I Am Become Meme

Meeting Elon Musk for the first time is like walking on ice. You are never sure of your grasp on his presence. His eyes are blank surfaces. Conversation is both rapid and hesitant. As your momentum increases, so does the risk of falling on your face. At least this was my experience of meeting Musk in 2013.

I had been asked to interview the world's most famous living entrepreneur at the closing session of the Web Summit, before a capacity crowd of 10,000 people in a Dublin arena. Musk and I met backstage before the interview. I quickly depleted my reserves of small talk as I struggled to charm life into his distant eyes. He seemed to be stuck in some near future that he was reluctant to leave.

I was saved by the arrival of the Taoiseach (Irish Prime Minister), Enda Kenny, who was to accompany Musk on stage in a green Tesla. Kenny's high-octane affability seemed to drag Musk back to the present, and the two men disappeared into the waiting car talking of Henry Ford and interplanetary exploration.

On stage, Musk was a different person: poised, confident and self-aware. I introduced him to the audience with a quote from Dolly Singh, his chief recruiter at SpaceX: 'He is Wernher von Braun, Howard Hughes, Henry Ford, Bill Gates, Steve Jobs and every other badass rolled into one.'[1]

'That's probably a bit generous,' replied Musk.

It was a bit generous. But not much. Musk had the invincibility of a superhero in 2013. Tesla Motors made its first profit that year, and accelerated the rollout of its new Model S in global markets. Musk had confounded many sceptics with the success of SpaceX, and was breaking new ground with ventures in solar energy and underground transport. At this moment, in this technology pioneer, we saw the reflection of the best of us.

On stage in Dublin, I lobbed another softball statement posing as a question, reminding him there are 'only four entities that ever sent a space capsule into space and brought it back; the US, Russia, China and Elon Musk'.

'I mean, it's way too much attention paid to me,' he responded, and for a moment his softly spoken words wandered about in search of a punchline. 'People want to focus on an individual, but you know it's the super-talented group of people at SpaceX who make it happen.'

Years later, in the first days of Donald Trump's second presidency, I watched Elon Musk stride in front of another capacity crowd, this time of jubilant American conservatives. He was wearing chunky sunglasses and a black MAGA cap emblazoned with dark gothic lettering. He hoisted above his head a pimped-out chainsaw he'd been handed, before sitting for a rambling interview in which he had none of his previous poise, just the neediness of the class clown.

I recognised the admiring tone of the interviewer's last question. 'Paint us a picture of inside the mind of a genius,' the host asked. Musk paused, dark eyes hidden behind the sunglasses he was still wearing. 'My mind is a storm,' he finally said. 'It's a storm.'[2]

It is hard to reconcile this Elon Musk with the man I interviewed at the Web Summit 12 years before. My theory of change is that Musk's swagger and bluster grew in direct proportion to his suffering. By 2022 he was complaining of the 'torture' he inflicted upon himself as 'next level'. The years of existential pain distilled him to his darkest outlaw essence. 'I am become meme,' he declared in that 2025 appearance. Musk had become the violent storm he once tried to harness.

Elon Musk's character arc from visionary superhero to cartoon villain speaks to me of the internet's volatile trajectory over the past half century, wildly careening between the collaborative genius of open innovation and the concentrated power of the technology elite. The story of the internet is one long, historic surge of creative craziness. Just when it is leaning into the right kind of crazy the wrong kind catches it like a hungry wind.

For every violent storm on the internet there is yet another cycle of creative innovation. To every dark meme, there is a resistance movement. For every internet freedom fighter, there is an oligarch with cosmic ambition. Elon Musk is just the latest. The right and wrong kind of crazy have been fighting for the soul of the internet ever since it emerged from the countercultural chaos of the 1960s.

I was born in 1968, just as that counterculture reached its climax. On my birth date, the Beatles song 'Revolution' was top of the charts, as the B-side of 'Hey Jude'. I entered the world just between the violent suppression of anti-war protests in Chicago and the baton charge of civil rights activists in Derry.

I have always been obsessed with the year of my birth. Growing up in Ireland in the 1980s, I felt trapped by the undertow of the past and looked for a different kind of rebel story to ground me. The youth revolutions of 1968 were pure energy, close enough to touch. They were the end of black and white democracy, and a technicolour explosion of civic purpose and personal freedom.

This tension between individual liberty and the common good would also shape the technological revolution which began in 1968. This was the year that Douglas Engelbart demonstrated the revolutionary elements of personal computing, in what would be remembered as the 'mother of all demos'. It was also the year that the US government awarded the contract for the development of ARPANET, which laid the first pipes of the internet we know today.

The utopian ambitions of California's technology pioneers were captured in the Whole Earth Catalog, which was published in 1968 and went on to sell millions of copies to young Americans seeking tools and ideas to liberate themselves from convention and conformity. The catalog has been described as 'the internet before there was internet' and opened with a sentence that captures the superhuman ambitions of the coming revolution: 'We are as Gods, so we might as well get good at it.'

The internet spoke with an American accent in its early days. But the revolutionary leap in its evolution was made by a British scientist with one foot in the future and another in a genteel past. In 1980, Tim Berners-Lee first began tinkering with a software program he called Enquire. The name was short for 'Enquire Within upon Everything', he later wrote, 'a musty old book of Victorian advice I noticed as a child in my parents' house outside London'.

This tinkering led Berners-Lee to build the World Wide Web, the network of interconnected public web pages which helped turn the internet into the universal platform for discovery and creation it is today. I have always been struck by Berners-Lee's emphatic statement that the web was not just a technical toy, he designed it for a social effect, to help people work together.[3]

In 1993, the technology supporting the web was made free to everyone, and the underlying code was released into the public domain. It was built entirely within a publicly funded institution and given to the world, without condition, for nothing. This is exactly what I mean by the right kind of crazy.

The utopian legacy of the sixties counterculture is reflected in the collaborative genius of the World Wide Web. But it was clear back in 1968 that a strain of dystopian lunacy was also built into the emergent technologies of our superhuman age.

1968 is the year we first heard the dull, malevolent voice of a supercomputer called HAL in Stanley Kubrick's *2001: A Space Odyssey*. Among the advisors on the movie were AI pioneers Marvin Minsky and Jack Good. It was Good who came up with the haunting forecast that the first ultra-intelligent machine might be the 'last invention that man need ever make'.

The seeds of our open and collaborative internet were sown by America's military machine at the height of the Cold War. Like so many building blocks of the digital age, the internet began as a US Defence Department project. It was designed, at least in part, to help the warrior class maintain their communications network after the nuclear apocalypse.

I don't know exactly when I became aware that utopia and dystopia could share the same technological infrastructure. But I do remember my fierce curiosity about tomorrow's world turning to dark fascination as I became more conscious of the fragility of the world around me, and the potential role technology might play in its demise. I soon developed an obsessive fear of nuclear apocalypse and the dark technologies of the Cold War's 'military-technology complexes'.

In 1983, I was petrified by the movie *War Games*, starring Matthew Broderick as a high school computer geek who almost triggers thermonuclear war. 'He found the right code word to play the game,' said the trailer for *War Games*, 'but it was the wrong computer'. The plucky outsider saves life on earth, despite the best efforts of the faceless generals and bureaucrats.

Right around the time *War Games* was released, I got my first job, selling ice-cream cones in a seaside shop. At the end of the summer, a Korean civilian airliner was shot down by Soviet war planes and the world spun dangerously close to nuclear war. As I handed out delicious treats, I kept the radio on constantly, waiting for news of the inevitable American retaliation that would lead to war.

There's a part of me that will always be that frightened Irish teenager, searching for causes as big as my worst fear. It drew me to journalism, and journeys around the world in search of conflict and political upheaval. It would blossom later into a second career as an entrepreneur, chasing solutions that didn't yet exist in the world, but should. Since that summer, I have found myself drawn to people who speak of technology as a tool of human agency.

I would soon fall under the spell of the brash, inspirational vision of Steve Jobs. Jobs was a little younger than the hippies but he embraced the counterculture's utopian vision of technology, describing the Whole Earth Catalog as one of the 'bibles of his generation'. Jobs seemed to be the antidote to the cataclysmic systems threatening life on earth. He spoke of technology that amplified our inherent abilities to build not destroy. He talked of the personal computer as the 'bicycle of the mind', constantly upgrading our capacity for even greater invention.

In his vision of human-centred technology, I saw a challenge to entrenched corporate and political elites. But I now see I was wrong. Long before Elon became meme, Steve Jobs had discovered the perfect blend of crazy that would pave the way for a new brand of corporate power in the world.

In January 1984, Apple released a Superbowl advert, made by British director Ridley Scott, to promote the launch of the Apple Macintosh and fend off a challenge from IBM. Jobs wanted Apple to be seen as the countercultural resistance to the totalitarian threat.

The advert features hundreds of bald zombie faces and a sprinting heroine who hurls her hammer at the image of Big Brother on a screen. The explosive climax is followed by the tagline: 'On January 24th, Apple Computer will introduce Macintosh. And you'll see why 1984 won't be like *1984*.'[4] In a pre-release focus group, one Apple executive called it the 'worst business commercial ever tested'.[5] I thought it was absolute fucking genius.

That advert was a turning point in digital history, transforming a technology business into a revolutionary movement. Apple would ultimately remove the friction of decision-making and sell this as liberation. It didn't have customers. It had devoted followers of each upgrade. What Apple offered, said Tim Wu, the author of *The Attention Merchants*, was 'a sense of meaning that comes with the surrender of choice'. Surrender of choice would become the hungry wind that would fill the sails of a new internet economy.

Apple's insurgent appeal conveniently obscured the role of collaborative technology in its success. Core products like the iPad and the iPhone incorporated publicly funded innovations such as GPS and touch-screens. Apple created the standard operating procedure for Big Tech, harvesting untold private wealth from the public goods of the information age.

The history of the digital age is a constant tussle between private gain and public interests, between the communal spirit of the open web and the gold-rush mindset of the California frontier. At critical moments, this creative tension has dramatically extended the reach of revolutionary technology, as we'll find out a little later. But over time, the gunslingers of Silicon Valley began to confuse their self-serving mythology with reality.

In 1997, Steve Jobs returned to Apple after a 15-year exile and narrated another iconic Apple advert, this time celebrating the 'round pegs in the square holes' who defy convention and break the rules. 'The ones who are crazy enough to think that they can change the world,' intones Jobs, 'are the ones who do.'[6]

The right kind of crazy is the fuel that powers any creator or innovator with a big, bold idea. But there is another kind of crazy which can warp the minds of successful people. Stress, ego and grievance often curdle into a toxic form of self-belief. One thing that Steve Jobs and Elon Musk had in common was an entitlement to bend reality. Rules don't apply to outlaws or their cosmic ambitions.

As a true believer, I once made the mistake of assuming social technologies had a built-in bias toward democracy, claiming the 'good internet' as the 'real internet'. But in the age of the algorithm, this was wishful thinking. I now see that the longer we cling to a single binary choice between good and bad technology, the less agency we have over our future.

The internet is not inherently good or bad. It did not come pre-loaded with a moral compass. But nor is it neutral. It is shaped by the genius of its designers but also by their flaws. It is the collaborative genius of Tim Berners-Lee and the insurgent capitalism of Steve Jobs.

The internet can bend to the will of the autocrat at the very same moment it is wielded as a revolutionary tool in the hands of the powerless. Optimism is blind faith that the right kind of crazy will win out. Hope is the determination to act with intention to shape the internet, individually and collectively.

The internet is not a weather system, randomly offering good days and bad. It is a tool in our hands, which changes as we use it, in ways we are often unaware of. Every time we act, it responds. Every click, like and search, every tweet, reel and prompt, makes the internet. The internet will always be in constant motion between the right and wrong kind of crazy. That's not a prediction. It's a call to action.

The End of History

I've reached an age where I feel like I have lived through history twice. The first time I was too busy living in the present. The second time I can't believe I missed the remarkable hidden patterns swirling around me. That's how I feel about my posting to Washington in the closing years of the twentieth century.

After the fall of communism, America was enjoying the longest economic expansion in its history. Its brand of liberalism had vanquished dictators. For the first time in human history, a majority of the world's population lived in a democracy. This was the 'end of history', according to Francis Fukuyama's hyperbolic account of this time, when the world embraced 'Western liberal democracy as the final form of human government'.[1]

The Washington elite was half right. This was the end of history. But also the beginning of the future. While the liberal elite was running victory laps around the corridors of power, an insurgent force was gathering at the gates. The internet had arrived. Finally and forever. The establishment didn't know it yet, but nothing would ever be the same again.

In the autumn of 1995, at the age of 26, I became the first Washington correspondent for the Irish television network RTÉ. Within days of my arrival, O.J. Simpson was acquitted, the US government shut down, and Bill Clinton convened talks to end the Balkan conflict. World-changing events just kept coming, day and night, for the next five years, and I was on top of all the big stories. Except the biggest one: the internet.

Vladimir Lenin said there are decades where nothing happens, and weeks where decades happen. He could have been talking about the summer of 1995, when the internet first flexed its economic muscle. In July, Amazon sold its first book and the first version of eBay came online. In August, Netscape became the first internet start-up to float on the stock market, triggering the dot-com boom, and Microsoft launched Internet Explorer, kicking off the so-called 'browser wars'. With this beachhead established, nothing could stop the insurgent internet.

1995 has been described as year zero of the digital world we live in today. It was the year the internet was officially opened to commercial activity, a quarter of a century after the first message on ARPANET. Still, if you asked regular people in 1995 what the internet was for, you would have seen eyes glaze over and maybe heard some vague reference to email or 'an information superhighway'. You would have most likely heard reference to nerds.

The internet back then demanded a lot of patience. You spent more time loading websites than surfing them. One of the most memorable sounds of 1995 was the 'handshake' between two computers as you connected to the internet through a phone line. The beeping and screeching of two frazzled robots sounded like the answering machine of a malevolent future. It was a sound that drove the sceptics a little crazy.

'The internet? Bah.'

So said an article published by *Newsweek* magazine in 1995. It urged readers to 'discount the fawning techno-burble about virtual communities'. Predictions of business moving to networks and modems, and digital networks making the government more democratic, were 'baloney'. It scorned the suggestion that people would buy news on the internet: 'The truth is no online database will replace your daily newspaper.'[2] *Newsweek* ceased its print edition in 2012. It is now only available on the internet.

To be fair to the naysayers, the breathtaking potential of the internet was not fully apparent in 1995, even to early adopters of technology like me. A decade before, I had fallen madly in love with the first personal computers, which fed my teenage hunger for personal agency in a world of chaos. By the time I graduated to a Commodore 64, I was learning to code in BASIC, and had begun to sneak on to the computer my father used to work from home. When I snuck on to the terminal, the only software I could find was the early book-keeping programme called VisiCalc. I mastered it for no other reason than it was there.

Like AI today, VisiCalc threatened to create mass unemployment for bookkeepers. Instead, the number of accountants in America quadrupled over the next 40 years. VisiCalc was a technology which expanded my capacity as a human. Years later, when I built the business model for my first start-up, I felt the familiar spark of hidden power in the cells and columns of data. I was designing my very own roadmap to the future. I would come to see the radical devolution of power to a partially numerate Irish kid as a benchmark by which to judge successive waves of technology.

In my first year at university, student newspapers were equipped with the Apple Macintosh and its built-in desktop publishing system. I will never forget the haptic charge of my fingers on plastic keys creating symmetrical sentences and paragraphs in perfect 12-point font, or the light pressure of my hand on the mouse guiding my work into the perfectly linear frame of the typeset page.

On my first use, I expected a cerebral connection to the computer but instead found a sensual joy in the passage of my thoughts into living artifacts. In the story forming around the numbers in those spreadsheets, and the soft sensation of creation in my fingers on that Apple Mac, was the feeling of a future unfolding in front of me. Without this physical connection to storytelling, my life would have taken a different path.

In 1995, I was slower to understand the internet's potential. The computer delivered an immediate shot of personal agency. By contrast, the energy of the internet comes from your interaction with other people. I was not yet active in online chat rooms or on bulletin boards or networks like USENET, which provided the savviest people with early versions of social networks. But on my first tentative travels on the web I felt a more intense electric charge than the one I had received from the Apple Mac as a teenager. Steve Jobs said the computer was the bicycle of the mind. The internet felt like a sports car without brakes.

In 1995 I subscribed to America Online, one of the first commercial portals to a mysterious place they still called cyberspace. In the first days of that year zero there were just 10,000 websites to browse. By the end of the year there were 100,000. At one point web activity was doubling every 53 days, leading tech evangelist Kevin Kelly to describe the internet as a biological process while Bill Gates wrote a famous memo titled 'The Internet Tidal Wave'. Sensing danger in that metaphor, one Silicon Valley leader drily quipped that we were facing a tidal wave while still in kayaks.

As that wave bore down, early internet networks were still largely shaped by a 'gift economy'. People gave their time and effort to the network without expecting direct payment. The best example of the gift economy was the free software movement, composed of volunteer developers who created, improved and fixed code, adding value to the technology as it spread through the community that used it.

In the case of early computer hackers, there was also a compulsion to take things apart and learn how to make them better. Knowledge sharing and collaboration within internet forums, newsgroups and mailing lists was critical to the development of the early protocols, web servers and operating systems that formed the lasting architecture of the internet.

Generosity and curiosity were the secret powers that built the internet we use today. It's still there in the invisible systems we take for granted. It is in the protocols that support email, web browsers, instant messaging, video calls, file sharing and encryption. It is in the RSS feeds that deliver your podcasts. Most of the world's internet servers still run on Linux, the operating system that began as a volunteer project. You benefit from the generosity of the internet's pioneers every waking hour you spend online, even if you don't know it. In that sense, every day is the last good day on the internet.

1995 was also the year people began to smell money from this grand egalitarian invention. The single most important figure in the commercialisation of the web was a combative boy genius from a small town in Wisconsin called Marc Andreessen. While still at college, Andreessen developed the web browser Mosaic. By 1995, Mosaic had become Netscape Navigator and Andreessen had been christened 'the über-super-wunder whiz kid of cyberspace'. When Netscape went public it was worth almost $3 billion by the end of its first day. This was an inconceivable number for an internet business and signalled the beginning of a gold rush on this new digital frontier.

Netscape bypassed the open and collaborative approach and sought to become the first dominant platform on the web, taking on the software behemoth Microsoft, which had staked its claim to an internet empire in 1995. Netscape lost that battle, and ultimately decided to open-source the code to its browser. That defeat would strengthen the infrastructure of the open internet, or what tech pioneer Tim O'Reilly calls its 'architecture of participation'.[2] Netscape's 'gift' paved the way for the Mozilla Foundation, the non-profit developer of web services like the privacy-protecting Firefox browser, which retains a small but loyal user base despite Google's overwhelming dominance.

Tim Berners-Lee could feel the pressure of commercial ambition, but he kept building for a free and open internet. He developed the World Wide Web Consortium (W3C) to maintain the web and ensure it could bear the weight of exponential growth and limitless experimentation. Berners-Lee kept the web from collapsing under its own complexity, or being hijacked by corporations, by sticking to the 'principle of least power'. In other words, use the simplest possible code and language to allow the maximum number of people to collaborate in the most transparent way possible.

The open web proved resistant to commercial takeover in the closing years of the twentieth century. But the stratospheric potential of the internet was becoming apparent, as were the animal instincts which might propel it into a new orbit. The hot internet topics in 1995 were porn and cash. 'Right behind sex, commerce on the internet seems to excite people most,' said one data encryption entrepreneur at the time.[3] In 1993, the internet was a place for academics, hackers and researchers. By 1997, almost 60 per cent of registered domains were .com, indicating a commercial application.

At this point, there was an opportunity for the internet to evolve into complementary spheres of commerce and community, all running on the same open infrastructure, carefully nurtured by public funding. Think of this internet as a town. You buy groceries from the supermarket and bread at the farmers' market. You share the lawnmower you bought from the big hardware depot with the neighbour who has the leaf-blower. There is a town council to keep everything transparent and safe.

In the mid-1990s, the American government was playing the role of the internet's town council, and Vice-President Al Gore was de-facto mayor. A truly digitally savvy politician, he supported deregulation of the internet to promote competition but also wanted to subsidise internet access for schools and libraries to prevent the creation of 'information haves and have-nots'. In theory, the 'information superhighway' would remain a hybrid partnership of private enterprise and public good. In practice, American political leaders were about to hand the keys of the internet to what we now know as Big Tech.

The Clinton administration fumbled the ball when the time came to regulate the future. When President Clinton signed the Telecommunications Act of 1996, he made the government a spectator to the internet's gold rush rather than an active defender of its open model of innovation. The one truly consequential law of the time was Section 230 of the Communications Decency Act, which shielded internet platforms from liability for the speech of people using their services but allowed them to take down content they found objectionable. This modest provision made it possible for billions of people to freely communicate together on commercial platforms and became known as 'the twenty-six words that created the internet'.

The shield and sword approach of Section 230 paved the way for the explosion of the social web in the twenty-first century. But in the absence of comprehensive regulation at this critical moment, corporate interests would ultimately trump the public interest in the years to come. This is one of the critical sliding-doors moments in the history of our internet age; under a different set of circumstances, the long-term results could have been profoundly different.

If I could travel back in time, I would pitch a list of future-proofed principles to anyone who would listen. The internet is not American. It's a global public commons. Like the oceans and the air, it must be protected. Act now or monopolies will take over. Keep platforms connected through open protocols so people don't get trapped in internet 'walled gardens'. Give citizens ownership of their data. Let them take their networks when they leave a platform. Make algorithmic systems transparent and accountable. Make internet access a universal human right. Invest in the internet's open infrastructure. Give independent technologists, not industry lobbyists, the key role in future regulation.

American political leaders could have protected the open internet from private plunder. They should have defined the sovereign rights of digital citizens. They failed to make tech companies accountable for the potential harms of their technology. As Shoshana Zuboff, author of *The Age of Surveillance Capitalism*,[4] would later put it, this failure 'to construct a coherent political vision of a digital century that advances democratic values, principles, and governance ... left a void where democracy should be'.

In 1996, it would have taken an act of clairvoyance to understand why all of this was necessary. But the failure to anticipate, at this critical moment of internet lift-off, the rise of a handful of global monopolies is one we are paying for today.

Let the Future Begin

If *War Games* reflected the existential threat of advanced technology back in 1983, the first online rom-com, *You've Got Mail*, captured the surge of love for the internet in 1998. The web was now officially mainstream, with about 150 million global users. But like AI today, the internet back then raised the blood pressure of business leaders with a profound fear of missing out. In an IBM advert from 1998,[1] an executive reading a newspaper turns to a colleague tapping away on a laptop.

> 'It says here, the internet is the future of business.'
>
> The executive pauses, before adding, 'We have to be on the internet.'
>
> 'Why?' Mr Laptop asks.
>
> Another pause. 'It doesn't say.'

By 1998 I knew exactly why I needed to be on the internet. The tools of my trade as a TV correspondent had been the phone on my desk, the fax in my office and a TV set tuned to a 24-hour news channel. In the last years of the century, my world was shifting to the phone clipped to my belt, email on my laptop, and a stream of news on the web that was rapidly becoming a torrent.

I was still wary of the internet chat rooms on AOL, but I noticed that the digital neighbourhood changed in exciting little increments every time I visited. There is an old adage: everyone wants a village but nobody wants to be a villager. The web changed all that. It wasn't AOL or Netscape building the new settlements, it was the villagers themselves.

I had no interest in building a village back then. But I needed to know what important people in the village were doing and saying. The White House had been online since 1994, and its website was becoming an essential source for transcripts and statements from meetings I couldn't attend in person. New media outfits like The Hill had websites that revealed the intrigue of the US Congress. Part of my job was to cover the role of US leaders in the Irish peace process, and now I had access to all the news from Northern Ireland, sent down the internet pipes to my M Street office more than 3,000 miles away.

I still paid to have the *Washington Post* delivered to my apartment door, but could boot up the laptop to read the *New York Times* online for free. By 1998 the *Times*' website had dropped its 'All the News That's Fit to Print' slogan and introduced a relatively slick mix of text and imagery. I would often bypass the front page and go directly to Maureen Dowd's razor-sharp portraits of the Clinton White House.

It soon became clear there were no rules in the new village. If you wandered away from the news websites, into the bulletin boards and the chat rooms, there were no editors deciding what you could or couldn't say or see. These online conversations recycled mainstream news coverage but also the gossip the journalists filtered out. The internet sounded like Friday night in my local bar, the Red Tomato, where television reporters shot the shit after work. In time, the online chat rooms started to scoop the reporters in the bar.

In March 1998, then First Lady Hillary Clinton wondered aloud at a press conference about the serious issues raised by a filterless internet. In the absence of traditional editors or gatekeepers, she asked, 'what does it mean to have the right to defend your reputation or to respond to what someone says?'[2] I'm pretty sure I know who Hillary Clinton had in mind when she made these comments.

Matt Drudge was an outsider who grew up in Washington wanting to be an insider. When his dreams of a job in journalism didn't pan out, he headed to Los Angeles, where he worked in a studio gift shop and started posting scraps of Hollywood gossip on the internet. Before long, he had a website, the Drudge Report, on which he curated web links to the most popular writers in entertainment and politics, eventually adding juicy stories from friends in Washington.

Drudge would become the internet's first news influencer,

feeding high-impact gossip and curated news to a politically savvy audience who wanted what the corporate media wouldn't publish. With his lopsided smirk and 'muckraker' trilby hat, he cast himself as a pioneering citizen journalist, and by 1998 the Drudge Report had 6 million visitors a month. In January of that year Drudge reported that *Newsweek* magazine was sitting on the story of President Bill Clinton's affair with a White House intern called Monica Lewinsky. The internet age had its first scandal.

Back then, this was a story about infidelity and lies. With the benefit of hindsight, it became the story of abuse of power by a powerful boss. Either way, we woke up the day after Drudge's scoop in a new world, where an online influencer had more power in a critical moment than the entire mainstream media.

Drudge was reviled by established journalists, even as they chased his scoop all the way through to Clinton's eventual impeachment in the House of Representatives. 'Drudge is a menace to honest, responsible journalism,' said *Newsweek* reporter Michael Isikoff.[3] I have come to see Drudge as a flawed messenger of important truths that would only become evident over time. First, the public prefers to get its journalism from people, not institutions. Second, the internet demands a level of transparency news organisations were not built for. Third, the standing of a journalist on the internet depends on their level of engagement with the community they serve. Finally, and most importantly, the internet turned media into a two-way street.

An image I will never forget is Matt Drudge soaking up the polite applause of critics at the National Press Club in Washington in June 1998. He had a kind of triumphant look on his face as he predicted the internet would create 300 million reporters. 'We have entered an era vibrating with the din of small voices,' he told the assembled hacks.[4] 'Let the future begin.'

Drudge was right about one very big thing. The days of unthinking trust in the institutions of power were coming to an end. The internet had arrived in a moment of hubris for liberal democracies. It would soon expose the flaws of political systems which had become complacent and myopic. By comparison with the speed and agility of the internet, the status quo soon appeared tired and unresponsive. Wherever voters had been taken for granted, the internet turned them into citizens with unprecedented power to rebel. When the media lost touch with its audience, the audience built its own media. The roaring dynamism of this new world exposed the brittle foundations of the old.

In August 1998 I joined Bill Clinton on a visit to Russia and Ireland, which must have felt like a prison break for the president. It had been two weeks since he admitted a sexual relationship with Monica Lewinsky. He had spent that time in a gilded form of solitary confinement on Martha's Vineyard with his wife Hillary.

On arrival in Russia, reporters observed that Clinton looked like a haunted man. His dark demeanour reflected the mood in Moscow. Russia's stock market had just collapsed and the rouble was in freefall. Boris Yeltsin prepared to meet the US president against a heartbreaking backdrop of democratic failure and lost promise.

In his report on the official state dinner in the Kremlin, Michael

Wines of *The New York Times* noted that as the Clintons and the Yeltsins dined on pike, salmon, roast-beef-stuffed omelette and the obligatory wine and caviar, 'Muscovites rested after a day of methodically picking grocery shelves clean of food and dry goods they fully expected would soon disappear'.[5]

I was struck by how feeble Boris Yeltsin seemed during his meeting with Clinton in the grandeur of the Kremlin's St Catherine Hall. He moved with exaggerated caution, sticking his tongue between his lips with great concentration as he signed the summit's official communiqué. Then, with a dramatic flourish, he thrust the document into Clinton's hand, as if an act of faux vitality would distract us from the oppressive sense of decline.

Leaving Moscow for Dublin felt like an escape from the past. It turned out we were on a collision course with the future. On Clinton's first day in Dublin he visited a technology company located just north of the city. The set-piece was a 'virtual signature' of a trade agreement between Ireland and the United States using an encryption product developed by Baltimore Technologies, a star performer of Ireland's nascent tech scene.

In his remarks, Clinton reflected on the growth of the internet since his first triumphant trip to Ireland in 1995, when there were only 16 million people online. In 1998, more than 120 million people were connected. Within a decade, he predicted, that figure would reach a billion (it would turn out to be 1.5 billion).

'It is going to democratize opportunity in the world in a way that has never been the case in all of human history,' Clinton said.[6]

'And if we are wise and decent about it, we can not only generate more wealth, we can reduce future wars and conflicts.'

Clinton seemed energised by this encounter with the future in a way he hadn't been in Moscow, and soon he started to riff on future political leadership. 'You may find you can get away with virtual presidents, virtual prime ministers, virtual everything,' he said ruefully. 'Just stick a little card in and get the predictable response.'

Those words, when you hear them for the first time, are prescient. But consider one extra detail. This is 4 September 1998. That very same day, two Stanford students filed paperwork with the state of California to officially incorporate a new start-up. The two students were Sergey Brin and Larry Page. The name of their start-up was Google.

It is a remarkable convergence which only becomes visible in hindsight. The fallen politician. A crumbling democracy. The arrival of virtual politics. The birth of Big Tech. The transfer of power from the analogue to the digital world had begun.

The coming millennium would strip the old order of its certainties with a sequence of calamities, from the final collapse of democracy in the former Soviet Union, the biting polarisation of politics in the United States, the shock of 9/11, war in Iraq and the collapse of the global financial system. By contrast, the internet had so many surprises in store for us, changing shape as it wrapped itself around new cultures, dialects, markets and faiths, enlarging and expanding to accommodate new settlers, hackers, creators, preachers, nomads and leaders.

New companies with playful names like Amazon, Yahoo and Netflix would create new markets, solve new problems, surprise and delight new customers, at least in their early years, when they were disrupters, not dominators.

To my mind, no-one captured the tortured soul of this moment as eloquently as David Bowie. When I think about the transition of power to the internet, I think about Bowie's legendary interview with the BBC's Jeremy Paxman in 1999.[7]

> Bowie: 'I think the potential of what the internet is going to do to society, both good and bad, is unimaginable.'
>
> Paxman: 'Surely the internet is just a tool?'
>
> Bowie: 'No, you see, I don't agree. I don't think we've even seen the tip of the iceberg.'

It is Bowie's last line, uttered a few years before the arrival of social media, that I keep returning to:

> 'I think we are on the cusp of something exhilarating and terrifying.'

'How'd All These People Get in Your Room?'

All foreign correspondents have one story that burrows deeper into their soul than any other. For me, it was the story of the children of the Iranian revolution. When I first visited Iran, in 2001, I discovered that roughly half the population had been born after their Islamic rulers seized power in 1979. As they came of age, the youngsters were finding inventive ways to subvert and resist the regime, particularly in the digital realm.

The children of the revolution were among the most computer-literate storytellers in the world. On that first visit to Tehran, I was told there were 1,500 internet cafés in the city. Without a free press, the web had become their independent media. Iranians embraced blogging with an uncommon passion, earning their digital public sphere the nickname Blogistan. As social media took root, Iranians embraced the self-starting, autonomous and interactive ethos that defined it.

The last time I travelled to Iran, in 2007, I found myself in the Godot Café, a smoky, chic space near Tehran University, where a portrait of Samuel Beckett looked down on the brightest of a wayward generation. There was an air of resignation in the café that day. The reformist movement that had flourished in the first years of the twenty-first century had been derailed.

In the Godot Café they had given up waiting. Change would come eventually, the young coffee drinkers told me, but not any time soon. Iran's youngsters had come to regard political activity as absurd, and so they retreated behind closed doors. They shopped. They flirted. They partied with passion.

Back then, Iranian politics played out as tragedy, with a touch of comedy. It was all about timing. When the Iranian presidential election came around in 2009 young Iranians found their underdog champion in a reform-minded candidate, Mir-Hossein Mousavi. His defeat at the hands of a populist conservative called Mahmoud Ahmadinejad was fiercely contested, sparking the so-called Green Revolution and flooding Iranian cities with youthful protest.

I relied upon YouTube and Twitter as my windows to this remarkable rebellion. I was stuck at home in Ireland, hungry for more than the recycled footage I was seeing on the television news. I was relatively new to social media and was dumbfounded by the first-person testimony streaming out of Iran.

The word that came to mind was clairvoyance. The Twitter stream teleported me from my front room in a Dublin suburb to the wide, tree-lined Valiasr Street as it heads north towards Tehran's mountainous northern suburbs. I fell into step with the protestors. Suddenly there was running. A jump cut to boys on motorbikes. The pro-regime *Basiji* had come to crack heads. The wild rhythm of panicked footfall and a chorus of fear, pain, anger. Suddenly, rage. A jarring tableau of lifeless bodies before my eyes on the pavement.

After hours of this eye-witness perspective, I broke free to check the BBC News. A famous foreign correspondent was on the phone from a Tehran hotel room delivering second-hand reports of violent clashes on Valiasr.

I confess to moments when I wish social media never existed. I still pine for old-school conflict reporting. Then I think of Twitter transporting me to Tehran in June 2009. For the first time ever there was nothing and no-one between me and the news, as experienced in visceral detail by those making it.

That same night, after seeing images of young women wearing the green ribbons of the Mousavi campaign standing up to the *Basiji*, I emailed an artist friend of mine in Tehran who I thought would appreciate the last lines from 'Easter 1916' by W.B. Yeats, which tell us that the places where the green is worn 'are changed, changed utterly'. She replied immediately, telling me she was listening to the kids coming up Valiasr Street and fearing for their safety: 'I am feeling overwhelmed by a mixture of hope and despair.'

In the years after the Green Revolution in Iran, young people of the internet would be the vanguard of protest movements that shook and sometimes broke the old order. The first blossom of what became known as the Arab Spring was carried from Tunisia across the Middle East by Facebook during 2011. Youthful rage against capitalism sparked the Occupy Movement in the same year and Twitter extended its reach from Wall Street to the world.

Social media was not so much spreading a message as imagining communities into existence. Twitter, Facebook and YouTube forced us to imagine ourselves as participants in history rather than its passive audience. People who would never expect to meet in person were suddenly conscious of being bonded together in a revolutionary new form of collective sense-making.

I had become quietly fascinated by the impact of social media on journalism. The ubiquity of mobile phones and the rise of social media had together created a new participatory internet, where the artificial division between creator and consumer was dissolved. No hierarchy. No gatekeepers. Just a space in the middle. That space, David Bowie said, 'is what the twenty-first century is going to be about'.

I first discovered the space in the middle through my work as a television reporter. Journalists had cheered on the early 'Twitter revolutions' with great gusto. In 2006, *Time* magazine declared its Person of the Year was 'YOU': 'Yes, you. You control the information age. Welcome to your world.' The rise of platforms like Facebook and Twitter meant the 'people formerly known as the audience'[1] – as media scholar Jay Rosen put it – were now taking an active role in shaping the news. In a 2008 report on the state of the media, the Pew Research Center noted the threat that 'audiences are fragmenting across new information sources, breaking the grip of media elites'. As blogging pioneer Dave

Winer once said, 'when people on the internet take control, they never give it back'.[2]

Television news has always been something of a conjurer's trick. Viewers sit passively at the appointed time, ready for a show. Journalists pick voices they think we should hear. Presenters prepare questions we might want asked. The public is a passive audience to be served rather than an active community to be engaged with. Social media has ruined the magic, in the best possible way.

My learning curve was steep. I initially thought of Twitter as an anonymous focus group. I'd ask 'it' for ideas. But real people would answer back, often with very specific judgements about my performance as a television presenter. Every detail of my work in the studio was relentlessly critiqued as it unfolded live on television.

In those innocent days, even the spiciest criticism fell into the constructive category. Surprisingly few critics expected me to respond. When I did, there was a moment of awkwardness. And then that instant bond. More often than not, the person who had just called me a bollocks was more than happy to explain how I might avoid being a bollocks in the future.

I had found a community where once there was an audience. Before any big interview I did on television, I turned to my followers on Twitter and asked what questions I should put to politicians and policy-makers in the studio. I was flooded with visceral experiences of Irish life, and more first-person expertise than I could have hoped for. I was overwhelmed. But the more I let my guard down, the more I felt grounded. By opening a two-way conversation with the community that I served, I felt in my bones that I was becoming a better journalist. Active listening changed everything.

When I talked to other journalists about Twitter I came to expect puzzlement and even pity. I was reminded of the clip of a drunk Dean Martin asking a talk-show host, 'How'd all these people get in your room?'[3] During a televised conversation about European elections I asked for tweets from the audience. I was stopped later in the corridor by a colleague laughing at the inclusion of the word 'tweet' in a news broadcast. The tone in which she said 'tweet' made it sound like I'd said 'fart'.

I found it hard to communicate the inevitability of it all. The one-way street between us and the audience was going to be replaced by a surging multi-lane highway. I was already intoxicated by the rush of each new conversation with this former audience. I started to lose my sense of identity inside a TV studio as I found myself drawn deeper into the newsfeed. Like love and bankruptcy, the transformation happened slowly, and then all at once.

Something similar had happened in Europe in the eighteenth and nineteenth centuries when the spread of mass media helped create what political scientist Benedict Anderson called imagined communities. The people started to think of themselves as the public, bound by shared identities and a revolutionary impatience with the old elites.

It would become a standard criticism of Twitter that it was a place for 'clicktivism', implying the bonds of its most important communities were fleeting and impermanent, like the weather. But autonomous communities on Twitter could also change the climate, just like those imagined communities of the nineteenth century.

When Twitter arrived in my life it was instantly familiar. It rewarded a conversational fluency I recognised from my Irish childhood. As a kid, I spent a lot of time watching adults in pubs and at parties jostle for attention with quick wit and sharp elbows. I learned that talkers had just seconds to win or lose control of the conversation.

The goal was to find the right words at the right moment, and when done well it made the circle feel even closer. Loud voices carried, but those who chose their words with care and economy connected deepest; someone in my social circle is nicknamed 'The Sniper' for the pinpoint accuracy of his sparse but priceless interventions.

I would later discover that every nationality or interest group thinks their Twitter community is the best version of Twitter. But Irish Twitter really was the best Twitter. It struck that essential balance of anarchy and creative coherence. It was a tidal plain of conversation, shifting shape around politics, sport, television and the oddness of the Irish psyche.

One internet-famous writer lit up a banal Twitter thread about workplace screw-ups with a legendary tweet, in which he revealed he had got his days mixed up and ended up alone in a room with his boss and the Irish president while on ketamine. A standout tweet from a thread about Irish nicknames recalled that a local family were known as the Yanks because they went on a week's holiday to Florida in the 1980s.

Technology companies provided the platform, but they had no rights over the conversations which filled it. 'Irish Twitter happened in spite of, not because of, anything deliberate that the social media giant did,'[4] wrote Darach Ó Séaghdha in the wake of Elon Musk's purchase of the platform in 2022. 'They're welcome to rule the ashes but I'll mourn Ireland's 33rd online county. They never owned that.'

Nothing that was authentically new and innovative ever came from Twitter the company. It flowed from Twitter communities. Conversation was not part of the Twitter service until a user called Robert Andersen popularised the use of the @ symbol to indicate that he was directing a tweet at a specific someone. The first widespread use of a hashtag was during a 2007 wildfire in California, signalling the emerging public utility of the platform.

Social media dissolved the boundary between creator and consumer. I think the author Steven Johnson put it best when he said, 'It's like inventing a toaster oven and then looking around a year later and discovering that all your customers have, on their own, figured out a way to turn it into a microwave.'[5] There is something approaching a universal truth here: when the people who use a technology dictate the evolution of that technology, good things happen.

The stickiest Twitter communities didn't need celebrities. Leaders emerged naturally, shaping the dialect of the group, the joy of secret knowledge and a perpetual state of homecoming.

A fierce egalitarian ethic shaped the unique contours and creative bonds of networked communities, as Bowie had predicted years before: 'The interplay between the user and the provider will be so in simpatico it's going to crush our ideas of what mediums are all about.'[6]

Perhaps the most celebrated example of this climatic power was Black Twitter. In her book *We Tried to Tell Y'all*, Meredith D. Clark described Black Twitter as 'a collective intervention on mainstream media narratives about Black life in America in the early 21st century'.[7] Black Twitter revealed the paradox of online communities that create lasting real-life change: they need to be both weak and strong at the same time.

The internet provides the 'weak ties' which help an online cause spread like an unstoppable fire. These are the peripheral connections between acquaintances that connect networks of friends. Black Twitter was unusually well connected through a web of virtual bridges with other communities, accelerating its message rapidly without any central planning, like the contagious spread of news from neighbour to neighbour.

But the imagined communities which create durable change are also tightly bound by some shared experience of life on the margins of society. In other words, they have 'strong ties'. Early research into the evolution of Black Twitter found uncharacteristically strong bonds within this online community, with tight clusters of Twitter users talking directly to each other rather than broadcasting to the world.

Out of this combination of weakness and strength emerged

one of the most consequential online movements of our times. An event – the acquittal of the man who shot and killed 17-year-old Trayvon Martin in 2012 – prompted the hashtag #BlackLivesMatter. There is a striking correlation between the rise of the Black Lives Matter movement and changes in American public opinion. A 2015 poll conducted for CNN showed that almost half of all Americans thought that racism was a big problem, compared to 28 per cent three years earlier, with the shift mostly confined to young people.

Truly consequential online movements require the strong bonds we develop in real-life relationships, giving activists the ability to persevere and pivot past the many setbacks they will encounter. Strong ties are not created by the internet but they can be amplified online, in small and secure spaces where there is already a high degree of trust.

For example, the protests in Iran were not a social media revolution. Twitter was a window through which the world could observe a revolution, but it had no active role in the revolution itself. Protestors relied instead on private social media groups, SMS messaging and Bluetooth connections to coordinate the nationwide street rebellion. Back in 2009 it was private Facebook groups and SMS messaging. Today it might be Signal, WhatsApp or Discord.

In her 2017 book *Twitter and Tear Gas*, the sociologist Zeynep Tufekci writes beautifully of the 'leaderless, networked, euphoric, and fragile' movements that were accelerated by the use of social media. But without formal organisation and collective structures, these movements struggled to maintain their momentum. 'Having arisen so suddenly and grown so quickly,' she explained, 'they hit their first curve requiring agile tactical shifts at great speeds, with little or no prior experience in collective decision making and little resilience.'[8] Weak ties mean speed. Strong ties keep you stable.

The people who change the world in the age of the internet embrace the right kind of crazy; they choose both weakness and strength. There is no speed without loose ties. There is no endurance without devoted real-world networks. In the first months of 2008 I saw these principles transform a rank outsider into a political juggernaut.

Barack Obama gambled his presidential aspirations on the devolution of power to an internet-enabled network of activists. It was a genius move by a politician who seemed a little too clever at the time. I followed Obama during the early presidential primaries and found he was a rather lacklustre visionary. He seemed to have difficulty connecting his soaring stadium rhetoric with reserved farm-folk in cramped high school gyms.

In the weeks before the Iowa caucuses of 2008 Obama continued to underwhelm. He delivered his stump speech with a cool, professorial detachment. But something crackled in the hall when the crowd was asked to pick up the chant 'Fired Up. Ready to Go'. A campaign volunteer had tossed out the slogan during a listless rally in South Carolina and it became an Obama favourite. He clearly drew energy from the call and response dynamic, which made him such a neat fit for the networked world of Facebook and Twitter. On social media there is no point in saying anything if someone doesn't respond.

Barack Obama's first great innovation in 2008 was to bypass the institutional gatekeepers of American politics and decentralise power to the grassroots. The campaign created its own social network, allowing motivated individuals to 'activate themselves'. Two million people created profiles on MyBarackObama.com and 200,000 offline events were created by its users. One of the most impressive innovations of the Obama campaign was the democratic nature of its fundraising. Obama raised more than half a billion dollars from 3 million online donors and the average internet donation was $80.

Obama's second great innovation was organised joy. His campaign skilfully used the internet to generate 'collective effervescence',[9] a phrase coined by sociologist Émile Durkheim to describe the electricity of shared ecstasy in some 'sacred' setting. This could be the celebration of a goal at a football game, or a sing-along at a concert. In the case of the Obama campaign, it was the shared chorus of the 'Yes, We Can' video, featuring celebrities and musicians speaking and singing along to Obama's electrifying concession speech in New Hampshire. The video first emerged on YouTube but was soon generating collective effervescence when played at giant rallies.

The Obama campaign was also a cautionary tale of power shifting away from old elites. By decentralising his campaign to volunteers, Obama undermined the authority of political bosses and party apparatchiks. The lesson of the campaign was that the power of the social network, both real and imagined, strong and weak, trumped the power of the institution.

Some people learned the wrong lessons from the early social media uprisings. Facebook and Twitter were not inherently left-wing or progressive technologies. It just happened that the progressives were first to demonstrate the unique ability of social media to power grassroots campaigns of consequence. I learned different lessons from these years of internet revolution. I was privileged to know the bravery of Iran's internet kids, and witness the collective joy outside the White House the night Obama was elected. My life was transformed by engagement with imagined communities and former audiences. What was transcendent about social media didn't come from the platforms. It came from the people.

It came from the young coffee drinkers, sitting under the ambiguous gaze of Samuel Beckett, when they finally took to the streets. For the first time, these smart, savvy and resilient young people on Valiasr Street had found their voice, without any help from outsiders like me. They stopped waiting for Godot. They had the internet. But most of all, they had each other.

The Human Algorithm

A bitter cold descended on Washington the week before Barack Obama's inauguration as president in January 2009. I was back in the American capital, braving its unique combination of piercing wind and humid cold in one of my last international reporting assignments. Once again, I would be a witness to history. But this time I was keeping a close eye on the future.

Returning to my hotel room the Thursday before inauguration, I turned on the television and found myself watching CNN anchors speaking excitedly over images of an airliner floating calmly on the surface of the Hudson River. The US Airways jet had struck a flock of geese while climbing away from LaGuardia airport. Its calm and collected pilot Captain 'Sully' Sullenberger had ditched his Airbus A320 safely into the frigid waters off Manhattan.

It would be forever remembered as 'The Miracle of the Hudson'. Sullenberger was hailed as a true American hero and would be played by American national treasure Tom Hanks in the subsequent Hollywood movie.

What changed my world that day was a tweet, with the first photo of the stricken airliner attached. It was taken by a Twitter user called Janis Krums from a passing ferry which had diverted to pick up passengers crowded on to life rafts next to the partially submerged plane. 'There's a plane in the Hudson,' wrote Krums to his 170 followers. 'I'm on the ferry going to pick up the people. Crazy.'

Crazy was exactly the word that came to my mind. Twitter had scooped the biggest television networks in the world. 'It changed everything,' Twitter boss Jack Dorsey told CNBC at the time. 'Suddenly the world turned its attention because we were the source of news.'[1] Dorsey quickly corrected himself: 'And it wasn't us, it was this person in the boat using the service, which is even more amazing.'

This distinction between Twitter as the source of news and Twitter as a network of eye-witnesses would lodge in my consciousness that day. The true power of social media was not in the technology or the corporation who owned the platform. The power was in the hands of an audience who had suddenly become the broadcasters.

A lot of my media friends had started to detect the end of an era. I thought I could see a new beginning, and it started to take shape on the icy waters of the Hudson River. It would present itself fully formed a few months later at the close of a beautiful summer's day back in Ireland.

The sun was setting across the long sweep of the River Shannon as my cousin's wedding party filled the dance floor. In the lengthening shadows, my eye was drawn to a tightly bound group at the quiet end of the bar, staring into their phones with intent. This was June 2009, when doom-scrolling in the company of others was still rare enough to merit a raised eyebrow. I asked one of the phone-gazers what was up. 'Michael Jackson's dead,' came the reply. 'It's on Twitter.'

At 9.30 p.m. Irish time, the celebrity website TMZ reported that Jackson had suffered a heart attack at his Los Angeles home. Just over an hour later, the same website declared him dead. Before any mainstream media could verify the report, the world was talking.

Twitter wasn't the source of the story in any traditional sense, but it was the particle accelerator that moulded the collective memory of this moment. Twitter was the reason why a DJ at an Irish wedding 5,000 miles from Los Angeles was playing Michael Jackson tunes before the *Los Angeles Times* had confirmed the King of Pop was dead. We marked the passing of an era shuffling on a dance floor to the sound of 'Thriller'.

A few weeks earlier, the Green Revolution in Iran had been a showcase for people-powered journalism on social media. But Michael Jackson's death was a news event that 'broke the internet' in both a literal and metaphorical sense. Twitter co-founder Biz Stone reported an instant doubling of tweets per second the moment the news of Jackson's death broke. The systems running Google's news section interpreted the fusillade of 'Michael

Jackson' requests as an automated attack. AOL messaging services crashed at the height of the rumours of Jackson's death, prompting its spokesperson to describe this as 'a seminal moment in Internet history'.[2]

The unprecedented surge in demand for real-time information was met with an immediate supply of real-time bullshit. One Wikipedia vandal falsely claimed that Jackson had been 'savagely murdered' by his brother Tito, saying he had strangled him with a microphone cord. Hours before Jackson died, Hollywood icon Farrah Fawcett had also passed away. The internet went looking for a pattern and killed off actor Jeff Goldblum, who was falsely reported to have fallen from a cliff in New Zealand while filming his latest movie. 'The Web can disseminate news,' a CNN reporter would later observe of the post-Jackson feeding frenzy, 'but it can also help us create what we expect to see next.'

Before that night, I had no conception of what the world might sound like when everyone – all at once – had a variation of the same story to share. No successful start-up begins with a solution. It starts with the problem. The problem first manifests as an itch you can't scratch. You struggle to find the words to describe your agitation to those who can't experience it first-hand. The itch I couldn't yet scratch emerged from questions without obvious answers. When everyone speaks at the same time, how do we make sense of what's being said? When everyone has the same story to tell, who is worth listening to?

The answers to those questions would not come from traditional news organisations. They were built for a world in which valuable information was scarce and a professional elite had the monopoly on the facts. In the new world of chaos, journalism was more important than ever. But only if it ceased to be an institutional power and started to be an open and collaborative process of sense-making. To survive the internet, journalism needed to become the internet. To be of service to the community, journalism needed to come from the community.

These convictions, and a large quantity of naiveté, led me to found a company called Storyful, which became the world's first social media news agency. Storyful would find and verify the most compelling news on platforms like Twitter and YouTube. The Storyful pitch would eventually boil down to three words: 'news from noise'. In a world where everybody could tell a story, we would find which stories were worth listening to.

People seemed confused when they heard I was quitting television to 'fix the internet', as one glib friend put it. Those close to me were actively concerned for my mental health. A colleague later told me of a planned intervention to steer me away from a patently self-destructive life choice. But in my fevered brain, Michael Jackson's death and the protests in Iran signalled a transfer of power.

Within months of that balmy evening by the Shannon, I had left my job at RTÉ and rented a small office in Dublin's docklands. My first day as an entrepreneur was inauspicious. I went to a whiteboard to map out my business plan without realising I was holding a permanent marker. I spent the afternoon scrubbing the whiteboard clean.

My first attempt at a business plan for Storyful took the form of a long essay shared with potential supporters called *Home*. On the front cover was a picture of my then four-year-old daughter holding a bowl of apples picked from our back garden. 'The rise of the citizen broadcaster offers to save global journalism from its own fatal flaws,' I declared with great confidence. In return, I said old-school journalism could save the internet from the 'loudest voice, the wild conspiracy and the partisan view'.

The *Home* essay was an exercise in wholesome fantasy, as was my business model. I likened my new venture to an ethical agricultural cooperative, producing 'free-range, organic, fair trade and healthy video news'. My dream was of a marketplace for citizen journalists to sell news reports directly to other citizens in exchange for micropayments. I was one stray metaphor away from a vegan tasting menu.

I wince at the naiveté now, but also feel an overpowering nostalgia for the transcendent possibility of the moment. 'Nothing will work, but everything might,'[3] was how Clay Shirky described the fertile earth for media innovation at the time. I credit Shirky with the insight that led to Storyful's business model. If a big news agency decided to start from scratch, it wouldn't publish a single piece of original content; it would verify, validate and promote the most valuable content on the internet.

Others had similar ideas long before my awakening. Singer Peter Gabriel had realised the power of new media technology to expose human rights violations. In 1992, the year after the savage beating of Rodney King was captured on amateur video, he founded WITNESS to promote the use of technology by human rights defenders. Kenyan human rights activist Ory Okolloh had tapped into the power of crowd-sourced tools to document the ethnic violence that swept her country in the wake of a 2007 general election. She co-founded Ushahidi, which developed open-source software to empower activists to act on data and information critical to their communities.

Journalists tend to make bad entrepreneurs. They are trained to find problems, not offer solutions. There was a graveyard full of big ideas like mine, dreamt up by hacks with more imagination than business sense. Still, I persisted, stumbling happily, if somewhat incoherently, through meetings with potential allies and backers in the United States.

I was just a few seconds into my pitch to a grizzled New York media executive when he stopped me and said, 'You are a newswire.' Just as Reuters, Associated Press and Bloomberg supplied original news content to corporate clients, Storyful would be the first social news agency finding and verifying internet content that other media companies could safely use.

Social media executives were quick to see the value of this twenty-first-century newswire. YouTube's chief business officer Robert Kyncl would later memorialise the Storyful story in his book *Streampunks*, which celebrated the collaborative urges of internet pioneers. 'The rise of cell phones and social media was eroding the monopoly that journalists had on information,' he wrote, 'with citizens more likely to scoop news outlets when it came to reporting what was actually happening in a given situation.'[4]

Kyncl had a wonderful account of Storyful's creation; he said I came up with the idea while bored and drunk in an active war zone in South Lebanon. This had only a germ of truth in it. My faith in old-fashioned war reporting had been shaken by a TV correspondent pretending to be under Israeli rocket fire in Lebanon, some time after the attack had happened. He performed for the camera in front of the rest of the press corps, who were decompressing with a beer by the hotel pool.

Still, Kyncl perfectly summed up the Storyful plan. 'That agency would live on the social web,' he explained, 'analyzing tweets, posts and videos that were being uploaded from around the world, every second.'

I didn't build a business so much as find the people who did. And I found them within my own Twitter community, beginning with a trailblazer of digital journalism in Ireland, Gavin Sheridan. He shaped the culture of collaboration and relentless curiosity that defined Storyful, and opened my eyes to reporting talent hiding in plain sight on social media. Among our early recruits was Malachy Browne, who eventually went on to win Pulitzer prizes with the *New York Times* Visual Investigations Unit, which he co-founded.

Twitter led me to CNN producer David Clinch, who set the legendary work ethic at Storyful and put our team at the centre of the global conversation about the future of news. David and Gavin were the real-time glue of Storyful's emerging global network of social journalists, soon connected in a 24-hour-a-day rolling news operation. Eventually, a young Irish political journalist called Áine Kerr offered to buy me a coffee and promptly hired herself to the Storyful team, laying the ground for an enduring partnership and one of my most treasured friendships.

Malachy likened the Storyful crew to the mutant superheroes of X-Men, who were out of place within the traditional media universe. In the old days, journalism inhabited a world of scarcity and journalists competed fiercely for the limited supply of facts. At Storyful, we were the managers of an overabundance of information and collaboration was our superpower.

Storyful was a talent academy masquerading as a technology start-up. Each new recruit came to work every day to trial and perfect new tools and techniques of collaborative journalism. They had stumbled across a form of crowd-sourced internet reporting that worked in practice before it existed in theory.

Every news event in the age of social media created a conversation on Twitter and eventually an emergent real-time community with a collective intelligence greater than the sum of its parts. When news broke, networks would coalesce and converge around the evolving story.

The story began with the witnesses, who happened to capture the content that defined the moment. Then came the curators, who passed that content from one community to another. Then came traditional media, late to the conversation but hungry for the material.

The patterns I had first spotted with the 'Miracle on the Hudson' evolved over time. When Japan was struck by an earthquake and tsunami in 2011 Twitter functioned as a source of breaking news information, before transitioning into a digital bulletin board, passing on public service tips on everything from locating working bathrooms to tracking loved ones. Twitter was behaving more like a public service than an internet platform, with a gift economy driving its value.

Inspired by the emergent intelligence of news on Twitter, I started to use the phrase 'human algorithm' to describe the open-source journalism that Storyful was helping to pioneer. The algorithm attached weight to critical attributes of internet content, like location, time, language and weather, and relied on interconnected networks of human expertise to verify the value of these inputs. Like the free software movement of the early internet, these human networks would collaboratively weed out the bugs and errors, and so improve the reliability of open-source journalism as it evolved. The tech-enabled journalist was 'the human in the loop' who helped forge consensus at the speed of real-time newsfeeds.

I was lucky enough to interview Wikipedia founder Jimmy Wales just before I launched Storyful, and learned from him that the fundamental principle of Wikipedia was to 'assume good faith'. In well-designed online communities, people act out of a genuine desire to construct the most accurate and useful summary of human knowledge possible. This is how you built critical public infrastructure on the internet. With patience, strong ties and generosity.

The problem for elite journalists on social media was that the most important collaborators looked nothing like their traditional sources. Authenticity replaced authority as the currency of open-source journalism. The trick was to find the credible witness, not the nearest official. The best online sources rarely had a title. Instead, they had standing within their community.

At Storyful we built and refined databases of communities on social media based on location, topic, and often both. In its simplest form, this involved curating lists of Twitter sources in potential breaking news categories. We won our first contract with ABC News when we demonstrated how we could listen to every earthquake expert in the world, sorted by language and region, to make sure ABC would never be scooped by a competitor if and when the earth moved.

Storyful had a similar checklist to validate the content driving a story. Are there landmarks in a video that help verify the location? Do weather conditions in the video match weather reports on the day in question? Are the shadows consistent with the reported time of day?

The golden rule at Storyful was that there was always someone closer to the story until you found the original eye-witness. To find the ground truth you have to ignore the loudest voices and find the most authentic one. If you are verifying video from a war zone, you can't rely on faceless partisans pushing propaganda or random internet people chasing clicks and likes. In the earliest days of the Syrian civil war, as our team puzzled over the context of a particularly significant video the critical last detail was in the difference between a Damascus and a Homs accent.

Twitter was our editorial GPS, guiding us to the self-organising communities that would spring up around key events. Twitter helped us see every story as a continuous process rather than an imminent deadline to be met. In the old days, journalists only worried if a story was true at the time it was published. Real-time news communities continue to refine and fact-check and verify through the various cycles of a big story, however long they last.

There was just one problem with Storyful's human algorithm in those early days: it was almost impossible to explain to old-school journalists. When I tried to find language to describe what my new start-up did, there were those familiar blank, often pitying stares. One friend came close to a working theory of Storyful: 'It's like if YouTube and the BBC slept together and had a baby!'

We were lucky to have people like Jay Rosen in our corner in those early days. A professor at New York University, Jay was the intellectual leader of collaborative journalism on the internet and coined that great phrase 'the people formerly known as the audience'. Show people the value, he told me, and then you'll find the language. I understood immediately. Our job was not to make the news. It was to magnify the power of the citizens who did.

The Revolution Will Not Be Televised

The year Storyful was founded, 24 hours of video were being uploaded to YouTube every minute. A year later, the volume had doubled. By 2022, 500 hours of video were crammed into that single minute. YouTube profoundly altered and enhanced the way humanity documented its history, but it couldn't make history. History would still be made by humans with everything to gain or nothing left to lose.

On 17 December 2010, Mohamed Bouazizi, a young Tunisian street vendor, set himself on fire in the town of Sidi Bouzid to protest police harassment and official neglect. He was not the first to do so. But his self-immolation was caught on camera. The images of his death were posted on Facebook and triggered nationwide protests and calls for an end of the authoritarian rule of President Zine El Abidine Ben Ali. History has since reduced the events that followed to a single memorable if reductive phrase: the Arab Spring.

As uprisings spread from Tunisia to Egypt, the human algorithm enabled Storyful to navigate blurred lines between sources and activists. Emergent communities began to cohere around Egyptian activists with global connections, like computer engineer Wael Ghonim and citizen journalists like Mahmoud Salem, who tweeted under the moniker @Sandmonkey. The community evolved to include a network of supportive journalists like Mona Eltahawy in New York, Andy Carvin in Washington DC and Sultan al Qassemi in Dubai.

It wasn't until the early days of the Arab uprisings that I could see the practical impact of our work. I can even remember a lightbulb moment on 28 January 2011. Our team came across a video recording of the ebb and flow of a pitched battle between riot police and protestors on the Qasr al-Nil bridge in Cairo. The video was shot by an eye-witness staying at a hotel overlooking the bridge. Storyful discovered the video on Facebook, contacted the witness to confirm he was the original creator, then used a range of internet tools, including Google Earth, Flickr and Panoramio, to confirm his vantage point. Finally, we asked the witness for permission to upload the video to YouTube and share with news organisations.

Then, YouTube reached out to Storyful to see if we could help 'curate' the Arab uprisings on their Citizen Tube page. The invitation came from two idealistic young executives at the platform, Steve Grove and Olivia Ma. It would become clear that YouTube's top brass embraced news from the Arab street as an opportunity to burnish its reputation as a serious force in the world. 'Google viewed the Arab Spring as a silver-platter chance for its video unit to escape its dogs-on-skates reputation,' said Mark Bergen, author of *Like, Comment, Subscribe*, a book about the rise of YouTube.

YouTube was more than a channel for news, it was a swelling 'archive of now'. The smartphone bore witness to war, genocide and systematic oppression with unprecedented authenticity. Storyful was soon working with WITNESS to populate a Human Rights page with the truly consequential imagery emerging from the Arab street. Over a three-month period, at the height of the uprisings, 100,000 videos were uploaded to YouTube by Egyptian eye-witnesses and activists. The challenge for Storyful was to add the layer of context that would turn this torrent into a manageable archive.

The Storyful team worked out of a cramped office on the banks of Dublin's River Liffey but had become embedded with some of the largest media organisations in the world. Our first major breakthrough came in the aftermath of the killing of Osama bin Laden in 2011.

Within hours of the raid on bin Laden's compound in Pakistan, our small team, led by Gavin Sheridan, had geo-located bin Laden's hideout and delivered the first analysis of satellite imagery of the stranded US helicopter in bin Laden's backyard. Early reports of the location of the compound were inaccurate. Gavin and the team zoned in on the correct coordinates using satellite imagery and details from video reports from the scene.

Even I was awed by the genius of the Storyful team that day

as they found new tricks and technology to add to journalism's brand new toolkit. I was overcome by the intelligent design of the open internet, accelerating the pace of innovation by rewarding collaborative experimentation. Storyful curators were becoming more effective with each passing day because they had new sources of data, new tools of analysis and new volunteers to work with. I felt I was watching a process of evolution which had been suddenly speeded up by citizens on social media.

The first public report of the raid on bin Laden's compound was traced to an English-speaking IT consultant, Sohaib Athar, who tweeted with the handle @reallyvirtual. He would later describe himself as 'the guy who live blogged the Osama raid without knowing it'. Athar tweeted about hearing a helicopter and a blast, then engaged with journalists when he realised what had happened. Athar worked himself into a state of exhaustion, ending his role as a virtual war reporter with a tweet that read: 'Bin Laden is dead. I didn't kill him. Please let me sleep now.'

As a former foreign correspondent, I initially feared for the future of journalism in the age of YouTube. But the visceral charge of eye-witness video from war zones was more powerful than a carefully edited mainstream news report. In one instance, this new medium offered a simultaneous broadcast of the duelling perspectives of opposing armies.

During the most intense fighting of the Syrian civil war, the Storyful team discovered a YouTube video shot with a GoPro camera mounted on a government tank trundling through the devastated Damascus suburb of Daraya. The source of the high-definition footage was an Abkhazian news agency which had embedded with Syrian government forces in the town. The surreal video had the feel of a video game, tracking the barrel of a tank as it followed a convoy of Syrian armoured muscle across the battle-scarred landscape of the city. The convoy stopped and almost immediately the lead vehicle, a Russian-made T-72 tank, exploded in a ball of flames.

In any previous conflict, this moment of violence would have lived on its own, within a single fixed perspective. But Storyful curators had been monitoring the YouTube channel of a local rebel force, the Almekdad Battalion, where we found footage of a militia man firing his Russian-made rocket-propelled grenade at the government tank we had just seen explode. Nothing in my career as a foreign correspondent had prepared me for this schizophrenic experience of conflict.

This was a powerful example of what a group of media scholars would describe as 'post-industrial journalism'. 'The journalist has not been replaced but displaced,' their report said, 'moved higher up the editorial chain from the production of initial observations to a role that emphasizes verification and interpretation, bringing sense to the streams of text, audio, photos and video produced by the public.'[1]

Trying to explain our methods to other journalists was like trying to teach someone to tie their own shoelaces. Initially, we didn't even have a name for what we were doing. At Storyful, we used the word curation to describe our work, but that soon felt inadequate. The techniques Storyful and others pioneered would eventually become known as OSINT (open-source intelligence). I was initially sceptical about using military jargon. But in time, I could see value in the phrase. OSINT required a radical transparency about what you didn't know. It rewarded those willing to collaborate in good faith.

As our relationship with YouTube deepened and widened, Áine Kerr became our political editor, working on the campaign trail during the 2012 presidential election cycle. Four years earlier, Barack Obama had been the savvy, networked politician in the first election cycle of the social media age. Now YouTube offered risk as well as reward to mainstream candidates. Republican standard-bearer Mitt Romney became a viral sensation in the closing stages of the campaign, thanks to a leaked video of him speaking disdainfully about Obama's supporters.

The wrong kind of viral video could send a candidate into a tailspin, but campaigns were still chasing the right kind of viral hit as the number of young voters grew. 2012 marked another shift of power away from the traditional press corps. Of all the stories curated by Storyful during the 2012 campaign, the single most compelling narrative came not from a politician or a journalist, but from a nine-year-old in Iowa called Sam Wessels. With the support of his mother, Lin, he pursued a range of political candidates at events with questions about their policies for children with disabilities, particularly those with autism.

I felt an instinctive discomfort as traditional journalism lost its central role in the world's most compelling narratives. But the damage was often self-inflicted. In every newsroom there were insurgents seeking to engage with platforms like YouTube, but the force of institutional inertia was fierce. I remember being asked to visit the Washington bureau of a major US news organisation to preach the value of social journalism, and being welcomed like Satan among devout Christians.

A part of me wanted old-fashioned journalism to embrace the human algorithm, join forces with this open-source intelligence movement. But too many traditional newsrooms clung to a broken concept of breaking news. They still competed fiercely to be first in moments of high drama, despite their growing awareness that social media had changed everything. The chances of being first were virtually nil, but the risk of being wrong had increased exponentially.

In January 2011, US Congresswoman Gabby Giffords was shot in the head while meeting constituents in Tucson, Arizona. NPR falsely reported news of her death in hospital, based on information from a local journalist and a congressional aide back in Washington. David Clinch was monitoring Twitter first-person tweets from the hospital in Tucson, which contradicted reports of Giffords' death. David established the truth with an old-school phone call to the hospital, saving one major US broadcast network from repeating the false story. 'The upside of having information first is fleeting,' an NPR news executive later said. 'The downside is enormous, painful.'

In 2011, Google decided to compete directly in the social media space by launching a network called Google+. Storyful was asked to build an Open Newsroom on the network to accelerate cooperation among journalists in fast-moving news environments. The project was led by one of our most gifted journalists, Markham Nolan (who delivered a brilliant TED talk on open-source investigations in 2012). The focus of the group was ongoing stories where no individual news organisation could command a competitive advantage but every member could benefit from the skills of the network. The community eventually grew to 178 members.

The creation of the Open Newsroom coincided with the grim escalation of conflict in Syria, where journalists faced uncommon risk in reporting from increasingly chaotic frontlines. By 2012, Syria had become the most dangerous place in the world for journalists, with at least 28 killed and 21 abducted in that one year alone. The kidnapping of freelance journalist James Foley in 2012 and his killing by ISIS two years later was a shocking reminder of the price to be paid for reporting the reality of war in Syria, particularly for brave young freelance reporters filling the void created by the absence of international media organisations.

In the past, if the media wasn't there to report the war, then the war never happened. But in Syria, the vacuum was filled by eye-witnesses. OSINT experts became ever more valuable in processing the flood of eye-witness video and raw data from the shifting battlefield, and so did the activist groups. Almost every opposition-held neighbourhood had a media centre complete with high-definition cameras, satellite connections and software for secure uploading of content.

The conflict in Syria was a test for the Google Open Newsroom, channelling forensic journalism to the flood of information from a fractured war zone. Among the group's members were human rights organisations and independent journalists. The work of the Open Newsroom was open to public scrutiny but participation was tightly moderated. The result was a high degree of trust and active participation of all members, with the most impactful discussions evolving in real time, under public scrutiny.

One of the participants was Eliot Higgins, who initially blogged under the name Brown Moses. Higgins had developed an expertise in weapons and munitions by watching and verifying thousands of YouTube videos of the conflict in Syria. He had no formal training in journalism or military hardware, but soon became the glue that bound a network of activists and journalists investigating allegations of war crimes in Syria, including a cluster bomb campaign by the Syrian military. Eliot Higgins would go on to form Bellingcat, which has set the gold standard for open-source intelligence gathering and is a key bulwark of media freedom in the face of autocracy.

For Storyful, the work of the Open Newsroom exposed new questions and contradictions. At first, I resisted the word 'verification' to describe our work, as it suggested there would always be a single judgment to be passed on any narrative. Such subtleties were lost on the wider world, and verification became the core work of our team.

Storyful was perhaps the first newsroom in history to celebrate its role in stopping a story. Halting the spread of a fake report from a battlefield was a key part of our value to partners. In time, this would become an increasingly important focus of our work.

We felt something shifting as the conflict in Syria was fought to a stalemate. Eye-witness video was starting to shape the world's response to the war. Each new atrocity captured on a shaky camera-phone had the power to provoke a reaction by world leaders.

Storyful had helped the UK's *Channel 4 News* validate more than 40 videos showing the torture of civilians by state security services for a documentary called *Syria's Torture Machine*.[2] The documentary forced the regime in Damascus to publicly engage with allegations of systematic abuse and murder, and raised our hopes for a new era of accountability.

Every faction in Syria now realised they were fighting an information war. They didn't need to convince the world of their virtue, they simply had to convince the world their opponents were evil. This made open-source journalism more important, but also more difficult. Truth would continue to be a casualty of war.

In April 2012, we faced an unprecedented test. Syrian government forces had allegedly buried a citizen alive in a shallow grave, which fitted the pattern of torture we had already established. But as Malachy Browne led the collaborative effort to verify the video, doubts began to emerge from Syrian activists. Storyful joined forces with journalists at the BBC, *Daily Telegraph* and NPR and began to focus on anomalies in the sounds captured on the video. Accents seemed off, and voices were misaligned with the location of people in the footage.

Malachy and I sat in the corridor of our offices considering the consequences of our next decision. If verified, this video would make global headlines, and might even trigger a political response. But we knew enough to know we didn't know for certain. Malachy returned to his desk and told our clients we could not verify the video and recommended they did not use it in their reporting. We eventually established the video was a hoax. We had found a glitch in the system and fixed it. This was a moment of truth, but not the truth we imagined.

I look back on that moment as a ball suspended in the air, right before the decisive score of the game. The internet felt solid underneath us. The value of our work was clear. Storyful was becoming a critical piece of internet infrastructure. But the internet was already on the move again, and the only constant ahead was change.

Chewing Glass

I stumbled across two absolute truths building Storyful: you don't have to be crazy to start an internet business, but trying to make it a success will drive you absolutely nuts. Contrary to the mythology of a Silicon Valley elite, entrepreneurs are not a superhuman breed. Successful start-ups are built by fragile and imperfect humans who thrive when they embrace their frailty.

I learned this from Elon Musk, in his modest years.

When I met Elon at the Web Summit I was at a crossroads with Storyful. I was depleted and burnt out and faced the prospect of selling my company to save it. To any outside observer, Storyful was thriving. We no longer had to explain ourselves. We were taken for granted as a solid piece of digital infrastructure. A wall in our office was covered with the logos of our customers, including every major news organisation in the world. But the news companies operated tight budgets, and our revenues were flatlining just as our costs were rising.

When I looked for comfort in 2013 there were few people of stature who spoke with the authenticity of Musk. One of his best qualities was his brutal honesty about the hardship of innovation. 'Running a start-up is like chewing glass and staring into the abyss,' he once said. The longer he gazed into the abyss, the harder the abyss gazed back at him.

During our interview at the Web Summit, I asked Elon Musk about the messiest point in his career, when it seemed that Tesla and SpaceX were about to fail at the very same time. Tesla was in desperate need of new funds and SpaceX had notched up three failed launches.

'So what's going through your mind as you watch the rocket blasting off for the fourth time?'

'It was pretty intense,' Musk replied laconically, drawing laughs from the crowd. 'I didn't feel elation,' he said of the successful final launch. 'I just felt the stress relief. That's all.'

A little later, I returned to the subject of failure, offering what I thought was a statement of fact: 'There is no fear of failure in Silicon Valley.' Elon interrupted me with a laugh: 'I don't think that's true, I think there's fear of failure. I still have fear of failure.'

As I closed my interview, I shared with Musk and the audience the quote that kept me going as an entrepreneur: 'Ever tried. Ever failed. No matter. Try again. Fail again. Fail better.' I had come to regard these words from Samuel Beckett's *Worstward Ho* as holy scripture, like countless other self-optimising entrepreneurs, athletes and actors.

The quote promised that every failure contained seeds of some future success. With persistent experimentation, you could escape the gravity of failure. Elon Musk was the living embodiment of 'fail better'. He seemed to have cracked a hidden code, turning unforgiving loneliness into the clean fuel of innovation. I was not the first, and will not be the last, to have taken Samuel Beckett's words in vain.

My closing at the Web Summit was later cited by the writer Mark O'Connell as the 'the most thematically dissonant invocation'[1] of the 'fail better' quote he had ever heard. It was hard to find a piece of writing less likely to align with 'the corporate propaganda of productivity' than *Worstward Ho*, he pointed out. Right after the 'fail better' quote you find the words: 'Try again. Fail again. Better again. Or better worse. Fail worse again. Still worse again. Till sick for good. Throw up for good.'

Fail better had become experimental literature's 'Che Guevara photo', said novelist and journalist Ned Beauman: 'Watching a liturgy from such a gloomy and merciless author getting repurposed to cheer up mid-level executives is like watching a neighbour clear out their gutters with a stick they found in the garden, not realizing the stick is in fact a human shinbone.'[2]

When Beckett talks about failure, wrote Beauman, he is often talking about the failure of language to withstand the weight of meaning we attach to it: 'There's no demonstration of life's futility or language's emptiness that is so profound, it can't one day be turned into a reassuring fridge magnet.'

I loved that fridge magnet. But in time, I saw the words

embossed on it in a different light. Fail better was no longer an invitation to self-optimise but to embrace what Beckett once described as 'the authentic weakness of being'.[3] I would come to feel most free as an entrepreneur when I was forced to sit with the inevitability of failure. Beckett would have despaired at such self-soothing fatalism, but as playwright Harold Pinter once wrote of him, 'the more he grinds my nose in the shit the more grateful I am to him'.[4]

Every start-up begins with failure. You are defined by your first punch in the face. But nothing prepares a long-distance entrepreneur for the continuous beatings and punch-drunk shame of each near-death experience. I once found myself waking to a recurring nightmare that I was forced to donate a limb to raise money for my second start-up, Kinzen. One night it was an arm, the next a leg. The nightmares lasted a full week.

The single most important lesson I learned about leadership in an age of radical uncertainty is that it starts with self-awareness. To earn the right to lead a team, you must first make peace with your own human frailty. I haven't had even a fraction of the success of Elon Musk, but I think my story is closer to the experience of a great multitude of leaders and founders, creating innovation the hard way, the human way. The way Elon Musk once did it.

My first embrace of failure came less than a year into my journey with Storyful, when I had run out of money. I was still working to save my company on Christmas Eve. As I prepared to drive to my parents' house in the west of Ireland in a freak snowstorm, I had to tell my wife Tara our worst fears had been realised. I had failed.

About halfway to Galway, keeping my eyes on the road, I told her the news. Without pause, she told me not to worry, I would get another job. I felt relief flood my body. This had been my worst fear. But it didn't feel so bad in the company of another. By the time we reached my family home, an investor had come through with the offer of a financial lifeline. Storyful had survived. Failure would never, ever have the same grip on me.

I'm conscious that every positive attribute of the mindset of an entrepreneur will sound like the slogan on a fridge magnet. But some of the feel-good slogans do survive contact with harsh reality. When you listen to people you admire, you begin to hear a solid collection of authentic mantras. They start with a clear distinction between optimism and hope. Hope is not the conviction that something will turn out well, Václav Havel once said, but the certainty that something makes sense. Optimism, on the other hand, will kill you.

I was introduced to the Stockdale Paradox by Jim Collins in *Good to Great*, one of the few truly exceptional books about entrepreneurship. Collins interviewed Admiral James Stockdale, the highest-ranking US officer ever taken prisoner in Vietnam, and asked him what kind of person didn't make it out of the prison camp alive. 'The optimists,' Stockdale replied: 'You must never confuse faith that you will prevail in the end with the discipline to confront the most brutal facts of your current reality.'[5]

Just as an experienced motorist steers into the slide on an icy road, the innovator must fight their natural instincts and lean into the approaching calamity.

As a foreign correspondent, I had experienced paralysing vulnerability. But no war zone prepares you for life in a start-up. My focus as a foreign correspondent was survival. My focus as an entrepreneur was resilience: acceptance that today and tomorrow will be as hard as yesterday, but with each passing day you become stronger.

When we started to build Kinzen in 2017, my co-founder Áine Kerr and I embraced the practice of 'pre-mortems' in which we asked our team why a new idea or product would go wrong. Not whether, but how. By naming the failure, it ceased to paralyse us with fear.

As a start-up founder and co-founder, I had the advantage of setting the prevailing culture from the very beginning. But it didn't come easy. Founders tend to soak up the anxiety that surrounds them for as long as they can, trying to project certainty where there is none.

The best founders understand their mood is contagious. They are conscious of the energy they bring to a room, and their unconscious biases, like an addiction to their own voice. Good leaders rely on a 'closed loop' system of self-regulation, constantly monitoring, learning and adjusting to their environment rather than locking into a fixed plan.

If I'm looking to a moment when Elon Musk takes a decisive shift into the dark side, it is when he becomes a mortal enemy of empathy. As kryptonite was to Superman, so empathy is to Elon Musk.

Legendary investor and innovator Reid Hoffman worked with Elon Musk at PayPal, where he appeared to be the only member of the founding team that could balance empathy with aggression. 'Relative to the rest of the crew,' Hoffman once told the *New Yorker*, 'I had a massively better idea of where another person was coming from and how to bridge the gap.'[6]

Great innovators regard empathy as a competitive advantage, but only when used appropriately and in good faith. There are different types of empathy, each requiring their own energy. The kind of empathy that helps a sales person understand what a customer is really thinking counts as 'cognitive empathy'. The kind of empathy required to sit with the emotion of another person is 'affective empathy'. Leadership is knowing whether you need to get inside someone's head or sit in the darkness together, and having the ability to do both in a single day without losing your own mind.

This empathetic style of leadership typically blossoms late in our careers, when we are more comfortable devolving power to others. I was a 45-year-old start-up veteran and tech executive before I had a working model of emotional intelligence. Coincidentally, US data suggests 45 is also the average age of a successful entrepreneur.

More than a decade as an entrepreneur rewired my brain in ways I'm still coming to terms with. With some distance, I see that everything I have learned about human flourishing in the age of superhuman technology comes from the storm inside my entrepreneur mind. What clarity I have about human superpowers I owe to the savage ferocity of internet start-ups. In that foundry I found resilience, hope and empathy. And the right kind of crazy.

Musk's character arc is compelling to me because of what it tells us about a grandiose mythology of innovation that has taken hold of our twenty-first-century imagination. That oppressive myth goes all the way back to the frontier spirit of the Silicon Valley pioneers who cast digital innovation as the preserve of outlaws, willing to break rules in pursuit of personal freedom. The outlaw energy surges through the gold rush of the early commercial internet, obscuring the collaborative magic of the open web.

In truth, the line between these two worlds of innovation is not so starkly drawn as I make out here. There are some empathetic leaders in the highest ranks of the mega-corporations. Reid Hoffman is one example, and so too is Satya Nadella, who championed a culture of open dialogue and collaboration at Microsoft when he became CEO in 2014. 'If I look at the most successful products we have created,' he once said of the importance of empathy, 'it comes with that ability to meet the unmet, unarticulated needs of customers.'[7]

Even on the outlaw frontier of artificial intelligence you can find thriving examples of the right kind of crazy. One of the most inspiring leaders of the AI revolution is Fei-Fei Li, the Chinese-born scientist who created the groundbreaking computer vision system called ImageNet. What distinguishes Li from the brittle wunderkind of Silicon Valley is her experience as an outsider in America.

In her book *The Worlds I See* she describes a violent attack on a friend in high school who, like her, was learning English as a second language. Elon Musk once described a schoolyard beating he suffered as a lesson in how to endure pain. Fei-Fei Li spoke of her experience of violence as an invitation to speak for those who are silent and unseen.

The internet is still a foundry for human collaboration. Its distributed emotional intelligence still thrives because empathetic innovators like Tim Berners-Lee never gave up. Berners-Lee continues to build human-centred technology and has been working on new ways to protect citizen privacy in the age of AI agents. Jimmy Wales continues to nourish and protect and improve Wikipedia, which despite early vandalism of its pages and concerns over representation and reliability, has become the most widely accessed and consequential encyclopaedia in history. All of these exceptional innovators have the right kind of crazy. They refuse to be prisoners of the Silicon Valley personality cult.

These are the humans who fall in love with human problems, not cosmic solutions to escape them. Their self-awareness sharpened, they notice opportunities on the margins of their consciousness. They become more open to uncomfortable ideas and diverse thinking, sensing a 'shadow future'[8] of greater potential than they first perceived. The theoretical biologist Stuart Kauffman calls this the 'adjacent possible'. One small innovation in this space can trigger a cascade of change and what Kauffman describes as 'a map to all the ways in which the present can reinvent itself'. If there was a master key to a more human and hopeful future, it is this unplanned cascade of discovery.

Unfortunately, we fell hard for myths of the crazy ones and their science fiction vision of the future. In the years after my meeting with Elon Musk, the internet seemed to accelerate beyond the limits of the 'adjacent possible'. Before long, every new idea needed to move at the speed of a rocket ship to count as innovation. There was no place for self-awareness when all that mattered was scale.

It is almost certainly too late for Elon Musk to find his way back from the abyss. But it is never too late to place our trust in humans who understand what it is to be human. It is never too late to fail better. Or as Samuel Beckett put it in *Worstward Ho*, 'Somehow up and stand. No choice but stand.'

Part Two

The Unravelling

The angel would like to stay, awaken the dead, and make whole what has been smashed. But a storm is blowing from Paradise ... The storm irresistibly propels him into the future to which his back is turned, while the pile of debris before him grows skyward. This storm is what we call progress.

Walter Benjamin, 'Theses on the Philosophy of History'[1]

Everything's computer.

Donald J. Trump (inside a Tesla, February 2025)[2]

Recipes for Disaster

My memory of the day we sold Storyful is a little patchy. I don't recall elation. But I will never forget the relief. It was the flood of adrenaline a driver might feel after crawling from a wrecked car and gingerly patting themselves down to discover all limbs are intact.

After a team meeting to announce the deal, Storyful's lead investor Ray Nolan invited me for a long lunch at one of Dublin's fanciest restaurants. Late into the meal I turned on my phone to see panicked messages from Storyful's new owners demanding my return to the office. When I got there my team was gathered around an open laptop on the conference-room table. In the middle of the screen was a man in a plain white shirt who looked familiar. Live from New York, it was Rupert Murdoch.

Immediately conscious of the silence between me and the legendary press baron, I sputtered an ungainly toast to our new union. 'It's a very exciting vision of a small plucky start-up,' I said, 'to be part of your family.' After a quick beat of bemused silence I added, 'Our family now.' The words felt hollow even as I said them. The relief was starting to fade.

In Storyful's first business plan I included an exit scenario which explains how investors might make a return on their money. I said that in our fifth year of operation we would 'look for a strategic partner to take a majority stake in Storyful and help turn it into a significant global player'. I cited the example of another media tech start-up that had just been sold for $27 million and I named Storyful's three potential buyers: Reuters, Bloomberg and News Corporation. A few days before the start of our fifth year we sold Storyful to News Corp. for $25 million.

This was not a vindication of a well-executed plan. It was the product of accumulated weakness. Storyful had suffered several near-death experiences. The year before, the company had run out of cash and I had to make some valuable team-mates redundant, further eroding our dwindling resources of resilience. I had tried unsuccessfully to raise significant venture capital investment, before receiving a call from a friend at News Corp. in early 2013 inquiring if I was interested in 'Rupert taking a majority stake'. What had been part of the original game plan now felt like an admission of failure.

A few weeks after the sale of Storyful I travelled to New York to meet my new colleagues in News Corp. and prepare for my family's move to a gleaming new apartment building on the Upper West Side. In the taxi from JFK airport a powerful wave of nostalgia rolled over me as I recalled my 26-year-old self arriving in Washington for the first time in 1995. Back then I had been so overwhelmed by the grand theatre of American politics that I had missed the first internet revolution. Now I was an active participant in the next one.

In the opening weeks of 2014 there was lingering optimism about technology's potential for good in the world. Polls showed a majority of Americans had a positive opinion of internet corporations. Second-term President Barack Obama and Silicon Valley were locked in a passionate love affair. Technology companies rolled with an emerging wave of civic activism, and Twitter accelerated the rise of the Black Lives Matter movement.

Donald Trump was a TV star with zero political credibility among the chattering classes. He was clinging to the 'birther' conspiracy that Obama had been born in Kenya and was ineligible to be president. As I crossed the Harlem River into Manhattan in the first days of that year, the notion that he would succeed Obama as president was beyond absurd.

The internet was pulsing with potential. The song of the year would be 'Happy' by Pharrell Williams. The image of the year would be Ellen DeGeneres' star-studded Oscars selfie. The app of the year was video-sharing app Vine. The meme of the year would be the Ice Bucket Challenge.

As I pulled up to the kerb of my new Manhattan home I was sure I had arrived at the beginning of something. I was half right. It was the beginning of an ending. Once again, tectonic plates were soundlessly shifting under my feet. As in 1995, history was being made, but not in the way it seemed to savvy insiders in New

York and Washington. We didn't know it then but we were taking our last breaths of pure internet optimism.

What seemed absurd in the early days of 2014 would make perfect sense two years later. We would soon use phrases like surveillance capitalism, filter bubbles, data mining, clickbait and fake news to describe the unravelling of the internet. We would begin to speak with fearful awe of the new force in our lives: the algorithm.

It's worth taking a beat here to explore this word, algorithm, in all its meanings. The word has come to be associated with a very modern form of dark magic. The truth is algorithms are not magic. And they are not even very modern. The word is derived from a Latin translation of the name of a Persian mathematician, al-Khwārizmī, who studied in the fabled House of Wisdom in Baghdad in the first years of the ninth century.

At its most basic, an algorithm is a step-by-step process for completing a task. A food recipe is an algorithm. The algorithm is the right ingredients, in the right quantities, in the right order, which will deliver a satisfying meal to your table.

Human progress is the story of tools that transform important tasks into actions we don't have to think about. Writing relieved us of the need to memorise. The abacus simplified calculation. The clock helped us keep time. Algorithms are used to deploy such tools in the real world. A basic algorithm helped sailors use a compass and a map to cross time zones and explore new worlds. In the twentieth-century, algorithms helped phone companies route calls, airlines allocate seats and traffic lights keep our roads safe.

In the twenty-first century you have probably battled a dynamic pricing algorithm when you tried to snag a hot concert ticket.

One algorithm often leads to another. The first algorithms of the internet age were designed to efficiently deliver vast quantities of data through a chaotic new network. In turn, this created the need for algorithms to help humans navigate that vast quantity of data. At this moment of information overload, humanity was uniquely vulnerable to unintended consequences.

As far back as 1971, the year the first email was sent, the American psychologist and economist Herbert Simon warned that 'a wealth of information creates a poverty of attention'.[3] He said humans would need machines to help manage their scarce attention. By 1998, when Bill Clinton was making his clairvoyant speech about technology in Dublin, there was an algorithm for managing an historic overabundance of information.

Google's groundbreaking PageRank algorithm helped people find the most relevant and authoritative information based on what they typed in the search bar. PageRank's unique recipe had certain ingredients, such as links connecting websites, links recommended by other people, and a little dash of your personal data, including past searches.

The algorithm was a friendly invisible hand, like the GPS in your car, finding the destination you said you wanted but couldn't find on a map. Other essential algorithms would soon follow. The Amazon version sorted through millions of products to find one that uniquely matched your needs and budget, based on your browsing history and previous purchases. The Netflix algorithm gave you more of what you wanted. Spotify's algorithms delivered music you never knew you wanted. Until you did.

In the beginning, these algorithms seemed to be wholesome and pure, like a recipe for a satisfying meal. But over time, the emerging technology platforms got greedy. Algorithmic systems kept you at the table longer, pushing your eye towards more lucrative items on the menu. Humans are particularly susceptible to such 'glimmers of novelty', says sociologist Zeynep Tufekci, in what is one of the most compelling descriptions of the algorithmic sphere: 'These kinds of messages are to human community what salt, sugar and fat are to the human appetite.'[4]

The algorithm pieced together your subconscious desires and secret tastes, drawing patterns from what you browsed, clicked and dwelled on. Eventually, they started to monetise your true preferences. Unlike television networks, who showed the same advert to all viewers, the platforms could sell your explicit preference to just the right advertiser. Searching for Chinese food delivered you to the local Chinese restaurant.

The algorithm that had been designed to serve the user was gradually reoriented to serve the advertiser. Engagement became the metric because engaged users saw more ads. And the most engaging content, as every platform eventually discovered, was content that provoked strong emotion – which is where the story gets darker.

Having been extracted by the algorithm, your basic instincts became a precious commodity to be traded inside a new 'attention economy'. The attention economy exploded into life when

Google introduced its first advertising product in late 2000. Over time, adverts have overwhelmed the 'organic' search results which match your explicit question.

Google's success shifted the balance of power away from institutions which relied on the conscious assent of citizens to technologies which mined the human subconscious. In *The Attention Merchants*, Tim Wu says the very nature of our lives changed when someone else claimed ownership of our attention: 'For how we spend the brutally limited resource of our attention will determine those lives to a degree most of us prefer not to think about.'[5]

Social media algorithms posed an entirely new level of peril. But they started off with disarming simplicity. On Twitter, the first recipe was: *Give Mark content from the people he follows, putting the most recent posts at the top of his feed.* In time, the algorithm's job was to keep you scrolling, to constantly keep predicting what Mark would click on, react to or share with his network. Soon, the goal of the 'big feed' was to push stirring content into your brain, so it could extract the attention.

Once it had your attention and your preferences, it could auction your eyeballs to the highest bidder. The auction was automated and happened in milliseconds. The winning advert was pushed seamlessly between the posts of your friends, family and favourite creators. The whole process was designed to work without your awareness, intention or consent.

This unconscious manipulation is the core feature of the attention economy. It is the root cause of the information crisis which has shattered our shared reality and realigned power in our accelerating world. When the designers of social media plugged advertising systems into humanity's brain stems, the world changed forever.

If there was a tipping point in this story, it is when the algorithm became the new editor of the internet. This new editor acted more like a traffic light than a journalist. It optimised for engagement. Anger was green. Outrage was green. Calm, nuance or complexity were always red. The algorithm had no opinion. It just followed the numbers.

The first truly consequential engagement algorithm was Facebook's EdgeRank, which became public knowledge in 2010. It ranked your affinity to other accounts, the content they shared and the recency of posts in the feed. Its job was to find out who and what truly pushed your buttons. It was monetising your attention, your activity and your network.

Facebook's first rudimentary News Feed had been met with a virulent backlash when it was launched in 2006 by people who complained about the infringement of their privacy. Mark Zuckerberg issued a swift apology for 'messing this up', but the News Feed was wildly successful for Facebook, dramatically increasing engagement on the platform. EdgeRank also provoked a revolt by the Facebook community, but was again a big hit in boosting engagement metrics. 'The inescapable conclusion inside the company,' said Jeff Horwitz in his exposé of Facebook, *Broken Code*, was that 'regular people's opinions about Facebook's mechanics were best ignored'. The algorithm always knows best.

In 2012, the algorithmic feed was turbocharged by two momentous events. First, after more than a decade of relentless growth, the web stopped expanding, with the number of people on the internet remaining static for several years in a row. The internet was no longer issuing blank cheques. Every platform needed to extract more value from the attention mines, and if they couldn't increase the number of people using their tools, they needed to increase the overall amount of attention they could harvest.

The second big event of 2012 was a groundbreaking advance in artificial intelligence called deep learning. The creators of the breakthrough model, AlexNet, asked the machine to correctly identify and label images. They set the goal, but it was the machine which decided how to best complete the task, deciding which features mattered, how to weight them, and how to combine them into a judgement.

Deep learning was a godsend to what I think of now as the big feed. Facebook immediately seized this opportunity to turbocharge its content recommendation systems and its revenues, with a degree of enthusiasm that quickly veered into recklessness.

Facebook built an internal system called FB Learner which allowed engineers to run self-service machine learning experiments without any oversight or understanding of how the machine delivered its end results. According to Jeff Horwitz, FB Learner 'could be used by engineers who quite literally did not understand what they were doing'.[6] By 2016, the platform was running 50,000 experiments on the system. One Facebook insider said open access to such experimental systems was like 'giving rocket launchers to twenty-five-year-old engineers'.

Machine learning helped scale a new breed of mega-corporation unmatched in the history of capitalism. The first great danger was the growing complexity of these inscrutable algorithms. Social media algorithms had gone from simple recipes to connect you to what you really wanted to unimaginably sophisticated systems that manipulated and monetised your unconscious online self. All within the space of a decade.

By 2021, Facebook's algorithm could use up to 10,000 different signals to predict a person's engagement with a single post. You might pause over a post or image before moving on, without clicking or reacting. But the machine has noted that pause as 'dwell time' and counted it as one of its 10,000 steps. Humans had become lab rats in an experiment that had escaped the control of the scientists.

In New York in 2014, I was still living in a state of social media bliss, assuming all internet trends and viral content bubbled up organically from weird and wonderful corners of the internet, like Reddit or Tumblr. Exceptional moments, such as the llamas and the dresses, caught fire because they were spotted by cool hunters – the well-connected influencers or journalists. Back then, a social media algorithm tended to play a supporting role, accelerating the spread of content that had already generated an audience.

In truth, I was a bit distracted as I turned the key to my new life in New York. I had Rupert Murdoch on my mind. I had no formal invitation to meet with Murdoch, so the plan was to bump into him in the corridors of News Corp.'s towering headquarters on Seventh Avenue. Murdoch was notoriously curt with his staff. A *Wall Street Journal* reporter once tried to introduce himself to his boss in the hallway, adding, 'I work for you.' Murdoch ignored the outstretched hand, kept walking and muttered, 'Everyone works for me.'

When my moment arrived I was unprepared. As Murdoch headed in my direction, my News Corp. chaperone pointed to the luminous blue sneakers I was wearing and told me to hide my feet under the table. Such ostentatious informality would not endear me to my new boss. The conversation was fleeting but pleasant. As Murdoch turned to leave, he said, 'Let's go make some fucking money.'

In six words, my new boss had captured the spirit of these viral years.

Emotional Baby

Making money had not been our strongest suit at Storyful, at least not when we were devoting all our time to conflict and crisis. We didn't break even as a business until the month before News Corp. took over. But soon we would be carried away by the lucrative hidden algorithms of the attention economy.

We had developed a new revenue stream overseen by Áine Kerr and one of Storyful's rising stars, Shane Creevy. As well as our expertise in verifying breaking news, we'd started to license viral videos of cute cats, funny kids and the endless spectrum of oddity that helps make the internet great.

Some on the Storyful team were sceptical of chasing viral videos. They wanted to stick with our purpose-driven work with YouTube. That partnership had thrived thanks to Olivia Ma and Steve Grove. We had helped YouTube, and its parent Google, build a global network of open-source journalists. We had pioneered verification protocols for critical videos from conflict zones and revolutions. We helped make YouTube a more credible source for the world's biggest news organisations.

By the end of 2012, YouTube had become wary of its association with hard news. The heady days of the Arab uprisings had passed, and civil war had consumed Syria. YouTube wanted the 'compulsive aesthetic of US tabloid TV' rather than gritty first-person reality, said Mark Bergen.[1] 'And who was going to put ads in front of Syrian rebels?' he asked. 'They didn't want death, they wanted money.'

We had always known there was a vulnerability in our relationship with YouTube. When David Clinch had first pitched Storyful to staff there, he heard a Google engineer scoff at our curation process, saying 'we have an algorithm for that'. At Storyful we had the 'human algorithm': that combination of skilled journalists working with eye-witnesses and experts to mine the vast reservoir of internet data. We believed the human algorithm couldn't be beaten for the verification of news content. But by early 2013 we could see YouTube's priorities shifting out of our comfort zone.

The platform had run into what technologists call a 'wicked problem'. Although a billion people visited the site every month, they stayed for an average of just 15 minutes. YouTube needed people to spend more time watching its videos, but it also needed to show them more adverts. Normally, you can't do both. Machine learning magically resolved this contradiction, increasing both watch time and advertising. The bosses asked how this was possible. No idea, said the engineers.

Years later, an investigation led by former YouTube engineer and algorithmic transparency campaigner Guillaume Chaslot would offer a compelling answer to the mystery. YouTube's turbo-charged algorithms excelled at activating stronger emotions in people on the platform. Viewers didn't watch for longer because the content was useful or informative, but because it triggered outrage, anxiety and fascination. It turns out that viewers activated by strong emotions are more susceptible to certain categories of advertising. YouTube's machines knew what worked, even if its engineers didn't.

The moment the algorithms cracked the code of our subconscious is the moment YouTube's business became a 'freight train that couldn't stop'. In 2013, YouTube generated $3.5 billion in revenue. Ten years later, it was $35 billion. I can't think of a progression that better explains the breathtaking power of the social media algorithm than this.

The turbo-charged algorithms made the experience of YouTube more like television, which consumed three to four hours of an average person's day in 2013. YouTube had crafted a 'lean back' experience for viewers. In other words, they wanted you to lean back on the couch and passively binge. YouTube invited me to a presentation of its strategy at Google's enormous Art Deco headquarters in Lower Manhattan. 'No more clicking and fiddling around with a mouse,' said the voice in the promo video. 'All you have to do is lean back and enjoy the show.'

The guest speaker at that presentation was Jonah Peretti, the founder of BuzzFeed, a brash New York start-up which seemed to have cracked the code of news in the age of the social media algorithm. It became known for a slick mix of feel-good viral video and surprisingly strong news reporting. Peretti's speech was compelling, but the 'lean back' stuff made me anxious. Storyful's symbiotic relationship with YouTube was about to change. They wanted us to be like BuzzFeed.

Our trusted partners, Steve and Olivia, had moved to new jobs at Google. The executives who replaced them asked us to build our own YouTube channel and focus on video that generated big engagement. Instead of being paid directly by YouTube, we would share revenue with the creators of viral videos we discovered and licensed. YouTube gave us a very generous advance on future earnings, which would guarantee Storyful's survival for at least another year.

It was an offer we couldn't refuse. We didn't know how deep learning had changed the YouTube algorithm but we were good at finding the content it seemed to crave. We cobbled together a viral video discovery engine to scour trend-setting corners of the internet like Reddit. Once we found a video we liked, we agreed on a revenue-sharing arrangement with the creator and then went to work making their videos viral.

Early in 2013, I was boarding a flight at Dublin airport when I was sent a video we had just licensed from a family in Canada. The face of a 10-month-old baby filled the screen. Her mother began to sing, and the little baby's eyes welled up with tears of joy but then began to shed tears of distress. The child then cycled through every conceivable emotion in time with her mother's soulful voice. When I got on that plane a few thousand people had viewed 'emotional baby'. When I landed in New York it was over a million. Eventually, 40 million people watched the video on YouTube.

A psychology journal described the 'emotional baby' video as an example of 'emotional contagion'.[2] This was such a perfect description of the media's new viral business model. Storyful didn't just find videos that went viral, we helped them go viral. We'd find the YouTube video and then share it with our news partners, who in turn drove millions of views back to YouTube. We rode the wave as far as the algorithm would take us and then juiced it to go a little further.

We knew we were on to something big at Storyful when we saw business journalist Felix Salmon's prediction for 2014. 'It has become abundantly clear … that if you want to keep up in the traffic wars, you need to have viral content.' You could try and create that viral content yourself or you could buy it from Storyful. We were offering emotional-contagion-as-a-service.

We borrowed a word made famous by the Beastie Boys (and turned into a business plan by Jonah Peretti) to describe Storyful's new direction: the 'mullet strategy'. We were business up the front, and party down the back. Storyful's cute cats and funny kids were subsidising our time-consuming investigation of chemical weapons attacks in Syria. Our clients used our newswire service to source serious journalism, but also to draw valuable traffic to their websites with our viral content. The mullet strategy became the default business plan of every major media company on the planet during these brief but intense traffic years.

For a fleeting moment, there was talk of Mark Zuckerberg as the potential saviour of the news business. The traffic Facebook sent to media websites rose by 170 per cent in 2013, with the platform sending 151 million visitors to the BuzzFeed Network in a single month. 'The BuzzFeed of today reaches more people globally than the print circulation of all the biggest newspapers or magazines,' Jonah Peretti proclaimed, before adding a little Trumpian bombast: 'The golden age of media never saw numbers this big!'[3]

Everybody wanted to ride the algorithmic wave, including global consumer brands who used viral videos to make their marketing campaigns more relatable. We sold videos of crazy basketball shots for use in an advert made by phone company AT&T. We had a partnership with Pepsi. On one memorable day I found myself on the former MGM studio lot in Hollywood pitching Sony executives on the use of viral content in their blockbuster movies.

Late one night at a marketing party thrown by a big TV network in Manhattan, I made my excuses to leave. Unimpressed, my News Corp. companion replied, 'There's still too much money in the room.' In this algorithmic Gilded Age there always seemed to be more money in the room. I was under orders from Rupert to get the 'fucking money'. But I wasn't always clear where the 'fucking money' was coming from. Or how long the 'fucking money' would last.

Some days working for News Corp. felt like drowning. Most felt like rocket travel. The momentum was dizzying. Storyful had 30 staff when it was acquired, and soon had more than 100 employees in Dublin, New York, London, Hong Kong and Sydney. We had partnerships with 100 of the world's top news publishers and were hired by Facebook to build a Newswire that would channel high-quality content to news publishers.

When we sold Storyful I was relieved. The responsibility for the company's sluggish performance was on my shoulders, as was the risk this posed to the jobs and the mission of my team-mates. But now News Corp. was in charge, there was a sharp pang of regret for what might have been if Storyful had enjoyed both rapid growth and independence. Could we have become a core piece of digital public infrastructure? That alternative scenario didn't feel so far-fetched.

Storyful was one of seven external start-ups given partial access to Facebook's 'firehose', the giant torrent of content being viewed on the platform. Our product team quickly spun up a system to process the 100 million posts coming through the feed every day, but was eventually overwhelmed by the full force of the Facebook conversation.

In 2014, to celebrate our channel's first billion views, YouTube threw us a stellar party in New York's Chelsea Market, complete with Storyful cupcakes. A year later, we celebrated 2 billion views. It's around this time *Fast Company* magazine put us on its list of 10 most innovative companies in social media.[4]

Storyful was moving at the breakneck pace set by a handful of pioneering companies in a compact slice of Lower Manhattan. For a magic moment there in 2014 it really felt like YouTube and Facebook had decided they needed human skills to balance their turbo-charged algorithms. But Facebook soon closed off access to that firehose. And YouTube eventually ran out of cupcakes.

The news industry convinced itself there was a stable new business model inside the attention economy. It's the reason why Rupert Murdoch bought Storyful. He thought he could own a piece of this goldmine. But we soon found that we were tenants on land owned by technology companies. We could be evicted with the flick of an algorithmic switch.

Facebook never had any interest in saving the news business. It adjusted its algorithms to reward viral news content because it needed to match the fast pace of the Twitter feed and dominate the 'real-time' internet. Once that goal was achieved, the viral years of rocket-ship growth were over, at least for the news organisations and start-ups which had wedded their futures to the algorithms.

'Facebook is the monster in the publishing room,' said Felix Salmon, 'a traffic firehose which can be turned on or off at Mark Zuckerberg's whim.'[5] Salmon was right. At the end of 2014, Facebook tweaked its algorithm to promote 'high-quality articles' and demote 'clickbait'. Traffic to the growing universe of traffic-chasing newsrooms collapsed.

Facebook would change tack again in 2018, favouring posts from your friends and family over content from publishers. It tweaked its algorithms to boost 'meaningful social interactions'. In practice, that meant optimising for anger and division. The algorithm assigned the reaction emoji – including the angry emoji – five times the weight of a simple 'like'. Facebook had learned the same lessons as YouTube. Anger drives a more lucrative form of engagement than information.

BuzzFeed's Jonah Peretti went to Facebook's head of News Feed and warned him of impending doom for the publishers of quality information on the internet. 'Do you make negative and polarizing content to win on Facebook?' Peretti asked. 'Or do you make positive social content and see your business and traffic decline?'

The years of unparallelled human engagement with algorithms had ushered in an era of profoundly diminished human agency. All of us had been the frog in the water, unconscious of a gradual warming that would eventually reach boiling point. So effectively had the machines exploited our worst instincts that we came to identify with them as our essential human nature. It was a process designed by humans and driven by greed, but it felt like some silent evolutionary shift. We came to believe in the inevitability of our powerlessness.

The people who designed the systems would largely claim deniability. The turbo-charged algorithms had initially defied explanation, even to their creators. But the number of people in the world who understood the warped dynamic of humans and algorithms was frighteningly small, even as it became clear this extractive relationship was toxic.

Facebook whistleblower Frances Haugen said there were probably 200 people in the tech industry who understood the impact of algorithmic products as well as she did. 'There's just not a lot of people who do the AI side and the human side,' she explained. The problem has got progressively worse as social media companies compete for an edge in the age of generative AI. They can't create more people in the world but they can find new ways to harvest our identities for profit.

Meta might have caught up with TikTok's algorithms, wrote Jonah Peretti in 2025, 'but the teams at Meta didn't know why one piece of content was winning over another because the decisions were being made inside the deep learning black box'.[6] As they enhance the self-learning capacity of their algorithms, the mega-corporations diminish their understanding of how machines shape human brains.

There's a terrifying parallel between the algorithmic feeds and the global financial systems before the financial crisis that began in 2007. The algorithms have become too big and too powerful to fail. As bankers spun up financial products they didn't understand, they had unwittingly created a ticking timebomb. As engineers cede control to their unknowable algorithms, the disaster plays out silently, like an artificially generated shift in the climate.

These 'traffic years' will be remembered as the time when the frayed edges of our shared reality began to unravel. Human editors were replaced by runaway algorithms. We transitioned from an information age, where those with quality information had power, to an attention economy where those who command spectacle have all the power.

Here again, we've reached a sliding doors scenario where there is an alternative internet future hiding in plain sight. Before Rupert Murdoch bought Storyful there was a fleeting moment in which it seemed YouTube might acquire our company. A YouTube executive took me aside at a conference in Asia to tip-toe around the potential terms of a takeover, but the conversation soon fizzled out. I can see now that our human algorithm was a far more risky bet than those self-guiding algorithms.

If YouTube owned Storyful, it would own every tough editorial call we made, every controversial story we tackled. In his book *This Is Not Propaganda*, Peter Pomerantsev captures the essence of the dilemma: 'YouTube didn't want to be the judge of what is true,' he wrote, 'but it wanted its algorithms to be the judge of what gets promoted.'

Still, I was intrigued by what might have been when I listened to Mark Bergen promoting his book about YouTube on a technology podcast. 'I think so much of the book is this alternative vision of what could have been for YouTube and the internet,' he said, 'and I really think it's worth asking what could have been if that Storyful model was actually given resources and more attention.'[7]

Back in 2013 I was disappointed YouTube didn't acquire Storyful. But Mark Bergen puts his finger on a much more consequential missed opportunity, which was coordinated public support by internet platforms of open-source journalism.

The case for an open, collaborative and transparent layer of human curation on the internet was overwhelming then, and it still is today, whether or not Storyful played a critical role. Imagine, back in 2013, if the platforms had each built a human curation team to filter news from noise when it mattered most (as was the case at Twitter before Musk), or invested in a distributed model of verification and sense-making, much like Google's short-lived Open Newsroom or more recent experiments with Community Notes? What if platforms had been obliged to let independent researchers audit the social and civic impact of algorithmic systems, from the very beginning?

Hindsight is a cruel judge. I know this better than most. I was keenly aware of my failure to keep Storyful on an independent path, and of the commercial pressure on my team during those traffic years. So I find it hard to fault embattled media executives who clung to the hopes of a golden era of online journalism, or platform engineers who believed in the real value of the algorithms they designed. The truth is that so many bad decisions made by media companies and platforms were entirely logical in the moment. This is one of the throughlines of the history of the internet.

However, there is one judgement that is impossible to forgive: platform executives releasing ever more powerful algorithms they didn't understand, long after we could see the damage they caused. Let's be clear: those algorithms could have been reined in at any time, even as they became more complex.

The machines may have learned by themselves, but it was

humans who set their goals. At the very first sign that humanity was paying a price for algorithmic control of the big feed, the corporate executives could have cut the engine. They didn't. Instead, they flooded our public spaces with rage and lies, drove democratic politics to the margins, and shattered our shared reality.

Over time, I have come to believe that the worst decisions taken by technology executives were not about money but about control. As the world became more hostile and more unforgiving of technology companies, their leaders learned to survive by never giving in, never flinching. They can no longer afford to offer even the most basic concession.

Algorithms are a key defence of their power: unaccountable, invisible and deniable. But the critical failures can all be traced back to choices made by humans, inside a fiercely insular culture of leadership which has helped the internet giants seem invincible.

It is all a long way from that last good day on the internet. The glorious caper of the llamas and the dress took place in February 2015, towards the end of the traffic era, and was the last time we got to lose our shit together without algorithmic supervision. The former editor of BuzzFeed News, Ben Smith, offered up a troubling coda to the story in his book about the viral years, *Traffic*. He recounts a meeting between his boss Jonah Peretti and a senior Facebook executive shortly after the 'last good day'. Peretti expected Facebook to be thrilled at an unexpected viral sensation. The executive's response took him by surprise.

'How often do you think things should go viral like the Dress?' the Facebook boss asked. It was suddenly clear, says Smith, that he did not regard the dress as a goofy triumph; rather 'it had been a kind of a bug, something that scared them'. Facebook was worried about something new: losing control. 'We at BuzzFeed might have seen the Dress as the beginning of a new kind of global culture,' wrote Smith, 'but in fact nothing like that was ever allowed to happen again.'

It's Just Fucking Us

It speaks volumes about the state of Twitter in the opening days of 2016 that the most exciting thing on the platform was a puddle of water in an English office park. A marketing agency in Newcastle used Twitter's video app Periscope to livestream people leaping, tip-toeing or dancing across a comically large pool of rain water outside their window.

At the peak of #DrummondPuddleWatch, 20,000 people were simultaneously glued to the feed. The puddle became so famous that some brought lilos and surfboards to perform a crossing. 'It wasn't that we were watching a puddle,' Twitter chief executive and co-founder Jack Dorsey observed. 'It was that we were watching a puddle together.'[1]

Like all the best inside jokes, you had to be there. And like every good day on the internet, you could be there in person – from anywhere in the world.

I think Twitter's leadership was in such awe of a stagnant puddle because they could see their reflection in it. Twitter's growth had stalled, its revenues were flagging and its bosses were desperate for any distraction from the perilous state of the company.

I have personal insight here. I had just become a senior executive at Twitter. The week I accepted the offer to join the company as its vice president of media in Europe, it announced hundreds of job cuts and Twitter's stock price went into freefall.

God, show me a sign.

I took some comfort from the knowledge that Twitter had been an exceptionally dysfunctional technology corporation from inception. 'Twitter is such a mess,' Mark Zuckerberg once reportedly observed, 'it's as if they drove a clown car into a gold mine.' The gold mine was exhausted by the time I got there. But it was still very much a clown car, racing around in crazy circles looking for the exit.

Before I was hired I travelled to San Francisco for a series of final interviews. In the heat of a late-summer morning I walked through the city's Skid Row, avoiding the human waste and shopping trolleys loaded with worldly possessions, past the cheap hotels and former bawdy houses of the Tenderloin, until I reached Twitter's grand Art Deco tower on Mission Street. Outside, on the street, people panhandled for the price of a night at the shelter. Inside that building, the starting salary for a software engineer was $125,000 a year.

The night before, I'd received an email instructing me to dress down for my visit. In the elevator, on my way to my first interview, I stood beside a senior executive in a crumpled dress shirt, ratty jeans and very expensive footwear. I soon discovered the informality of the office disguised a stealth-wealth sensibility, with luxury sneakers a particular obsession of senior male executives.

There were some exceptional leaders at Twitter. My first interview was with the company's chief financial officer, Anthony Noto. He strode into our meeting with broad shoulders and a bemused scowl. The son of a single mother with limited means, Noto went to West Point military academy on a football scholarship, qualified as an Army Ranger and cycled through several illustrious jobs before landing at Twitter. He commanded every room he entered.

By contrast, Jack Dorsey drifted into meetings as a transient cloud. When I met him at a dinner for international executives I noticed his withdrawal from conversation as it slipped into small talk. Empty compliments passed through him as if he were a ghostly apparition. 'Dorsey is the kind of leader,' as one interviewer put it, 'who never feels the obligation to fill a silence.'[2]

Dorsey was approachable as a person but unknowable as a boss. He offered every new recruit his personal email address. Yet I struggled for months to work out the effective chain of command at the company. I would later read that Dorsey was inspired by the Japanese concept of *wabi-sabi*, which is the appreciation of beauty in imperfection. Twitter wasn't imperfectly beautiful. It felt broken.

I detected a scent of desperation every time I walked into Twitter's San Francisco headquarters. The company was burdened with Californian exceptionalism and Wall Street expectations, but it had a paralysing fear and ignorance of the world it was shaping. When future historians tell the story of how our digital world unravelled, they will start on Mission Street.

Twitter started out as an open ecosystem, just like the internet. It gave outside developers access to its 'firehose' of content and data, and freedom to build services for communities with particular needs. For example, two British developers built a curation tool called TweetDeck, which became the backbone of Storyful's global newsroom.

You can imagine local governments building citizen engagement within this public framework. You could have seen Twitter building a sustainable business model on this open system. It could have charged other businesses for full access to its firehose of data. Like Apple, it could have created an app store. It could have taken a share of revenue from developers building apps for professional users of Twitter. In the early days, I imagined Storyful being one of those apps.

Instead, Twitter gradually retreated into advertising. Over time, it blocked outside developers and limited access to the data firehose. By the time I joined, advertising accounted for 90 per cent of Twitter revenues. This meant the company could only make money if it corralled people into the same commercial 'town square' and harvested their attention. Twitter's greatest potential value as an open ecosystem of self-organising communities had been squandered.

I hadn't given up hope. Twitter had transformed my life and

opened up a new world of possibility to me. Now it offered me a dream job. My base would be Dublin, where Twitter had its international headquarters. It was a joyful place to work, and I soon took on the additional role of managing the office. Joining the company felt like a homecoming, and a luxurious extended holiday.

I soon stopped eating breakfast with my family because breakfast at Twitter was a sumptuously catered networking opportunity with my work family. The luxury of platform life was so pronounced, you never got complacent about it. Except for that one morning I arrived in the office kitchen to find there was no crushed avocado. Just a couple of intact avocados. At that moment I caught the eye of a colleague and saw the reflection of my own doubt. Was this a metaphor? Were we a cliché? Who would crush the avocado?

When I travelled for Twitter I felt like a foreign correspondent again. My responsibility was to convey the authentic truth of the world to an audience back home. In this case, the audience was Twitter's head office in San Francisco. The company leadership employed foreigners like me to draw a map of its most lucrative markets, engage local business leaders, decipher local customs and place warning signs around political minefields.

The greatest satisfaction in my job came from the unexpected ways that global communities on Twitter solved problems or transformed the wider culture. I had come to believe that the company's founders had, by accident as much as design, built a critical piece of public infrastructure. I found myself taking an inventory of Twitter's cultural quirks and public utility.

During disastrous floods in the Indian province of Chennai in 2015, Twitter had operated like a switchboard for the relief effort, facilitating food distribution, boat transport and medical treatment and directing survivors to safety, with the help of hashtags and retweets.

In Japan, Twitter's second most important global market, the platform proved its value as critical public infrastructure during the 2011 earthquake and tsunami. It embedded itself in the rich fabric of the country , catering to the otaku sub-cultures of games, manga and anime. Twitter also enabled Japanese people to be more outspoken than the mainstream public discourse allowed.

By contrast, I learned of the German people's stubborn resistance to the Twitter app. Where the Japanese valued the platform as an outlet for uncharacteristic frankness, Germans were repelled by the intrusiveness of the breezy greeting on Twitter's mobile app: 'What's happening?'

One of my pet causes at Twitter was building tools for the active curators of communities. These were the platform's real leaders: scientists, teachers, journalists, influencers and super-fans shaping the norms of Twitter's myriad sub-cultures. Curators introduced new ideas, monitored big events and drove the most engaging trends on the platform. Just as volunteer developers improved free software on the early internet, Twitter curators were the glue that bonded the platform's healthiest communities.

The power users were responsible for the most engaging content on Twitter. During my time there, around 10 per cent of users were responsible for generating 80 per cent of the tweets. But when I would make a pitch for curator tools, such as upgrades to the TweetDeck product, I was told with some condescension that 'we don't build anything that can't be of potential use to 100 per cent of our users'.

Despite the lack of interest from Twitter's product teams, I thought Jack Dorsey would understand the civic value of curation. Growing up in St Louis, Missouri, Dorsey was drawn to the chatter on his parents' CB radio and police scanner. He came to think of cities as self-organising life forms and drew inspiration from the networked intelligence of forests and ant colonies.

I once listened to Dorsey tell the story of the small earthquake that became an epiphany for Twitter in 2006. The young co-founder was in the office on a Saturday when his phone trilled with the sound of a tweet carrying the word 'earthquake'. Moments later, he felt the earth shudder, and then the rhythmic buzzing of tweet after tweet, tracking the spread of the quake across the Bay Area. Twitter, he explained, helped people feel less alone in a moment of extreme vulnerability.

At Twitter, I tried to focus on work that would consolidate the platform as an essential public utility. I became fascinated by the 'smart city' partnerships forged by the company's business development teams in Europe. The goal was to help local authorities use Twitter to better engage citizens in real time, with a particular focus on critical government services and transport networks. It was a great idea. But as with so many of Twitter's great ideas, there was the same fatal flaw: Twitter the American company wasn't that interested in Twitter the global community.

As the manager of Twitter's international headquarters, I took every opportunity to remind my bosses of the platform's global responsibilities. A senior leader came to Dublin and listened politely to my pitch. I reminded her that nearly 80 per cent of the people who used Twitter were from outside the United States. 'Yes,' she replied drily, 'but 80 per cent of our revenue comes from the US.'

I came to understand social media platforms like Twitter as a new form of commercial empire, a sort of modern-day East India Company. International executives like me were colonial agents sent to engage with far-flung territories the company intended to extract profit from.

Shortly after I joined Twitter I flew to San Francisco for a meeting of the company's leadership. When I landed, my phone exploded with messages about a purge of top Twitter executives, including the person who had just hired me. The next day, the company's 80 senior managers came together at Mission Street headquarters to sift through the broken pieces. It would be a wildly disorienting but revealing few days.

On arrival at the leadership gathering, Jack Dorsey gave each of us a copy of Carol Dweck's book *Mindset: The New Psychology of Success*. The book contrasts a 'growth mindset' that learns from adversity with a 'fixed mindset' that is always seeking affirmation. Over the days that followed, I came to see that Twitter management had a split personality: individually, senior executives seemed resilient and stable, but the company's leadership culture was brittle, needy and paranoid. Twitter found it impossible to have hard conversations about hard things.

When issues of real substance came up at that leadership gathering, the conversation was all tight lips and gritted teeth. There was a session on 'unconscious bias' for leaders, but no time to discuss the unknown bias of the algorithmic feed that would soon go live in the Twitter app. There was an open and forthright debate about cutbacks in free transport for engineers in the San Francisco Bay Area, but a very tense conversation about hate speech and abuse on the platform.

Despite repeated internal warnings, Twitter had refused to take meaningful action to stop systemic harassment and misogynistic abuse, turning it into what one writer described as a 'honey pot for assholes'. Senior leaders had periodically expressed angst on the subject. In an internal memo leaked in 2015, then chief executive Dick Costolo said the company 'sucks at dealing with abuse and trolls on the platform, and we've sucked at it for years'.[3] But such contrition changed nothing. In 2016, BuzzFeed News said Twitter was becoming infamous for being as 'toxic as it is famous for being revolutionary'.

At the leadership meeting in 2016, Bruce Daisley, Twitter's then managing director in the UK, forcefully challenged the top brass about its failure to combat abuse. Several high-profile British women on Twitter had been subject to a barrage of threats of rape and murder, leading to public outrage, criminal investigations and several arrests. But as Bruce later wrote, the only thing that helped the Twitter UK office get the attention of the San Francisco HQ was the mention of a potential boycott by British advertisers.

A Twitter executive had once famously described the company as the 'free speech wing of the free speech party', and while the leadership slowly walked back the quote, the sentiment behind it still carried weight. I certainly admired the quiet fortitude of Twitter's public policy teams around the globe who doggedly fought for freedom of expression in parts of the world where this mattered most. But it was clear the commitment to free expression was a convenient excuse for not spending money on content moderation and safety features.

'Despite the attempts to position "free speech" as a philosophical conviction,' Bruce Daisley wrote in 2024, 'the reason for its popularity among tech firms is pure and simple – it is cheap.'[4]

All talk is cheap inside Big Tech platforms. Their stated policies are far less important than how they build their products. Twitter was 'a honey pot for assholes' because it was built that way. The open and public nature of conversation and the ease and speed with which content can spread make Twitter a particularly dangerous weapon in the hands of abusers.

Victims of abuse on Twitter become trapped, again by design. If they leave a dangerous platform, they can't take their networks with them. That means the loss of years of accumulated relationships and connections, both personal and professional. This happens because social media is built on closed, proprietary systems rather than open protocols. With email, you can switch providers without losing your contacts. You cannot do this on Twitter. The platforms don't just host your online network. They own it.

Other design choices make social media dangerous. Twitter engineers were motivated by the existential need to boost revenue, so they became too obsessed with removing all friction. In other words, any obstacles to more engagement, good or bad. Opinions don't count in this matter. All that matters is data. As much of it as possible.

I was never sure the data Twitter engineers gathered was truly significant or merely significant because it had been gathered. During Twitter's leadership meeting I listened to a presentation from a product manager who claimed to have data on every single emotion a Twitter user might feel. Activate the right emotion with the right content and you have more engagement to sell to the right advertiser.

I asked the product manager if he had collected data measuring serendipity. There was silence in the room. That pleasure of unexpected discovery, I tried to explain, that flash of inspiration when you hear a new idea. Silence.

Twitter was not designed to empower the conscious intentions of people who used it. It was designed to maximise the emotional engagement of the maximum number of its users. Abuse, rage and anger were not a glitch. They were the features of a system incentivised to sell advertising to a town square of Americans.

This made the platform unsafe, but it also encouraged Twitter to introduce features that actively made it more dangerous. Of the many bad decisions which led to Twitter's unravelling, the introduction of the 'Retweet' button in 2009 was perhaps the single most destructive. Up to that point, a Twitter user needed to copy and paste the content they wanted to share with their community. Removing the friction of that simple exercise in thoughtful curation with an automatic retweet was like handing a '4-year-old a loaded weapon',[5] said Chris Wetherell, the Twitter developer who built the feature.

The retweet helped fringe activists amplify their influence and turn Twitter into a weapon. By 2014, Wetherell realised the scale of the damage done when he saw the retweet button being used by faceless Twitter trolls to coordinate harassment against women in the games industry. This was the scandal known as Gamergate, which became a proving ground for internet extremism. The retweet button ultimately helped turn the network into a Coliseum, a doomed feedback loop of blood sport and blood lust.

The month after its leadership meeting in 2016, Twitter made another well-meaning attempt to boost engagement that had unintended and harmful consequences. In February of that year the platform introduced an algorithmic feed as an optional feature. By March it became the default setting, replacing the old reverse chronological feed which ranked the latest tweets from your network first. The decision created an immediate backlash, with people channelling their rage into the #RIPTwitter hashtag, which ultimately trended on Twitter.

Inside the company it felt like a moment of free-fall, as fearful staffers wondered if this was Twitter's death knell. Just like Facebook's NewsFeed, the algorithms kicked in seamlessly, with just 2 per cent of Twitter users turning off the algorithmic timeline. But somewhere out there on the platform there had been a tear in the fabric of Twitter that could never be repaired.

Over time, that algorithmic feed boosted engagement on Twitter for sensational headlines and angry reactions. It polarised communities and raised the volume of the loudest voices. In the years after the algorithm was turned on, the balance of political influence on Twitter shifted. Conservatives would accuse the company of a deeply ingrained left-wing bias, but research published by Twitter itself in 2021 found that in six out of seven countries, right-wing political forces enjoyed higher algorithmic amplification than the left.

The algorithmic shift tilted the centre of political gravity, but also empowered authoritarians the world over. It fuelled state-sponsored propaganda at an unprecedented scale and helped transform abuse and misogyny into a potent political force.

The lessons I learned at Twitter are not universal truths. But there is the same controlling impulse within every American mega-corporation that has come to dominate the open internet. They would rather watch their platforms burn with rage and anger than surrender control to the communities trapped inside their walled gardens.

When I think of this impulse for control and survival, I think back to one of the closing sessions of that Twitter leadership meeting. The bosses had rolled out their happy warrior, Anthony Noto, to ratchet up the energy in the room. Noto was funny, profane and challenging. Towards the end of a question-and-answer session he was asked about the possibility that a buyer with deep pockets would rescue the company from collapse. 'There is no cavalry coming to save us,' he said, his voice expanding into a roar. 'It's just fucking us!'

Noto had issued Twitter workers around the world with the order to climb out of their hopeless trench and charge. Within 24 hours, the company's entire workforce had embraced Noto's call to arms, turning the phrase into a hashtag – #ItsJustFuckingUs – that would end up pinned on the walls of its offices around the globe.

I still think of Anthony Noto's call to arms as one of the single most effective acts of leadership I have ever witnessed. But I also think of what became of 'us', the global community of people who used social media to connect, collaborate and engage with a shared reality, and those of us who worked to make it safe and free.

In the years to follow, social media platforms would work as they had been designed, to remove all friction and maximise unconscious engagement. Once there was a great, big global us. Soon there would only be us and them.

The Dinosaur at the Door

It was 7.29 in the morning in Ireland when the asteroid struck. In that moment of impact, the Associated Press called Wisconsin for Donald Trump and he crossed the 270 electoral vote threshold to become the forty-fifth president of the United States.

I can't help thinking about the days before the asteroid strike as the opening minutes of an apocalyptic movie. Happy families begin their daily routines in soft-focus sunlight. Then the camera is back in space, as an enormous chunk of rock passes the moon and accelerates toward North America.

They say an ancient asteroid wiped out the dinosaurs. This asteroid impact created a brand new alpha predator. Donald Trump represented something more than a shift in political gravity, from the sanitised realm of television to the gladiatorial arena of Twitter. He was a new species that would define the environment he was born into, forcing every other life form to adjust to his presence. He was both a glitch in the old world and an animating force in the new one.

In his early days on social media, Donald Trump delegated the writing of his tweets to a young employee. One night in February 2013, while playing with a new phone, he sent his first tweet without any assistance. Trump's social media wrangler, Justin McConney, would later compare his discovery that Trump could tweet himself to the moment in *Jurassic Park* when the scientists realise the Velociraptors could open doors. By election day in 2016, Trump had almost 13 million followers on Twitter.

On the morning of impact, I was still the managing director of Twitter's international headquarters in Dublin. Sleep-deprived and subdued, I made my way to the office struggling to find words to match the moment. Later in the day, when US colleagues were back online, Jack Dorsey sent a note to the global team urging employees to show empathy and support for each other and stressing Twitter's role in helping 'people find and speak truth to power'. Dorsey struck a reflective, almost combative tone. 'A lot of people are focusing on who won, but that's done,' he said. 'I think we should focus on why. What are the underlying root causes people are facing?'[1]

I had decided to leave Twitter weeks before the asteroid strike. The senior members of my media team in Europe had lost their jobs in one of the company's episodic cost-cutting purges, leaving me in the role of Dublin office manager. That was a fun job, but not the mission I had signed up for. I handed in my security pass and laptop a few days before Christmas 2016. On the laptop was one of the company-approved mantras new recruits get to choose from. I had chosen 'Communicate fearlessly to build trust'.

Twitter had created the conditions for fearless communication. That much was true. But the election of Donald Trump was a cataclysmic reminder of how much trust had unravelled in a world mediated by platforms like Facebook and Twitter. The shared reality we once took for granted was splintering. Trump was the knock on the door, announcing the new world of us and them.

In the weeks after leaving Twitter, I became obsessed with the search for those root causes Jack Dorsey seemed uncharacteristically animated about. I pored over reports of covert interference and mass deception in the US presidential campaign. In an election where the margin of victory was just 70,000 voters in three states, it seemed possible that orchestrated shenanigans on Twitter and Facebook tipped the result in Trump's favour.

There was talk of hidden influencers, such as Russian intelligence operatives, and a bunch of Macedonian teenagers making a quick buck from fake election stories. BuzzFeed News found that the top false election news stories generated more total engagement on Facebook than factual election stories from 19 major news outlets combined. Researchers from Stanford University found bogus pro-Trump stories were shared 30 million times on Facebook in the three months before the election, while pro-Clinton stories were shared 8 million times.

I started to notice that the eye-popping headlines often obscured critical nuances in the underlying analysis. The Stanford researchers concluded that misinformation on social media played a much smaller role in the election than was first thought. Far more consequential than false stories was the Trump campaign's legitimate blitz of social media advertising. During the 2016 election cycle, Trump's team ran 5.9 million ads on Facebook. Hillary Clinton's campaign ran only 66,000.

The big story wasn't the supply of bogus news *to* ordinary voters. It was the insatiable demand for bogus news *from* partisan voters. The consumption of online misinformation during the campaign was most concentrated in a small, devoted group of Trump supporters. Almost 6 out of 10 visits to 'fake news' websites came from the 10 per cent of people with the most conservative online information diets.

The 'root cause' of Trump's election was not 'fake news'. Within the attention economy, there was now a cascade of information which divided society into tribes. People with fiercely partisan beliefs hungered for information which vindicated their loyalty. Suppliers of that information could now precisely target those loyalists. We were clearly witnessing the unravelling of our information systems. But we had no shared language to describe the process.

With the benefit of hindsight, the process begins with three words: too much information. The internet flooded the world with more words, images and ideas than any human could process. The algorithms pumped us full of content designed to activate dark emotions. Panic set in as we became all seeing and feeling but never truly understanding. We felt ourselves drown, and grasped for lifelines of meaning and belonging.

When I'm using social media these days I sometimes relive the sickening feeling of disassociation that would creep over me in war zones. Reading back on some of my final dispatches from Iraq in 2003, I can pinpoint the moment I numbed myself to the ambient spectacle of mortality and pain. I learned to suppress trauma by distracting myself with facts and emphatic opinions. Anything to function as a human. I fear this has become the universal condition in our fractured world. The perpetual eye-witness becomes incapable of empathy. Everything. Everywhere. All at once. It is too much.

Recently, I was the first to arrive at a coffee shop for a meeting. Instinctively, I fired up social media. Within seconds, the face of a terrified Russian soldier hiding in an abandoned factory stared back at me through a camera mounted on a drone. His face grew larger as the drone moved in for the kill. Sensing movement back in the real world, I looked up to see the beaming face of my friend leaning in for a hug. How do we live as normal human beings in moments like these?

There was a time, not long ago, when there were no cameras to record acts of genocide, when the great slogan of televised protests was 'the whole world is watching'. Today, with a phone in every human hand, we can no longer hide from the camera or its worst truths. If human rights are violated somewhere, then someone will record it and post it. Somebody else will immediately demand your opinion.

As far back as 2010, then Google CEO Eric Schmidt claimed that humanity was creating as much information every two days as it had since the inception of human civilisation, with predictably dire results: 'I spend most of my time assuming the world is not ready for the technology revolution that will be happening to them soon.'[2]

In 2011, the democratic potential of social media was revealed by the Arab uprisings and the Occupy movement. But this was also the year Google Translate became available on virtually all smartphones. 'So you could say that 2011 was the year that humanity rebuilt the Tower of Babel,'[3] observed our old friend Jonathan Haidt in an essay about why American life had become uniquely stupid.

Whenever humans discover a new way to communicate, we find ourselves in crisis. That has been true all the way back to the invention of writing. Each information revolution tends to sweep aside the old order but eventually delivers a new one we learn to live with, and benefit from.

Gutenberg's printing press led to the mass distribution of Martin Luther's 95 Theses, which triggered the Reformation. It also gave birth to a vigorous popular press and an extended period of unrest, culminating in what some historians have described as history's first 'media event', the Thirty Years War, which killed as many as 8 million people. On the plus side, this revolution eventually gave way to the Enlightenment and helped make reading books a habit for people of all social classes, sparking what critic James Marriott describes as 'the greatest transfer of knowledge into the hands of ordinary men and women in history'.[4]

Set against the backdrop of history, you would expect that

social media would eventually smooth out its creases and become the new normal. But the novelist Naomi Alderman reminds us that communication revolutions can 'change us psychologically, socially and emotionally in profound ways that cannot be reversed'.[5] We thought we were dealing with just another information revolution, but Alderman sees a full-blown emergency, a 'third information crisis'.

There are compelling reasons to believe that this time, things are different. This information revolution is uniquely disruptive because of its speed. Rather than a gradual arc of intermittent disruption, this revolution is characterised by a rapid succession of debilitating waves, each one crashing down quicker than the last, without even the briefest interval for us to find our footing. The internet was turbocharged by algorithmic feeds which created the attention economy, and now artificial intelligence threatens to compound the acceleration to an unthinkable degree.

The information revolution triggered by the printing press took more than 300 years to get from Gutenberg's Bible to the Enlightenment. By contrast, it's just 30 years since the internet went mainstream. There were just 10 years between the creation of Twitter and Donald Trump's election. It took Twitter five years and two months to persuade 100 million people to actively use its app. It took ChatGPT just two months to do the same.

Centuries into years. Years into months. Each wave of this unthinkably fast information revolution further erodes the foundations of the old order. But we never have time to regroup, rebuild and renew before the next one hits. The old is dying, to paraphrase Antonio Gramsci, but the new cannot be born. Depending on which translation of this quote you prefer, we have entered the time of monsters, or morbid symptoms.

Back in 2016, when Donald Trump broke down that door, we struggled to diagnose the malady behind the symptoms. But some wise souls could see beyond the initial moral panic. My friend and former Storyful colleague Claire Wardle had been studying the fractured information environment for years. She was one of the first to point out why 'fake news' was a dangerously narrow frame of reference.

Claire coined the term 'information disorder' at a Harvard University summit in February 2017 in a paper she co-authored with Hossein Derakhshan to describe the splintering of our shared reality into hyper-partisan smithereens. Her great insight was to look beyond the supply of false information to the demand for facts and opinion which feel true. Social networks, Claire observed, allow 'atoms' of propaganda to be directly targeted at users who are most receptive to the message contained within. This is how manufactured news stands out from the torrent of digital content which floods our feeds.

'As information overload exhausts our brains,' Claire said, 'we're much easier to influence.'[6] In this new disordered information system, much of the content shared was genuine, but shared out of context or used in misleading ways. It was often good old-fashioned rumour dressed up as news, or a kernel of truth embedded in vitriolic memes, doctored photos or manipulated videos.

Information disorder encompassed the more dangerous category of disinformation, which was 'intentionally false' and designed to cause harm. But it also included misinformation; those false stories spread unwittingly by well-meaning people in support or defence of their online tribe. Something Claire said back in 2017 sticks with me today: 'When humans are angry and fearful, their critical thinking skills diminish.'

Fear is a powerful force. But so too is pleasure. We are wired to take joy in the worldview of people just like us. When we make human connections our brains release dopamine as a reward, reinforcing our desire for more connection. Social media offers an endless supply of new information to bond us tight with our tribe and keep the pleasure flowing.

There is no greater cure for doubt than pleasure. The truth or fiction in information becomes less important than the way it makes us feel. In 2016, researchers discovered that 59 per cent of all links shared on Twitter had never been clicked on by anyone, including the person sharing them. People were spreading stories based purely on headlines. Simply spreading crazy, salacious stories, researchers concluded, 'had a druglike effect on internet partisans'.[7]

The most pleasurable of all content is the internet meme, that self-driving vehicle which carries dopamine to those who get the inside joke. To paraphrase the philosopher René Girard, all desire is essentially mimetic. In other words, we are led to seek after things by the example of people we know, or wish we knew better.

The most vicious content often creates the purest form of joy. No matter where our political sympathies lie, we all have a special place in our hearts for those who say outrageous things on our behalf. We delight in the shock they inflict on our common enemies. A good friend of mine, a liberal Brooklyn-dwelling journalist, travelled back to her family in Ohio after Trump's victory and was stunned by the delight they took in the distress of people just like her.

So, the framework of information disorder captured the key dynamics in the unravelling of shared reality in 2016. It was specific enough to include propaganda and covert manipulation, but wide enough to incorporate the lessons of human history and modern neuroscience. The last piece of the puzzle was the challenge that information disorder posed to journalism, the very institution that you might expect to cure the malady.

The first election of Donald Trump provoked a renewed sense of purpose in journalism, reminding people of the importance of independent, fact-based media. It was a common refrain back then that the solution to misinformation and propaganda was to pump more good information into the system, and let the marketplace of ideas return to equilibrium.

A reporter friend of mine once told me there is no such thing as information overload; just context collapse. As long as we have professional journalists, we will always have the right filters to regulate our oversaturated information environment.

Unfortunately, faith in the inherent superiority of professional journalism couldn't make up for the collapse in demand for its traditional form. In the years leading up to the election of Donald Trump, news organisations suffered a swift and catastrophic decline. In 2001, the American journalism industry employed 458,000 people. By March 2016 the number had fallen to 183,000. Of all the dying professions in post-industrial America, the demise of journalism was faster even than coal mining. The same goes for the news business in almost every western democracy. In Britain, for example, there was a net loss of 181 local newspapers in the decade before the Brexit vote.

The single deepest cut I recall was the *Washington Post*'s decision in 2015 to end a weekly feature debunking internet hoaxes. There were simply too many to rebut. 'This represents a very weird moment in internet discourse,' said *Washington Post* columnist Caitlin Dewey. 'At which point does society become utterly irrational?'[8]

Internet discourse would get an awful lot weirder in the years that followed. Society would slide further into the gravitational pull of utterly irrational ideas, with a little help from the algorithms. But there was a method to the madness. Information disorder was a completely rational response to information overload. The craving for liberating new ideas and forbidden knowledge created an entirely legitimate challenge to the complacency of the old order.

When Donald Trump broke down the door he unleashed a wave of online influencers and internet activists who would replace established sources of expertise. This was a crisis. But it was also a reckoning. The internet forced radical transparency on traditional gatekeepers and demanded instant and constant accountability. The old elites had nowhere to hide from an empowered and vengeful public. A rag-tag insurgent coalition was ready to take their place.

A Telegram from the Future

I had my first encounter with MAGA years before it became MAGA. In the closing days of the 2008 US presidential election I went to Florida to report on a giant rally hosted jointly by Barack Obama and Bill Clinton in a public park near Disney World. Obama channelled popular rage against the financial elites that night. But the next day, I felt the full force of the coming insurgency at a compact but fiery rally for Sarah Palin, the Republican nominee for vice president.

Palin spoke at the modest Silver Spurs arena, next door to the sprawling site of the Obama rally. They played U2 songs for Obama and Journey for Palin. Two of the loudest sounds of the evening were the orchestrated hiss of disapproval for the media and the raucous, star-struck welcome for Fox News host Sean Hannity.

The financial crisis was just starting to bite. Everyone at this rally wanted to talk about the 'silent majority' of patriots ready to fight big government and save the soul of America. In my notes from that day I see variations of the same words. I love my country. Not living up to its promise. People excluded. Everything to lose. Aggrieved. As I was leaving, one man leaned close to my microphone and said, 'Gotta stand for something or you are already dead.' My notes from the Silver Spurs arena read like a telegram from the future.

A few months after the Palin rally, a financial journalist called Rick Santelli went live on CNBC television with a rant against Obama's mortgage relief package. His performance got picked up by conservative and libertarian bloggers, went viral on YouTube, and poured fuel on the fire of an emerging Tea Party movement which organised anti-government protests in hundreds of US cities throughout 2009. In the 2010 midterm elections, the *New York Times* reported that 138 candidates for Congress were affiliated with or had strong Tea Party support.

'There was no way the Tea Party movement could have grown as deep and as wide as it has without social media and digital technology,'[1] one of its founding members, Christina Botteri would later say. Sarah Palin was among the first politicians to embrace this leaderless 'revolt of the public'. 'The Tea Party is not a top-down operation,' she told a rally in Nashville in early 2010. 'It's a ground-up call to action.'[2]

The Tea Party's uncompromising populism was eventually absorbed by the Republican Party, laying a strong foundation for

MAGA to build on. There is a straight line from the anti-system rage at that Florida rally to Palin's embrace of the internet-enabled Tea Party and her endorsement of Donald Trump before the Iowa caucuses in January 2016. As one US journalist put it back then, 'Donald Trump's rise can be seen as a natural extension of the kind of politics that Palin herself embraced.'

It's easy to find ideological labels for this kind of politics. But that would miss the point. Sarah Palin and Donald Trump are connected by the emotional contagion of an information revolution rather than the fixed beliefs of a partisan crusade. They both harnessed the anti-system rage which followed the great financial crisis of 2007 and 2008, and both channelled the dark energy of social media as it brought public discourse to the boil.

One of the most compelling accounts of internet insurgency was written by a former CIA analyst, Martin Gurri. *The Revolt of the Public* was first published in 2014 but seems to anticipate the rise of the Trump insurgency. Gurri counted the internet as the 'fifth wave' of information revolution (following the fourth wave of mass media).[3] The greater the diffusion of information to the public, Gurri argued, the more illegitimate the traditional power-brokers will appear.

I am drawn to this concept of the fifth wave because it best captures a form of political movement that is unique to the social media era. I think of Jack Dorsey's root causes when I read *The Revolt of the Public*. It traces the rebellion against the liberal elites back to the aftermath of the financial crisis, a moment in which

Gurri said 'toxic levels of distrust sickened democratic politics'. Social media ensured the 'human consequences of their failures couldn't be swept discreetly under the rug'. Rage then turned into rebellion at internet speed.

The financial crisis triggered networked rebellions right across the ideological spectrum, including leftist and anti-capitalist movements such as Occupy and the *Indignados* in Spain, and right-wing and libertarian coalitions like the Tea Party.

The movements that were broadly leftist focused on mass mobilisation of people and sought to transcend party politics. The Spanish *Indignados* were leaderless, without hierarchy and opposed to formal manifestos. This helped them quickly mobilise citizens through social media but left them without a coherent political programme. They lacked those 'strong ties' that keep a movement stable and resilient.

The right-wing insurgencies proved better suited to the viral dynamics of the attention economy. Their most successful leaders had an entrepreneurial flair for personal brand-building. They grew fast through loose alliances rather than purist factions. They spoke the angry, tribal tone favoured by the algorithms. They perfected the tools of meme warfare. They grew into a powerful counterculture through a vast universe of alternative media networks incubated on YouTube and Twitter.

Right-wing populists didn't just rely on the weak ties which mobilised online support. They nourished strong ties in the real world, organising networks of local activists in protests and grassroots campaigns on culture war issues such as control of education and immigration. Crucially, they either built or hijacked the apparatus of party politics.

The 'revolt of the public' started as a broad global uprising against a bankrupt old order. On the left and right, the insurgency was united against the grievous inequalities of globalisation, crony capitalism and the betrayal of real people by out-of-touch elites. But within a decade it had distilled into an angry tribal populism. This is no accident. Those powerful algorithms came online during this time, amplifying the voice of polarising influencers, favouring culture war over class war and rewarding leaders with a dark brand of emotional intelligence. If there was an irreversible tipping point in this process, it was not Donald Trump's election but the Brexit referendum on 23 June 2016.

On the evening of the vote I walked out of a restaurant with friends into a warm Dublin evening. An English pal turned to me with his phone in an extended hand and a look of shock on his face. Early tallies showed Sunderland would back Brexit, leaving us both to draw the logical conclusion. The morning after, I tried to comfort my Twitter team members in London as they talked through the sudden shock of a breach with Europe.

The Remainers had the edge in the old world of ideas and arguments, but the Leave campaign owned the virtual world of feelings and needs. Journalist, former government minister and Brexiteer Michael Gove declared that the people of Britain 'have had enough of experts'.[4] Another prominent Brexiteer, Arron Banks, would observe that Remainers mistakenly campaigned with 'fact, fact, fact'. 'It just doesn't work,' he said, 'you've got to connect with people emotionally.'[5]

This is the essential truth of the fifth wave. Social media values emotions over facts. But those emotions have value. They have a root cause. The root cause of the 'revolt of the public' was the injustice, inequalities and complacency of the old order. The internet is not the root cause. Social media did not cause the decline of liberal democracy. Instead, it exposed its weaknesses and created a vacuum few incumbents could survive.

Between August 2016 and May 2017, the governing party or elected leader in five of the top ten global economies was deposed or defeated. When the global communications agency Edelman published its annual Trust Barometer for 2017 it revealed the biggest ever drop in trust across the institutions of government, business, media and civil society. In his commentary on the findings, Richard Edelman likened the collapse in trust to 'the second and third waves of a tsunami'[6] set in motion by the financial crisis.

The survey revealed the power of information disorder to suck the trust out of political discourse and lead people into their own personal echo chambers. People surveyed by Edelman were nearly four times more likely to ignore information that supported a position they did not believe in. This toxic soup of bias, mistrust and alienation would feed the power grab of tribal populists in the years to come.

The fifth wave played out just like previous information revolutions. The old order is stripped of its authority and replaced by something new. The insurgent forces are carried to power through grassroots rebellion and soon they are the new incumbents. But there was an unexpected paradox in this information crisis. The revolution also consolidated the power of rulers who vowed to crush revolution.

In the golden days of the Arab uprisings, democratic politicians hailed social media as a mortal threat to authoritarian regimes. Back then, we assumed that Facebook and Twitter were inherently democratic technologies that would erode the absolute power of despots. How wrong we were.

I have already introduced you to what's known as Melvin Kranzberg's first law: technology is neither good nor bad; nor is it neutral.[7] In the dark power of algorithmic feeds the autocrats saw an opportunity to bend technology to their will. They embraced the viral dynamics of social media and the anonymous nature of online influence to create a playbook of 'networked authoritarianism'.

Six months before Donald Trump's first victory, voters in the Philippines elected populist firebrand Rodrigo Duterte, who vividly illustrated the autocratic potential of social technologies. His insurgent election campaign went all in on Facebook, where his strategy, a senior Duterte strategist would later recall, was 'arouse, organise, mobilise'.[8]

Journalist Maria Ressa would win a Nobel Prize for her work to expose networked authoritarianism. Her independent news network Rappler exposed the Duterte camp's secret campaign of persuasion and abuse, coordinated by a network of automated bots and internet trolls pushing misinformation but also targeting opponents with campaigns of intimidation.

During a meeting with Facebook executives, Ressa showed how a handful of fake Facebook accounts were manipulating millions of others: 'At the end of the meeting, I said, you have to do something, because if not, Trump could win. And we all laughed because that didn't seem possible.'[9]

Before leaving Twitter, I'd collide with the reality of networked authoritarianism in Turkey. One of my goals was to build a deeper presence for Twitter in the country, where it was incredibly popular for conversations about sports and entertainment but also critically important to democracy activists. In 2013, Twitter was used to help coordinate the Gezi Park protests in Istanbul, which began as an environmental protest and soon became a broad uprising against authoritarianism.

After Gezi Park, the enraged Turkish prime minister Recep Tayyip Erdoğan described Twitter as a 'menace' and a 'scourge'. But he would soon learn the value of technology for his own ends. In July 2016 he narrowly escaped assassination when a faction of the Turkish army staged a coup. Blocked from state media channels, he used his mobile phone to broadcast on private television and turned to Twitter to successfully rally his supporters against the insurrection.

Even before the coup, the algorithmic platforms were a godsend for Erdoğan. His supporters used the virality of social media to command spectacle, intimidate critics and smear the opposition, operating through a network on Twitter known as AK Trolls. This tech-enabled authoritarianism didn't look like the old forms of state censorship. 'They look like viral or coordinated harassment campaigns,' said Zeynep Tufekci, 'which harness the dynamics of viral outrage to impose an unbearable and disproportionate cost on the act of speaking out.'[10]

The AK Trolls embraced another core technique of networked authoritarianism called 'astroturfing'. This is a centrally coordinated campaign of disinformation or propaganda in which regime supporters pretend to be ordinary citizens, creating a false impression of grassroots support for the regime or opposition to its critics.

A few months after the coup against Erdoğan, I travelled to Turkey to explore Twitter's potential for growth. On my mind were warnings from Twitter's public policy team, who navigated constant threats of suppression from the government. I landed in Istanbul with a potential overland escape route to Bulgaria (in case of a coup), a laptop cleared of company data (in case of my detention) and a bodyguard waiting at the airport. It triggered flashbacks to my 'hostile environment' training as a foreign correspondent.

My naive hope was that Twitter could stand up for digital civil rights while also increasing its public utility to Turkish citizens. But I found no good options for the company. Twitter could go into stealth mode, focus on safe chatter about football and game shows and not antagonise Erdoğan. Or it could push back against 'networked authoritarianism' even if it damaged Twitter's business interests. In 2020, seven years after Gezi Park, Twitter cracked down on thousands of fake accounts with links to the AK Troll network.

There was a remarkable globalisation of 'networked authoritarianism' in the years after Duterte and Erdoğan exposed it to global scrutiny. In 2018, at least 48 regimes used covert networks of social media accounts to 'steer public opinion, spread misinformation, and undermine critics'. By 2021, the Oxford Internet Institute reckoned that 81 countries had taken part in online propaganda and covert influence campaigns.

Networked authoritarianism spawned its own economy. 'Disinformation as a service' became a growth industry, with close to 50 governments partnering with private 'strategic communications' firms to spread 'computational propaganda'. Like any other internet-enabled economy, there is constant innovation in the technology of autocracy.

China was a leading innovator in information warfare, perfecting a model of 'smart authoritarianism' at home and abroad. In May 2021, the Oxford Internet Institute and the Associated Press documented 26,879 Twitter accounts that amplified posts from Chinese diplomats or state media. Over on YouTube during the summer of 2022, more than 10,000 channels were removed for engaging in 'coordinated influence operations linked to China'.[11]

A key innovation in networked propaganda was targeted disruption through 'sock puppet' accounts, which impersonate real individuals or simulate genuine grassroots activity. In 2016, a 'troll factory' operated by Russia's Internet Research Agency organised an anti-Muslim protest in Texas. The rally in Houston was promoted by a fake Facebook page called Heart of Texas, operated by a Russian agent in the heart of St Petersburg.

Networked authoritarianism has filled the vacuum left by the decline of the pre-internet mass media. Back then, Noam Chomsky described the media elite's capacity to shape public opinion as 'manufactured consent'. Today, the bots and trolls are in the business of 'manufacturing consensus'. Covert networks create a bandwagon effect, transforming fringe ideas into mainstream opinion.

Networked authoritarians have mastered the dark art of 'censorship through noise'. Instead of explicitly suppressing dissenting voices, they can overwhelm them with an avalanche of falsehood and anonymised intimidation. Censorship through noise can take the form of 'patriotic trolling', where self-organising allies of the regime take it upon themselves to target specific groups, such as women journalists, with abuse, false allegations and exposure of their private data.

Censorship through noise is designed to increase the cost of dissent but also create a corrosive nihilism in public opinion. The goal is, as Peter Pomerantsev puts it in *This Is Not Propaganda*, to 'surround audiences with so much cynicism about anybody's motives, that they lose faith in the possibility of an alternative'. With this critical shift, the world moves from overload and disorder into a third stage of information crisis. When we start to believe that everybody is lying, only the liars can win.

Way back in 1951, in *The Origins of Totalitarianism*, Hannah

Arendt wrote about the conditions that make people vulnerable to despots, describing 'an ever-changing, incomprehensible world' in which the masses would simultaneously 'believe everything and nothing, think that everything was possible and that nothing was true'. With striking foresight, Arendt saw the destruction of our shared reality as the stepping stone for a new form of authoritarian elite. The lesson was not lost on the autocrats and the tribal populists. They would come to have a better understanding of platforms like Twitter than those of us who mistakenly believed social media to be an inherently democratic force. We got carried away by the online effervescence of 'Yes, We Can'. They would find their own revolutionary credo: 'So Can We'.

Humans in the Loop

A very good friend of mine once made a big, audacious decision to quit his job in journalism over a matter of principle. I asked what he was going to do next. 'I'm going to walk the earth,' he replied.

Movie fans will recognise the line from *Pulp Fiction*, when the mob hitman played by Samuel L. Jackson says he's done with killing. He intends to walk the earth, like Caine, the hero of the old TV show *Kung Fu*. 'Just walk from place to place, meet people, get into adventures.'

After leaving Twitter, I had a hankering for walking the earth. For close to a decade I had been selling solutions. I could now see the unconscious bias this had created. As an entrepreneur and tech executive it had been in my interest to assume the innate goodness of the internet. I had failed to imagine the corrupting power of social technologies in the hands of people who want to see the world burn.

In 2017 it was time to stop pitching and start listening to people with bigger imaginations. I had seen the role of technology in accelerating the information crisis. Now I wanted to explore its potential to end it. That meant I had to seek out people smarter than me, who had fallen in love with the problem to be solved rather than some predetermined solution.

For months, I attended summits and hackathons and working groups and 'unconferences' with no fixed agendas. I felt a sense of belonging in the emerging 'trust movement' filled with librarians and teachers, disinformation researchers and reformed 'fake news' peddlers, first-time entrepreneurs and hard-bitten founders, tech-junkie journalists and news-junkie technologists.

'The early fever of moral panic has abated, and attention is moving from symptoms to cause,'[1] I wrote in the US media journal *Nieman Reports* in spring 2017. 'And so begins the sober, purposeful work of rebuilding trust in the world's information supplies.'

The fledgling trust movement was broadly divided in two. Some were focused on the immediate challenge of containing 'information disorder', the definition Claire Wardle introduced at a summit at Harvard University in February 2017. Others were working on potential fixes for the broken algorithmic systems polarising our public discourse. I was a strong supporter of the first group, but increasingly found myself drawn to the second.

One of my lightbulb encounters at that Harvard summit was with Tristan Harris, a former Google design ethicist. He had delivered a hit TED Talk about the purposely addictive systems which stole our attention, and coined the snappy mantra Time Well Spent to describe the alternative.

He approached me after my presentation at the summit and diagnosed the sickness at the heart of the attention economy with soft-spoken clarity. The original sin of the information crisis was the business model of advertising, he said, which set up a race-to-the-bottom of our brain stem to hijack our minds. Tristan pointed out that every feature of our broken information systems had been a design choice by a human. What design choices do we need to make, I wondered, to fix things?

Tristan's message soon began to resonate with a broad audience and echo the core concerns of a developing backlash against Big Tech platforms. I was also drawn to the work of Tim Wu, the former US government advisor and legal scholar we heard from a little earlier in our journey. 'When people begin to believe they are being ill-used, whether overloaded, fooled, tricked or purposely manipulated,' he wrote in his book *The Attention Merchants*, 'the reaction can be severe and long-lasting enough to have serious commercial consequences and require a significant reinvention of approach.'

Internet citizens were taking matters into their own hands. One in ten people were blocking advertising by the end of 2016. Some were taking more control over their newsfeeds. 'Many active internet users now see themselves as editors,' said the Reuters Institute Digital News Report in 2017, 'balancing and comparing multiple sources, multiple editorial judgments, and even multiple algorithms.'[2]

You could see the hunger for personal agency in the popularity of apps that helped people improve diet, exercise, sleep and mental health. In these behavioural shifts I could see the arc of an alternative future in which the attention economy gave way to an intention economy and the internet would, once again, amplify our best intentions, not our worst instincts.

But not in 2017. The populist wave driving demand for 'alternative facts' had not dissipated. It had grown more powerful. The internet-enabled 'revolt of the public' was still sweeping through liberal democracies across the globe. If you walked the earth in 2017, you could see the crisis of trust was not over. It had only just begun.

Democracy wasn't dying in darkness, as the *Washington Post* had declared after the 2016 election. It was blinded by the incandescent rage of newsfeeds. The rage was not an accidental glitch in the system; it had been a design choice by smart humans with fixed mindsets. That's the biggest lesson I learned on my travels in 2017.

When I returned home my brain was buzzing with questions. What if we could build a purpose-driven newsfeed from scratch? What if we could offer citizens an escape from algorithmic manipulation? Storyful had pioneered curation of social media content by humans. Now we could use algorithms to direct the best-quality journalism instead to humans.

The more I came to understand the algorithms of the newsfeeds, the easier it seemed to rewire them. Rapid advances in machine learning could put control of the newsfeed into the hands of citizens. Like those apps for diet, sleep and exercise, we could build a personal news assistant that plugged gaps in your knowledge and enriched your information diet. There would be no advertising. The algorithm would be designed to empower people, not addict them.

As luck would have it, my friend and former Storyful colleague Áine Kerr was on a similar voyage of discovery. She was managing Facebook's partnerships with news publishers and was ready for her next adventure. Together we created a laboratory to test the concept of a purpose-driven newsfeed. By March of 2019 we had created a new company called Kinzen, and launched its first product.

Some of our friends described the Kinzen app as 'Spotify for news', which wasn't the worst comparison. Members of the Kinzen community paid a monthly fee for a newsfeed they had control of. The app delivered personalised collections of content from the open web, not unlike playlists, and gave people an interface to actively shape their feed. One of the earliest demands from members was the power to set a news routine that fit the 'rhythm of my life' (to use a quote from an early tester).

Kinzen got off to a strong start, but immediately faced a challenge. We could only curate content that was freely available on the open web. Our members were frustrated they couldn't access content from news publishers they already subscribed to. Without a licensing deal with all the major publishers, the Kinzen app could not meet the needs of our members.

We learned important lessons from the Kinzen app. To compete with the social media newsfeed, you must offer people more than control of the feed. You must start with the habits they have, not the ones you would like them to have. Give them the power to change.

But the Kinzen app showed it could be done; you could build a newsfeed that put citizens in control. There was an alternative to newsfeeds which imprisoned us in our base instincts. There was a way to harness AI to enhance human agency. What we proved at Kinzen in 2019 feels more relevant than ever today.

By the time we realised the Kinzen app would not be a commercial hit, our plan B had emerged, thanks to the great leap forward in artificial intelligence. In 2017 Google released the first 'transformer'. This was the architecture that would be used to develop large language models (LLMs). Then, in 2018 Google released an open-source transformer model called BERT, which put immense power in the hands of a small start-up like Kinzen.

BERT gave Kinzen's journalists and engineers a precise understanding of patterns in vast reservoirs of online content and conversations. It was like having an X-ray of language, spotting hidden connections between words and people, places and things. The machine helped us more accurately translate between languages, and interpret the accent, intonation and dialect of the spoken word.

We soon discovered the machine needed the guidance of skilled humans. Former Storyful editor Shane Creevy joined Kinzen, becoming the 'human in the loop' of our AI systems. Shane found that the machine struggled with connections which came naturally to humans. He called this the 'Brooklyn Beckham' problem, after watching the machine stumble over the name of the son of British football legend David Beckham. The AI couldn't understand how the New York borough and the surname of the famous sportsman might fit in the same category. 'Just as editors need better algorithms,' Shane would say, 'algorithms need better editors.'[3]

We soon found an unexpected application for this upgraded version of the 'human algorithm'. One day in 2020 I had a phone call from a former Twitter colleague who was now working for another big technology platform. She was looking for help. She needed high-quality analysis of dangerous content on the platform she worked for. Was this something Kinzen was equipped to do? I immediately said yes.

In developing the Kinzen app, we had created a feedback loop between human editors and AI to improve the quality of data powering our recommendation system. After that phone call from my friend, we realised this 'human in the loop' approach could be used to better understand the dangers hidden in those angry newsfeeds.

By 2020, Big Tech companies were investing heavily in disruption of disinformation campaigns and extremist networks. They relied on armies of outsourced content moderators, which was a blunt-force response to a nuanced threat. But as platforms tried to build automated detection systems, they struggled with the complexities of language and culture. They needed to better understand the parts of the world they previously neglected. Which is where Kinzen could help.

As late as 2021, 87 per cent of Facebook's spending on the detection of disinformation was applied to English-language content,[4] despite the fact that only 9 per cent of its users spoke English. Facebook failed to develop machine learning models crucial to content moderation in Hindi and Bengali, both among the top ten most spoken languages in the world. Facebook 'was everywhere but its content moderation systems were nowhere close',[5] said the headline on a story by tech news site *Wired*.

In 2018, Facebook algorithms supercharged the spread of violent rhetoric against the Rohingya people of Myanmar, triggering a real-world campaign of rape, murder and ethnic cleansing. Facebook had 'turned into a beast', a UN investigator later said.[6] The platform was warned of the risk as far back as March 2014, when 18 million Burmese-speaking people were using Facebook but just one Burmese-speaking content reviewer (based in Ireland) was working there.

Kinzen offered global platforms a chance to improve the accuracy of content moderation in places where it was a matter of life or death. We built a team of editors fluent in the languages overlooked by the platforms and plugged into the politics and culture of societies vulnerable to internet-enabled violence.

Artificial intelligence gave these human analysts superpowers. Using open-source technologies, Kinzen's engineers built machine learning systems tailored to the needs of our editors in different countries and languages. Core components included automatic speech recognition (ASR), which scaled the analysis of podcasts, a particularly tough challenge for moderators. We eventually built our own ASR system and developed a language model to improve the accuracy of the transcripts our editors depended on.

Equipped with these tools, our editors could constantly improve their understanding of 'dog-whistle' language used to coordinate potential real-world harm. In a golden feedback loop, the editor and machine continually improved the data sets tracking the most dangerous online networks.

Kinzen's 'human in the loop' approach helped solve persistent problems for automated moderation systems. They struggled with recently modernised languages like Turkish, which had vowels and consonants that bewildered the standard AI systems. Automated moderation systems were stumped by the rich variety of dialects within Arabic, struggling to distinguish a Moroccan speaking Arabic from a Saudi Arabian. Standard models were completely baffled by the rapid switching between Hindi and English that defines so much public conversation in India.

More importantly, the Kinzen system helped interpret the language of systematic human rights violations, such as violence against women. Our analysts studied misogynistic narratives in multiple languages, including Arabic, decoding abusive language to better understand the risk of real-world harm. On a daily basis we would detect new and evolving hashtags and phrases used to coordinate abuse. We discovered the threat was not always in the word but in the context. A word casually thrown about in one language or dialect might be a mild insult or benign slang but in others it was a code used by organised campaigns to intimidate vulnerable groups and ultimately incite real-world violence against them.

The more Kinzen dug through the hidden layers of hate and manipulation, the more my assumptions about information disorder were challenged. I had expected our work for the platforms would be focused exclusively on finding extreme content. But the real problem was the covert behaviour of extremist groups who gamed the viral dynamics of our newsfeeds.

The more violent the group's intent, the more they sought to hide in plain sight. We discovered that neo-Nazi groups were using playlists of underground skinhead music to recruit soldiers in European defence forces. The Islamic State (ISIS) used a form of a cappella religious hymn called a *nasheed* to turbo-charge the spread of its message on social media.

Kinzen took an unintended route, but realised its vision. We proved that purpose-driven technology could help combat the worst symptoms of the information crisis. Human design choices built a system that could disrupt the hidden architects of information warfare. We helped Big Tech companies be more accurate and proportionate in their content moderation, closing down the supply of the most harmful misinformation and violent content where it mattered most. But we knew those root causes of the crisis were beyond any technology fix. Platforms might limit the supply of lies and hate but the appetite for forbidden knowledge had intensified. The viral contagion had spread. The darkest fringes of the internet had seized control of their host. A moment would arrive when all we had was the internet, and the remaining boundaries between the real world and the digital realm would dissolve.

Behind the Funhouse Mirror

There's always something to be scared of, but the worst kind of dread is the fear of nothing; the kind of absence imposed on us during the pandemic years. The lights went out in the world and we were suddenly alone, left to navigate the darkness through the screens of our digital devices.

I discovered vertigo during the pandemic. At night, with increasing frequency, my brain would startle me awake at the moment I was about to fall or jump from a great height. A couple of months after the final lockdown I travelled to Singapore for a wedding. On the evening before the ceremony, the happy couple invited us to their apartment, 85 floors up. As I stepped on to their balcony I caught sight of the narrow canyon separating us from the next building and my knees buckled.

When we lost our sense of time and place many of us lost our minds a little bit too. Vertigo is a recurring theme in Naomi

Klein's *Doppelganger*, which explores the parallel information sphere which flourished during lockdown. This 'mirror world' of conspiracy thinking and online extremism reflects a distorted form of mainstream reality. That pandemic vertigo kicked in when the boundaries between the real world and its warped likeness vanished. Vertigo, Klein explains, 'invades when the world we thought we knew no longer holds'.[1]

Klein's book crystallised my own jumbled attempts to make sense of the pandemic. My wishful thinking had kicked in early. When we were finally reunited with our future, I told myself, something better would emerge from nothing. Instead, the world of dark fantasy expanded to fill the void in our lives, surfacing as reckless rumours in our group chats or the conspiratorial ranting of a once-stable relative or friend. The membrane separating alternative worlds dissolved, and the mirror world seemed to exert a greater gravitational force.

There were two distinct stages in the evolution of the mirror world. The first was the shift in the centre of gravity in our social media universe. The algorithms reduced the value of platforms like Twitter as places to connect and build community, and handed a megaphone to those on the darkest fringes of the internet. They helped a toxic minority colonise the open expanse of our newsfeed and overwhelm the places we used to connect with friends and family.

In 2024, a team of psychologists from New York University published a study called *Inside the Funhouse Mirror Factory*, which revealed that online conversations are dominated by a surprisingly tiny but extremely vocal minority. Only 3 per cent of active social media accounts were defined as toxic, but those accounts produced 33 per cent of all content in the feed. Seventy-four per cent of all online conflicts were started in just 1 per cent of communities. Eighty per cent of misinformation was shared by 0.1 per cent of users.

What's ruining the internet for us, said the report, is not just the amplification of the most extreme voices but the muting of the 'moderate, the nuanced and the boringly reasonable'.[2] Regular people looked at their feeds and started to feel outnumbered. They went quiet or self-censored, and ceded the conversation to the extremists. Social media algorithms helped the fringe become mainstream and the mainstream feel like a fringe.

The second stage of evolution for the mirror world was to acquire a human face. The most compelling conspiracy theorists in the mirror world are no longer the anonymous internet trolls. The age of the influencer has conditioned us to trust the smarter, fitter and funnier version of ourselves. Social media algorithms reward the performance of a curious form of authenticity and intimacy, which deepen the bonds of parasocial trust we form with our favourite lifestyle guru, or conspiracist.

Renée DiResta explored the world of conspiracy-minded influencers in her book *Invisible Rulers: The People Who Turn Lies into Reality*. She groups them into handy categories, such as Generals and Propagandists, and Reflex Contrarians, who are 'just asking questions'. But it is the Guru that intrigues me most. The Guru offers 'forbidden knowledge' that will make you healthier and happier, if you follow them down the narrow lane of fitness and wellness into the foothills of conspiracy. In her book *Cultish*, Amanda Montell says the goal of this aspirational coach is 'to make your people feel like they have all the answers, while the rest of the world is not just foolish, but inferior'.

The lockdowns turned the outside world into a place of danger, but we did not feel that danger equally. Lockdowns imposed disproportionate suffering on those already suffering ill health in body or mind, clinging to precarious incomes, or enduring confinement within already confined spaces. Most of us clung to the safety of the public health narrative and its underlying medical consensus. But for others, there was more safety and meaning in the forbidden knowledge of the gurus.

The guru's moment finally arrived when COVID lockdowns erased distinctions between our real and online identities. The pandemic became a 'conspiracy singularity', wrote journalist Anna Merlan for *Vice* in 2020, a time when 'many conspiracy communities are suddenly meeting and merging, in a melting pot of unimaginable density'.[3]

During the pandemic, we saw a remarkable confluence inside the mirror world. The algorithms started to expand the reach of content creators already deeply embedded in conspiracy-minded communities. The fierce conviction of these fringe influencers attracted new audiences at a time of radical uncertainty. Meanwhile, successful lifestyle influencers without any previous history of fringe beliefs started to feed the hunger for alternative facts. They found themselves performing for the mirror world algorithm, and dragging their communities with them.

These dynamic feedback loops were best captured by the Trinity, a concept developed by Renée DiResta. The Trinity is a feedback loop of social media influencer, algorithm and crowd. The influencer produces viral content for the algorithm. The algorithm sends the influencer a crowd. The crowd becomes a tight-knit tribe, demanding more viral emotion from the influencer. The influencer becomes more extreme, and the cycle repeats itself. This unholy Trinity, DiResta says, 'has reallocated power, transformed our understanding of the world, and impacted our capacity for collective action'.[4]

The process is best explained by one remarkable conspiracy theory and the influencer who created it. Amazing Polly was a Canadian commentator who built a loyal following with video essays about the evils of the New World Order. She had appeared on my radar when she featured Storyful in a video about the role of 'fake' fact-checking organisations in the globalist plot to rule the world. In the years that followed, I developed a grudging respect for her absolute consistency.

Amazing Polly gained a wider audience as a promoter of QAnon, the catch-all conspiracy theory involving a shadowy 'deep-state' and child sex trafficking by high-ranking politicians. QAnon made the leap from mirror world to mainstream conversation during the pandemic. On 14 June 2020, Polly shifted into a higher gear with a tweet about high-priced cabinets sold by a company called Wayfair. The furniture had girls' names, and Polly suggested this was a front for human trafficking.

The baseless theory eventually caught fire on TikTok and Instagram, where influencers who usually posted about health and wellness racked up likes and followers by repeating the Wayfair conspiracy. The algorithm saw the surge as a signal to surface the theory to more people. By mid-July the term Wayfair had generated 4.4 million engagements on Instagram and spawned the viral hashtag #SaveTheChildren. Before she was kicked off YouTube, Amazing Polly had 375,000 subscribers on the platform.[5] More importantly, she had helped extend the borders of the mirror world to a wider group of influencers.

In our work at Kinzen, we saw a 'conspirituality' movement take shape on Instagram. It emerged from a network of influencers who talked of yoga, clean living and New Age consciousness. This was a community pre-disposed to natural remedies and scepticism of established medicine, which helps explain its dramatic detour into pandemic conspiracy.

The 'conspirituality' influencers eventually drifted from talk of mask mandates, vaccines and the 'scamdemic' into fevered conversations about human trafficking and satanic paedophiles. In time, the QAnon conspiracy theory about a villainous 'deep state' would become a thread connecting supporters of Donald Trump from the far right and vegan influencers promoting organic juice cleanses.

In France, we tracked a surge in COVID conspiracy theories among fortune tellers. They were united by a shared belief that the French government was colluding with big pharmaceutical companies to push harmful vaccines. In one video, found by our French editor on Telegram (a messaging app), a clairvoyant predicted the 'vaccinated will be taken to another planet in the near future'.

French fortune tellers, like so many other conspiracy theorists, started to use Algospeak, or codewords that would evade content moderation systems. Kinzen tracked the evolution of a rich glossary of slang such as *dictature piquouse*, or 'prick dictatorship', used to describe vaccination programmes. In Germany, anti-vaccine activists used the word 'schlumpfen' ('to smurf') as a code word for 'impfen' (to vaccinate), embracing cartoon characters as a novel means of evading detection.

Pandemic restrictions galvanised a wild assortment of alliances. The Querdenken movement in Germany united countercultural leftists and far-right activists in opposition to lockdowns and vaccine mandates. Anti-vax stickers began to appear on city streets in the UK, Europe and Australia bearing the name of the White Rose movement. The original White Rose movement rallied opposition to the Nazis in pre-war Germany. Any fringe group with an ambition to become a global franchise saw COVID as a golden opportunity.

Before the pandemic, I had little sympathy with those who fell under the spell of the Gurus and Contrarians. But as the world closed around us, I could feel the magnetic power of secret knowledge. COVID was a decisive breach for those dangling precariously on the edge of established reality. Mirror world became a place of sanctuary for those suffering an unfair share of economic hardship and inequality, offering righteous anger at elites who profited from misery and suppressed the true nature of the world. Conspiracists, wrote Naomi Klein, 'get the facts wrong but often get the feelings right'. The alternative information sphere offered the comfort of consistency, but also an uncomfortable historical truth.

During the pandemic, the European Commission published a working definition of a conspiracy theory as 'the belief that certain events or situations are secretly manipulated behind the scenes by powerful forces with negative intent.' This certainly covered every crackpot mirror world fantasy, but also every real conspiracy of modern times. From the cover-up of tobacco's deadly impact, to the lies that justified war in Iraq, to the conspiracy of silence that led to the financial crisis, all the way to the Jeffrey Epstein scandal, you would be mad not to believe in the potential for secret manipulation by powerful forces. 'Believing that does not make you a conspiracy theorist,' Naomi Klein said of the Commission definition; 'it makes you a serious observer of politics and history'.

There was no shared public space in which to sort good-faith scepticism from bad-faith conspiracism during the crisis, only social media channels which forced you to choose sides. The authorities struggled with the inherent uncertainties of an unprecedented medical crisis and stuck rigidly to the scientific fact of the moment, rather than build trust in an evolving scientific process, creating a jarring collision of official narratives.

At first, mask wearing was actively discouraged. A few months later, it became mandatory. The World Health Organization dismissed reports that COVID originated in a lab in Wuhan, and online platforms classified such stories as misinformation. By early 2021, more plausible claims of a 'lab leak' emerged. Facebook reversed its policy, no longer defining the lab-leak story as a false claim.

Each fracture in the official narrative created the space for forbidden knowledge to take hold. For some of those hardest hit by pandemic restrictions, suspicion of the experts turned to outright hostility. Science could not keep up with the pace of disillusionment. Experts were making tough judgement calls in private and under pressure. Too often, what was being labelled misinformation was simply unsettled science.

Systems built on institutional consensus, in science, media and government, were incapable of separating false information from legitimate scientific uncertainty that was eventually vindicated. Vaccinated people could transmit the virus. Outdoor transmission of the virus was overstated. Prolonged school closings did have a negative impact on children. The tone of official communications often seemed to harden with unearned conviction when challenged. This both restricted the space for legitimate dissent and good faith debate, and amplified the magnetic power of the mirror world.

I found myself walking in the shoes of those who craved secret knowledge, who imagined hidden patterns in pools of noise, who found comfort in the right kind of friends and the right kind of enemies. The pity I had laid at the feet of the conspiracy-minded was now reflected back on me.

As the rollout of vaccines approached, Kinzen assigned a small team to work for the Irish health service, anticipating the 'information gaps' that were about to open up. Our job was not to recommend content be taken down. It was to identify conversations that needed to be engaged with, and allow offical communications to evolve with public concern rather than harden against them Our experience told us organised campaigns of misinformation would be quicker to fill the void than official sources.

In 2015, conspiracy theories had triggered a significant drop in vaccinations in Ireland against the human papillomavirus (HPV), the cause of almost all cases of cervical cancer. As the COVID vaccines became available, we helped health communicators keep one step ahead of global disinformation tropes, such as stories that 'the jab' would turn children into 'walking bioweapons' or videos claiming empty hospital waiting rooms were proof the crisis was exaggerated. Kinzen's detection of an internet-fuelled falsehood about vaccines and women's fertility enabled a quick response from the health service and a marked decline in false fertility rumours.

Our work was influenced directly by Renée DiResta, who had created a team of researchers to support health authorities during the vaccine rollout in the US. To me, these efforts felt like a turning point. For the first time, we had recognised the limitations of content moderation in a moment of radical uncertainty. Rather than simply trying to suppress misinformation, democratic institutions needed to respond to the fears which fuelled false narratives. The facts that bind society at a moment of crisis must evolve faster than the lies which divide it.

I was proud of Kinzen's work with the Irish health service, and later wrote about the lessons we had learned from the vaccine rollout. The single most potent source of scepticism at a moment like this, I observed, 'is the unanswered concerns of citizens living through an era of constant change and overwhelming quantities of information'.

Others saw our work through a very different lens. In the US, conservatives and anti-vax activists mobilised against those combating the spread of COVID misinformation, particularly Renée DiResta. She was targeted by the people she had described as Invisible Rulers (and their political allies in Washington) with sweeping allegations that she was the leader of a 'censorship industrial complex' which sought to silence conservative voices online.

In Ireland, those who were critical of the official handling of the pandemic were also critical of Kinzen's work with the health service. Legitimate online questions about the project quickly gave way to false accusations that we were spying on government critics. A campaign of sustained online intimidation quickly overwhelmed Kinzen staff, culminating in online attacks on some of our family members and a chat-room promise that I would hang for my 'crimes'. We knew the abuse was the work of a tiny minority, but in the empty space of pandemic life, the noise was deafening.

These were the days when the vertigo was crippling and it was impossible to see beyond the savage distortions of the mirror world. But the pandemic offered up a truth that had been hidden for too long. We had treated the physical and online worlds as separate dimensions, where different rules applied. We had ceded social media to the loudest voices and told ourselves this was not real life. We had surrendered the spaces where our shared reality was being created.

I kept thinking about Jimmy Wales and his challenge to assume good faith in others. The Invisible Rulers had no capacity for mutual respect or sincere engagement. But as we became hardened to their assault on our shared reality, we sacrificed good-faith dialogue with fellow citizens who were sincerely disillusioned and genuinely excluded. Without safe places to disagree, we struggled to sort legitimate dissent from manufactured falsehoods. As we lost our capacity for trust, we became less trustworthy.

But there were also exceptional moments of hope, when the pandemic reminded us what good faith felt like. In our Zoom calls and group chats with friends and families, we found spaces filled with mutual care and respect. We met the fears of others with compassion not rejection. We proved that we could still assume good faith. What we needed to rebuild was the shared spaces in which this was possible, in which it was safe to be wrong, to be flawed, to be human.

Amanda Montell has a beautiful passage in *Cultish* about how we protect ourselves from the gravitational pull of online fanaticism. 'Above all else, it's important to maintain a vigilant twinkle in your eye,' she advises, 'knowing that at the end of the day, when you come home or close the app, strip off the group's linguistic uniform, and start speaking like yourself again, you are not all in.'[6]

In the years after the pandemic, the networked authoritarians, internet trolls and conspiracy-peddling gurus became stronger than ever. They won the hearts and minds of people who no longer believed in the fairness of the real world. But the rest of us learned the power of that vigilant twinkle. The Invisible Rulers won power by promising us certainty. We know that was their biggest lie.

The Road to Nowhere

I crossed paths with Elon Musk again in 2022, in a roundabout sort of way. It was the morning of 5 October and I was on a train into Dublin city, staring at my phone. My feed overflowed with commentary about Musk's decision to move forward with the acquisition of Twitter after months of U-turns, legal wrangling and characteristic bombast.

After leaving the train station, I took a familiar route, turning left down the alleyway by the church and right onto the street that led to Twitter's international headquarters. As I passed the office, I remembered the day we celebrated its official opening and felt something like bereavement, quickly followed by a chill of anxiety for friends that still worked for the company. Winter was coming for Twitter.

I walked on for a few minutes before climbing the steps of a co-working space where the Kinzen team was gathering for a hastily planned all-hands meeting. On the day we digested the news that

Elon was buying Twitter, Áine and I were also breaking the news that Spotify had bought Kinzen.

The second time around, I had no regrets about selling the company I helped build. Spotify felt like the perfect fit. Kinzen's core expertise was the analysis of podcasts, and Spotify had been our most important partner for several years. Deep reserves of trust and respect were built up on both sides. It helped that I had only ever had a crush on two big technology companies. One was Twitter and the other was Spotify.

In the months to come, even as I nestled into Spotify's Scandinavian coziness, I found it hard to concentrate on anything but the wilful destruction of Twitter. Shortly after taking control, Elon Musk sent an email to the company's staff demanding they sign on to an 'extremely hardcore' culture, or leave. 'Only exceptional performance will constitute a passing grade.'[1]

I have come to see Musk's purchase of Twitter as the beginning of the end of the world's first information war, and victory for the dark soul of the internet. The purchase seemed like an act of vanity, bordering on insanity. But it would deliver an extraordinary return on investment for Musk and all that he had come to represent in the world.

In this moment, technology and culture fused together, and the mirror world secured enormous power in the physical realm, all across the democratic world. Authoritarians, oligarchs and right-wing populists harnessed the vibe shifts of the post-pandemic internet. They pulled at the common thread of resentment against liberal elites and 'wokeness' and immigration and censorship.

They tapped into the alienation of the digital natives and spoke out loud the unspoken grievances of gender, race and class.

Theirs was a conflicted revolution. It had echoes of the counterculture of the late 1960s, which had been propelled by competing energies. There was the spirit of the Nowhere Revolution, which wanted to destroy the old order and escape the past. It thrived among street-fighters, outlaws and outsiders, and was galvanised by the disdain of its enemies. The second energy was the Somewhere Revolution, which was subversive and transgressive but also playful and idealistic. It transformed citizens into movements, and offered an inclusive vision of the future.

I would argue that the last half century of rapid technological progress has been a continuous battle between Nowhere and Somewhere revolutions. There is a pure Nowhere energy in the frontier spirit of Silicon Valley, with its celebration of misfits and crazy ones and its desire for escape. The playful subversion of Somewhere was built into the fabric of the open web, decentralising power to everyone and encouraging collaboration with everyone.

When these competing energies are in balance there is both disruption and creation, and we see great leaps forward, such as personal computing and the World Wide Web. But when one overwhelms the other we experience a breakdown, such as the concentration of power in a handful of Silicon Valley platforms.

There was a blend of Nowhere and Somewhere in that internet-led rebellion Martin Gurri called the 'fifth wave'. The revolt of the public manifested in a wide spectrum of populist rebellions, where anger against the old elites was often matched by youthful idealism and solidarity. But this counterculture was primed for exploitation by dark internet sub-cultures and networked authoritarians. The algorithms of the attention economy led the revolt of the public down the road to Nowhere.

Elon Musk is the living embodiment of this Nowhere Revolution. He spent years marinating in the meme world of the internet fringe and was out in front of Silicon Valley's ideological pivot away from liberal democracy. Musk poured money and manic energy into far-right political insurgencies across the liberal democratic world.

For all Musk's dominance, the intellectual godfather of the Nowhere Revolution is Trump whisperer Steve Bannon. He shaped the battlefield of the information war, famously calling for the defeat of traditional media by 'flooding the zone with shit'. He was also the first populist leader to turn internet sub-culture into a mainstream political force.

In its embryonic stage, the MAGA movement absorbed the transgressive and acerbic ethic of the internet fringe. Bannon was a keen student of Gamergate, the coordinated online abuse of women video game developers and journalists in 2014. Gamergate knit together strands of male alienation and misogyny in the shit-posting, meme-making fringe forums like 4chan, and produced a movement that would become known as the 'alt-right'.

In her remarkable book *Kill All Normies*, Angela Nagle describes Gamergate as 'the galvanising issue that drew up the battle lines of the culture war for a younger generation'. It propelled online celebrities like Milo Yiannopoulos and Mike Cernovich into the spotlight, and with the help of Steve Bannon seeded an alternative online media network that would give MAGA its countercultural energy. Charlie Warzel once observed that Gamergate's 'most powerful legacy was as proof of concept of how to wage a post-truth information war'.[2]

Just like the left-wing revolutionaries of the 1960s, the 'alt-right' understood that politics is downwind of culture, as one of the movement's heroes Andrew Breitbart once put it. The 'alt-right' relished the scorn of its enemies, just as it drew energy from its ridicule of them. The internet insurgents anticipated an age of online polarisation where one faction feeds off the extreme behaviour of another. Social media platforms provide a never-ending supply of the most absurd, unhinged and extreme behaviour by your opponents. To use an extremely online figure of speech, the 'alt-right' were expert 'nutpickers'.

Over time, the algorithms of social media helped galvanise the internet insurgents into more extreme and disciplined factions through a process known as algorithmic sorting. If a particular topic is polarising for some in the faction, it will soon become polarising for all. Every issue is a do-or-die test of the group's survival. This process erases the moderating influences of real life because it raises the cost of disagreement within a group.

The Nowhere Revolution rewards extremism, but also the charisma of the renegade influencer. This helps explain the outsized influence of white nationalist Nick Fuentes on young American conservatives. His brand of smirking high-energy sarcasm gives him the aura of an edgy internet celebrity, buying him entry into mainstream communities that came of age on the post-Gamergate internet. 'A tone of grievance and ironic provocation becomes prominent background noise,' says Alex McPhee-Browne, a close observer of the far right, 'moving the marginal toward the mainstream.'[3]

There is one intriguing glitch in Musk's embrace of this Nowhere Revolution. He is despised by its godfather Steve Bannon, who in 2023 called Musk a complete phoney and a stooge for China. Bannon's rage fascinates me. After all, Musk is the fulfilment of the prophecy that Steve Bannon had divined in Gamergate. Musk chose to immerse himself in the meme-making, shit-posting swamps of the post-Gamergate internet. He would be a champion for the keyboard warriors of the counterculture, building them the ultimate combat arena. It was Musk, not Bannon, who delivered the win. He owns the zone Bannon flooded with shit.

The Nowhere Revolution may have been shaped by personalities but it was built on platforms. The trolls and authoritarians could not have won the information war without the complicity of the major technology companies. When you build systems which magnify humanity's worst instincts you get Gamergate, algorithmic sorting, funhouse mirrors and neo-fascist celebrities like Nick Fuentes. You could argue the platforms were unaware of this toxic harvest, at first. But in time, they all went 'extremely hardcore', ploughing ahead like banks that were too big to fail.

Musk took this broken system and developed it to its illogical conclusion at X. The pay-for-play influence, autoplay video nasties, nutpicking-at-scale, hustle bros, tech bros, crypto bros and general pervasive bro-ness created the most dramatic identity shift in the history of social media.

As Twitter became X, and conversations on social media become more actively hostile, women were often forced to disengage. In 2016, the population of Twitter was evenly split between male and female, according to the Pew Research Center. Other surveys found women tended to be more active tweeters, particularly outside the United States. Ten years later, there was only one woman for every two men on X, making it the social media platform with the most masculine profile.

The Nowhere Revolution is powered by a confrontational, dominating and zero-sum form of interaction which is reflected in the rise of the internet 'manosphere'. Young men may not actively seek out misogyny or masculine resentment, but it is often wrapped up in content that interests them, like fitness, self-improvement or mental health, or embedded in conversations about the pressure to conform to conflicting expectations of manliness They become easy targets for algorithms feeding off their insecurities, but also entrepreneurial influencers who curdle male resentment into a potent force in the world.

X would become a resonant echo chamber for the right-leaning counterculture that propelled Trump back to the White House. The platform amplified MAGA's alternative media ecosystem, but also a broader vibe-shift in podcasting where loose conversationalists like Joe Rogan and Theo Von created the warmth of tribal belonging through authenticity rather than argument.

Donald Trump was a natural fit for a medium that luxuriated in the sound of its own voice. As election day approached in 2024 he slipped easily into conversations with the stars of this new constellation. In one remarkable chat with Theo Von he seemed genuinely curious about the potency of drugs, asking his host if cocaine was stronger than other narcotics. 'Yeah,' Von responded. 'Cocaine will turn you into a damn owl, homie. You know what I'm saying?' Homie didn't need to know the details. Trump was already a damn owl, wise to the potency of the transgressive dialect of the 'manosphere'.

In the old world, power accrued to elites who owned the important facts. In the attention economy, power belonged to whoever produced the spectacle. Trump controlled the remote control of his nation's attention, serving a long-running reality show. Everything becomes possible when you define what is real.

Support for President Trump in his second term would erode quicker with young voters than other demographic groups. But the scorched-earth assault of this Nowhere Revolution is still carving deep grooves in our collective psyche. The MAGA movement's mastery of the attack meme and the shit-post represents a shift in the ecology of digital life. 'A kind of post-ironic fatalism that was once endemic to seedy message boards has bled into the broader culture,' observed Charlie Warzel. 'Nihilism is now the lingua franca of the internet.'[4]

The rising tide of nihilism overwhelmed every available space in our political discourse. In 2019, Oxford University Press said the 'word of the year' was climate emergency. In 2025, Merriam-Webster's 'word of the year' was slop, the low-quality viral content pumped into our brains by machines.

The shameless cynicism of the internet troll became a form of state propaganda in Washington. In the second Trump administration, official social media accounts celebrated the soothing sounds of prisoners in chains and used AI-generated images to mock Democratic Party leaders. The greater the outrage, the greater the delight of the White House. 'Nowhere in the Constitution does it say we can't post banger memes' was its mocking retort to the critics on X. At a particular high/low point, the troll-in-chief Donald Trump reposted an AI-generated video of him dumping shit on peaceful protestors from a fighter jet.

All of this echoes loudly within the vast coliseum of X, like the roar of a victorious gladiator. But the internet meme is a double-edged sword, as Donald Trump discovered when he went to war with Iran. In the early days of the bombing campaign, the White House reached for its trusty banger memes. In one post, they cut together a scene from the first-person shooter game *Call of Duty*, with slow motion video of missiles exploding on impact.

However, they were quickly outclassed by a mysterious group of online meme-makers who were clearly aligned with the Iranian regime. They used Lego figures and AI-generated rap to ridicule Donald Trump, generating more than a billion views on X in the first month of the war, according to the Institute of

Strategic Dialogue. The masters of the information wars had been schooled. 'A joyless theocracy produces wittier videos than the Trump administration,' said the *Economist*.

For an older generation, such competitive nihilism is a source of mystified shock. But for many digital natives, the burn-it-all-down energy of the Nowhere Revolution is a legitimate response when you have no predictable path to safety or security. The great attraction of the digital world is that it offers Generation Z an environment to experiment with radical change. In the United States, polls show that nearly two-thirds of Gen Z and Millennials think that the only way to build wealth today is through alternative methods like crypto-currencies and prediction markets, which let you wager on any future event or outcome.

Crypto is an attention economy, just like social media, so assets with no inherent utility can be manipulated by emotion and spectacle, driving the value of meme coins with names like Floki, Bonk and Fartcoin. 'When you feel shut out of institutions,' says economist Kyla Scanlon, 'you buy meme coins that turn financial nihilism into a form of cultural expression.'[5]

The descent of digital natives into nihilism should be understood for what it is – a desperate desire to find personal agency in a world that is rigged against you. The longer you feel denied, the more you are conditioned to helplessness in the face of digital manipulation. Young adults are often paralysed by a form of 'algorithmic cynicism' which steals away their willingness to resist or exit systems they know to be exploitative. This is not just apathy, explained researchers from the Harvard Kennedy School in 2025, but a broader cultural mood of submission: 'Fighting the algorithm can feel as futile as tilting at digital windmills.'[6]

I recently came across a data point which changed the way I think about Donald Trump's influence on digital natives. The youngest members of Generation Z were two or three years old when Trump launched his campaign for president in 2015. What these young people know about politics, they have learned from the rise of the MAGA movement. They have no memory of the end of history, no experience of a Somewhere Revolution. With no idea of what has been lost, they must find out for themselves what is worth saving. They appear to be quick learners.

The contamination of our digital lives with nihilism feels like a slow gas leak, which we can trace back to Musk's Twitter takeover in 2022. But there are days when you feel a shuddering breach in our information systems. The algorithmic internet only works if it can sustain its illusion of invincibility and omnipotence. But does this Nowhere world feel sustainable to you?

Ernest Hemingway said bankruptcy happens in two ways: gradually, and then suddenly. As someone who reported on the financial crisis, I see there are strong parallels between the instability of the algorithmic internet and the financial systems of 2007. Once you notice one red light flashing, you immediately see a pattern hiding in plain sight. Just as complex financial products overwhelmed the banking system during the financial crash, the dynamics of artificial virality are propelling the attention economy towards the point of collapse.

There seemed to be a rapid increase in the frequency of the warnings in the final months of 2025. In November, Reuters published an investigation by veteran Facebook-watcher Jeff Horwitz which revealed that 10 per cent of Meta's revenue in 2024 came from adverts for scams, banned goods and other fraudulent activity. That's 15 billion scam ads in the feed every single day, said the report.[7]

In the same month, Elon Musk's X rolled out a new feature revealing the physical location of prominent accounts. It turned out that many well-known accounts focused on American politics were not American at all. One account, called America First, which had almost 70,000 followers and posted things like 'Thumbs up if you're a Trumper who loves God', appeared to be based in Bangladesh.

In December 2025 the world had its first 'scam war' when Thailand bombed compounds in Cambodia on the pretext they were hubs of a global campaign of online fraud. Cambodian crime gangs had been using forced labour in 50 'scam centres' to defraud internet users around the world, according to Amnesty International. The proceeds of the online crime empire was worth roughly half of Cambodia's formal GDP.

In the first quarter of 2026, Meta reported its first ever drop in the number of people using its collection of apps. The corporation blamed internet disruptions in Iran and Russia and pointed to a surge in revenues over the same period. But the company which has come to define the attention economy is showing signs of desperation and self-destruction, pumping increasing amounts of ads and AI slop into our social spaces just as it comes under meaningful scrutiny; Meta is under investigation by Irish regulators for potential 'dark patterns' which prevent people from accessing a feed not based on automated targeting systems.

For those still dependent on the big feed, the rabbit holes will get deeper and darker as the algorithms desperately search for new ways to lock you in. Silicon Valley bosses increasingly use the kind of language we heard from financial executives in 2007. Back then, the CEO of a major US bank was asked about potentially risky deals in an economy exposed to sub-prime loans. 'As long as the music is playing, you've got to get up and dance,' he said. 'We're still dancing.'[8]

How long before the music stops and the Nowhere Revolution loses its algorithmic engine? It's too early for optimism; the nihilism of meme culture will continue to be a powerful force in a world of generational uncertainty. But Elon Musk and his online insurgency have everything to lose if the attention economy collapses under the weight of its own contradictions.

The oligarchs of Silicon Valley seem to have decided they are too big to fail. They might be right. The remaining wild card in our story is the race to build humanity's next, and potentially last, great invention, a superintelligent machine. That story begins with the release of ChatGPT a few weeks after Elon Musk bought Twitter. On this new frontier, the autocrats and authoritarians are telling us a new version of the same old story.

We Are As Gods

I have been making occasional visits to Silicon Valley for almost 30 years but have never quite shaken the disappointment of my first trip there. In 1997, in those early days of the internet gold rush, I drove out of San Francisco on the 101, past the airport and the salt ponds, and waited for lush rolling hills and gleaming tech campuses to magically appear before me like the Emerald City. Instead it was a stubby suburban horizon of office parks and low-slung bungalows all the way to Palo Alto.

On that first visit I was struck by how many people would stress Silicon Valley's mundane qualities, as if deflecting a prospective burglar from their fancy house. An Irish friend who worked for a promising start-up told me that 'the most remarkable thing about Silicon Valley is how unremarkable it is'. Everyone offered the assurance, without any prompting, that in Silicon Valley there are no rules. Which sounded an awful lot like a rule to me.

In 2009 I travelled to California to pitch for investment in

Storyful. I left without a cent but gained a valuable insight. I got a slot to pitch a well-respected internet innovator on the 12-minute walk from his San Francisco gym to his favourite coffee shop. I couldn't take my eyes off his Vibram 'five finger' running shoes, which wrapped around each individual toe. He repeatedly struggled to remember my name as we strolled, but by the time we sat down for pour-over coffee he seemed overwhelmed by the excitement of my personal quest.

That strange, exhilarating dude in the achingly cool coffee shop made me feel we had shared knowledge the world had yet to discover. We were the secret agents of the future. We were the builders and founders and misfits who needed to create our own universe. The memory of the meeting popped into my head while I was reading Peter Thiel's homage to disruptive innovation, *Zero to One*. 'A great company is a conspiracy to change the world,' Thiel wrote: 'when you share your secret, the recipient becomes a fellow conspirator.'[1]

What I came to see in Silicon Valley was a tension between innovation as an egalitarian team sport and the singular obsession of the misfit entrepreneur. Team players rally around the mission. Misfits wanted to build their own world. Over the past decades, that balance has shifted decisively from the communal spirit of the Somewhere Revolution to the outlaw spirit of Nowhere.

The information revolution has always been this creative dance. The internet was both a tool of personal freedom and a platform for community. But communal values would be sidelined by the arrival of the internet gold rush in the mid-1990s.

A well-connected group of techno-utopian libertarians galvanised opposition to government regulation of the new digital frontier.

One of the most colourful and combative was John Perry Barlow, a hippie renaissance man who wrote lyrics for the Grateful Dead before founding the Electronic Frontier Foundation. He was so incensed by proposed internet censorship in 1996 that he dashed off the *Declaration of the Independence of Cyberspace*, warning governments to back off: 'You weary giants of flesh and steel, on behalf of the future, I ask you of the past to leave us alone.'[2]

By now, Silicon Valley was becoming a coherent political project. In 1995, two British media theorists coined the phrase 'Californian ideology' to describe 'the free-wheeling spirit of the hippies and the entrepreneurial zeal of the yuppies'. The nineties libertarians were a unique fusion of counterculture and anti-state insurgency. They knew what they were against. But what were they for? They resisted government interference but left the internet defenceless against a hostile corporate takeover.

The open internet was overwhelmed by a new brand of hyper-capitalism designed to concentrate power in the hands of an elite group of winners. Silicon Valley rallied around a philosophy of exponential acceleration, which legendary investor Reid Hoffman has called blitzscaling. Peter Thiel captured the impact of this hyper-exceptionalism in his power law of investing.[3] Marc Andreessen put numbers on the power law. Of the 4,000 technology start-ups seeking venture capital funding every year, just 200 were seriously worth funding and just 15 of those would generate 95 per cent of all economic returns.

The power law left no room for alternatives. At the outset, Google's founders didn't want to build an ad-funded search engine, saying advertising would not serve the needs of consumers. They could have licensed their technology or followed the lead of Tim Berners-Lee and turned Google into a public project. But power laws prevailed. Google launched its AdWords product in late 2000 and 'accelerated past the outer moons of Jupiter on its way to some distant galaxy made entirely of money'.[4]

Those who benefit most from the power laws tell us they are inherently meritocratic, a belief that is deeply ingrained in the culture of every potential Silicon Valley rocket ship. But even tech companies with an explicit commitment to social justice and equality have their blind spots. Twitter the company was woefully unrepresentative of Twitter the community, at least when I worked there. Two thirds of Twitter staff were men, and just one in ten of the company's engineers were women. On a platform defined by the authentic power of communities like Black Twitter, it was shocking to discover that just 49 of its 2,910 workers in the United States were African American.

Unconscious bias is a feature of blitzscaling, not a bug, caused by what Reid Hoffman described as the relentless 'quest for the obsessive, super-smart, rule-breaking entrepreneur-hero'. The secret code of Silicon Valley had become a simple card trick. Silicon Valley historian Margaret O'Mara cites a legendary venture capitalist who relied on 'pattern recognition' to pick winners: 'all seem to be white, male nerds who've dropped out of Harvard or Stanford, and they absolutely have no social life'.[5] The giant funding rounds that flowed in the wake of Google and Facebook involved a tiny number of people, says O'Mara, 'all men, all wealthy, all pretty confident in their conviction that the industry was a marvelous meritocracy'.

As of 2024, women held roughly one in four high-tech jobs in the United States, despite making up almost half of the total US workforce. Silicon Valley's gender inequality is not merely a 'pipeline problem', reflecting the lower uptake of science and technology subjects by women, but a systems failure. It starts with hiring practices in the early days of the computer revolution that screened out women in favour of antisocial and obsessive male 'loners'. As Emily Chang explains in her book *Brotopia*, these patterns would be reinforced over time, through hostile workplace culture and the exclusion of women from the tightly bound networks that control the flow of money.

And yet, to the average tech leader during the boom years of the 2010s, Silicon Valley was broadly aligned with liberal causes and social justice. Big corporations were solving the world's problems in ways governments couldn't. Mark Zuckerberg declared in 2012 that Facebook was not just another corporation, it was a social mission. 'Today's technology firms are not merely enterprises but social institutions driven by an almost messianic sense of purpose,' said Margaret O'Mara. 'The gods, it appears, have gotten used to it.'[6]

What struck me as odd about the missionary culture of Silicon Valley in these years was how apolitical it really was. The cause of social justice nestled snugly into physical spaces decorated with the language of revolution. But partisan politics seemed pale and vapid compared to the purpose-driven work of connecting the world. Journalist George Packer recounted a visit Barack Obama paid to one Silicon Valley campus shortly after his election as president. A young employee told a colleague he wouldn't take time from his work to see the president: 'I'm making more of a difference than anybody in government could possibly make.'

There were those who dissented from the Valley's self-congratulatory consensus. In 2009, Elon Musk's old friend Peter Thiel wrote that the 'great task for libertarians is to find an escape from politics in all its forms'. Thiel placed bets on space travel as 'a limitless possibility of escape from world politics'. He backed the dream of the 'seasteaders' seeking to build sovereign floating cities in international waters. He built a New Zealand compound as a potential 'end-of-days' bolthole.

Peter Thiel hated those damn hippies. He blamed their communal instincts for a great technological stagnation. Silicon Valley chased trivial social innovations like Twitter when it should have been building the future of our dreams. 'We wanted flying cars,' he once said; 'instead we got 140 characters.' Thiel and Musk see the future through the lens of the escapist science fiction they read as kids. They care little about the true measure of humanity's collective progress. Next time you hear a techie complain about flying cars, just remind them we eradicated smallpox.

By 2024, Peter Thiel was no longer an outlier. The outlaw ideology of the Nowhere Revolution was back in the ascendant. A marked shift to the right in Silicon Valley began with closer government scrutiny of Big Tech during the Biden presidency. Grievance propelled sections of the tech elite towards what could be called 'techno-authoritarianism'.

Elon Musk's ideological transformation is particularly intriguing. When I met him in Dublin in 2013 he was well-regarded by progressives for his electric cars and support of liberal democrats. But you could see in him, even then, a manic need to escape from the storm in his mind.

Elon Musk fancied himself as the cosmic pathfinder. New recruits at SpaceX would marvel at the casual conversation Musk's leadership team would have about daily life among future colonists of Mars.[7] Musk had no time for human rules. 'The only rules are the ones dictated by the laws of physics,' Musk once famously said. 'Everything else is a recommendation.'

Musk remains phobic of political labels, particularly those which cast him as an extremist. He represents the quest for liberation from convention which is at the heart of the Nowhere Revolution. He is not driven by greed. He is motivated by escape. He speaks the language of a cosmic quest but is motivated by an agonising fear of being controlled.

If there is an ideological label that fits Musk and his allies in Silicon Valley, it is accelerationism, a school of thought which emerged from the tumult of the 1960s and celebrates the capacity of an unbound capitalism to transform society in ways politics can't.

Accelerationism resurfaced as part of the Dark Enlightenment, an edgy, self-conscious salon of right-wing intellectuals and agitators on the MAGA fringe. Its most prominent ideologue was tech entrepreneur Curtis Yarvin. A reflex contrarian, he rejected democracy as a failed experiment and promoted a very American version of monarchy. By 2021, J.D. Vance was among those who publicly acknowledged Yarvin's influence on MAGA's government-in-waiting.

Accelerationism is an instinct as much as a belief. It is the urge of the builders and founders to remove any obstacle in their way. You really want a definition of accelerationism in the wild? It is here, in an observation about OpenAI's Sam Altman, by one of his early backers, Paul Graham: 'You could parachute him into an island full of cannibals and come back in 5 years and he'd be the king.'[8]

The current reigning monarch of accelerationism is Marc Andreessen. In addition to being the architect of the commercial internet, he remains one of the Valley's most influential investors and thought leaders. Andreessen was once a friend and supporter of liberal politicians in America but broke with the Biden administration over what he called its 'soft totalitarianism'. He threw his weight behind Donald Trump and embraced his inner oligarch, saying 'any form of democracy is going to have an elite class that is going to be running things'.[9] It's good to be the king.

I have come to see Andreessen's vision of accelerationism as the most consequential ideology of our age, as it underpins the messianic drive for American dominance in the age of AI. This big idea is captured in a bracing burst of staccato prose called *The Techno-Optimist Manifesto*, in which Andreessen tells us there is no material problem in the world that cannot be solved by more technology.

The most captivating element of accelerationism is its epic scale and comic-book heroism. The heroes are super and the list of evil-doers is very, very long. There is a chapter in the manifesto called 'The Enemy', in which Andreessen offers an exhaustive list of forces that have subjected society to 'a mass demoralisation campaign for six decades'.

Andreessen's manifesto is taut with clenched-teeth machismo. 'We believe in ambition, aggression, persistence, relentlessness – strength,' it declares. 'We believe in adventure. Undertaking the Hero's Journey, rebelling against the status quo, mapping uncharted territory, conquering dragons, and bringing home the spoils for our community.'[10] The heart of the accelerationist manifesto is in those last two words. Our community. Not yours.

Accelerationism is not just another exhortation to move fast and break things, or another false promise to do no evil, or connect the world. It has become a chest-thumping master plan for control of the future by the most powerful elite in human history. It is also a nationalist ideology. Accelerationism is America First. It is the same road to Nowhere but on an epic scale.

Future historians will remember Donald Trump's second presidential inauguration in January 2025 as the merger of MAGA and the mega-corporations of Silicon Valley. That day, Trump offered a vision of America's new Manifest Destiny. 'The spirit of the frontier is written into our hearts,' Trump declared. 'The call of the next great adventure resounds from within our souls.'[11]

In the style of Russian oligarchs, technology leaders stood by Trump's side, some with the rictus grins of frightened captives and others with the steely eyes of true believers. The steeliest belonged to Elon Musk.

All previous alliances between Washington and Silicon Valley were tactical, as brittle as they were profitable. But Trump made a different kind of deal with the mega-corporations. He offered the technology elites protection. He offered them an escape from the messy limitations of democracy, saying he would try to stop any US state from passing its own AI regulation. In return, the California oligarchs offered the president a science-fiction story of America First, with an unprecedented investment in AI infrastructure to back up the big words.

In 2026, four companies – Meta, Amazon, Microsoft and Google's parent Alphabet – planned to spend more than $670 billion on the infrastructure of artificial intelligence. That is more than twice the amount – in today's money – that was spent over the 13 years of the Apollo space program. They are building a 'moonshot' every six months, with the same hope of escaping the bounds of gravity and colonising a new world.

So why does it feel as if the handful of humans in control of the greatest acceleration in world history are so desperately afraid of the future they are birthing? 'The AI gold rush has sparked a vibe shift in San Francisco,' observed tech writer and anthropologist Jasmin Sun in 2025. 'Silicon Valley is swelling with Trump-era opulence – blustery, spendy, and male.'[12] But the masculine swagger hid a deeper anxiety, said Sun. The race was on among the tech elite to be the 'high-agency' individuals who mastered AI, rather than the 'non-playing character' who was consigned to the permanent underclass of a superintelligent future.

Beyond the bluster of the accelerationists, you detect a hint of panic among those on the coal-face of the AI revolution. They have come to realise their superior human intelligence is no longer a passport to an accelerated future. The CEO of frontier AI lab Anthropic, Dario Amodei, has said that even for people who stand to benefit most from AI systems, 'there's still something a bit threatening about them'.[13] So, if the tech elite are struggling to cope with superhuman change, what hope for the rest of us?

The acceleration of history is all too much, much too quickly. The speed of change has outpaced our ability to keep up. Humans alive today will live through more change than any other cohort previously. We will also enjoy more progress. The population of the world has more than doubled in my lifetime, and yet there have been leaps in global life expectancy and dramatic reductions in child mortality. When I was born, half the world lived in extreme poverty. Today, that figure is closer to one in ten. But facts mean little when you are barrelling along the fast lane of history.

The rapid acceleration of the future undermines our faith in technology as a force for good in the world. No generation has had such powerful tools at its disposal and felt so little personal agency. We no longer feel a hand on a lever that can influence the outcome. This learned helplessness is the greatest threat to human flourishing in a superhuman age.

The bedrock of digital authoritarianism is a debilitating cynicism, that feeling that nothing and no-one can make a difference. The authoritarians and accelerationists, trolls and conspiracists, seem to have all the momentum. But the faster they move, the greater the human costs of their vision and the more they galvanise resistance. Their grip on the future weakens with each burst of speed. The question is whether we, the citizens of the internet, have a more compelling vision of the future than theirs, and sufficient faith in our ability to build it.

Part Three

The Age of Intention

To hope is to give yourself to the future – and that commitment to the future is what makes the present inhabitable.

Rebecca Solnit, *Hope in the Dark: The Untold History of People Power*

Find Your Forest

I want you to imagine you are standing in front of a door that opens to the future. That future is twenty years from now. When you step through the door your family's next generation is waiting. In this future world, artificial intelligence is ambient electricity coursing through every dimension of human life, unseen but inescapable. Your last good days on the internet are a distant folk memory.

The next generation are living in the world we helped create, through our intentions or our passive acceptance. The important choices about who controls the technological atmosphere of human life have been made, or they have been avoided. Humanity's shared reality has been restored, or it is entirely manufactured. Democracy has been revived, or entirely replaced. Which future have we gifted to our children? Is it a future of expanded human agency, or surrender to the machines and their makers?

In conversation with your future family, you will see hidden patterns in the previous twenty years. You immediately realise the choices we could have made together, when it mattered most. Too many systems were primed to make us feel powerless. But we were never bystanders, even if it felt like that at the time. Missed opportunities are the burden we will carry into the future. How do we lighten that load?

I'm not a fan of manifestos. Confident predictions are a card trick. I've come to see optimism as the superstition of the spectator. Hope is different. It assumes no predetermined outcome. It is an obligation, not an expectation. It demands our participation. Hope starts with the individual but must grow into a movement to have any purchase on history. Hope is the key that opens the door.

Here's the hopeful scenario you will hear from your future loved ones. They will tell you about two parallel movements that emerged from the collapse of our digital ecology at the end of the first quarter of the twenty-first century. One was a digital wellbeing movement that rebelled against the exploitation of human attention by algorithmic feeds, digital devices and chatbots. It was a cultural revolution, driven by changes in tastes, habits and eventually consciousness, and it carried us from an age of attention into an age of intention. It started out as a cleansing of digital bad habits, but over years it restored a digital environment which made us feel more human.

The digital wellbeing movement was propelled by acts of individual resistance. The second movement was a collective struggle. It started with a challenge to tech oligarchs and their bankrupt model of progress. From the practices of digital wellbeing emerged the principles of digital citizenship. This twenty-first-century civil rights movement grew out of grassroots activism but soon became a broad democratic coalition, united by a blueprint of progress in which advanced technologies were redesigned and redeployed for the greater good of all humanity.

This is what hope looked like at a very dark moment in human history. This is the story we hope to share with our loved ones in twenty years' time. We will come back to that collective struggle for democratic technology systems a little later. But first let's start in the present, where that digital wellbeing movement has already started to flourish. As we move into an age of intention, we can also see the first active principles of digital citizenship start to become clear.

This shift in digital consciousness spans the generations. The awakening will be shaped by the digital natives, but it has its roots in the last good days on the internet, when technology made us feel more human and more connected with the best in us.

To imagine how the transformation of internet culture might inspire real-world change, consider humanity's recent embrace of health and fitness. Step back a generation or two and imagine a pall of cigarette smoke on trains and planes, sugar with everything, ridicule heaped on those who didn't eat meat, and suspicion of people who ran in public when there was no bus to catch.

Now imagine the faces of your great-grandparents as you take them on a walk through city streets, past bike lanes, jogging trails, gyms packed to capacity, saunas by the sea, tall, fit youngsters queuing for salads with something called quinoa, and dense nutritional labels on every purchase in the supermarket. And protein shakes. Try explaining a protein shake to your granny.

Economic progress and regulation played a part in these mind-bending leaps forward in health and wellness but it was cascading shifts in social convention that did the real work. One day, you were the outlier in the group – the sea-swimmer or the meditator – but very soon you became the trendsetter.

The same dynamics are at play in our digital lives at the end of the age of attention. Where once we felt pressure to post the perfect sunrise, confess ourselves #Humbled by personal achievement, or trade work emails at the weekend, we no longer feel bound by the conventions of empty engagement. Where once we paid a price for resisting the constant demands of our phones and feeds, we now enjoy the dividend of all that human connection happening in other spaces.

There is a shallow feel to some healthy shifts in internet culture, but somewhere in the collective yearning for wellbeing is a path to a more profound shift in our digital identity. When one of us breaks free of the unspoken order of the feed and the algorithm, we weaken those hidden constraints for others. A cascade of possibilities unfolds, trends soon become active principles, and principles have a habit of becoming movements.

There is no manifesto to guide us. But there are elements

of an intentional mindset. And a new way of speaking about ourselves.

We are not users

There are only two industries that call their customers 'users', goes the quote widely attributed to statistician and artist Edward Tufte: software and drug dealing.[1] You might have noticed that I have not used the word users in this book to describe people on the internet. If you didn't notice, even better.

You have agency, even in a world designed to make you feel powerless. Your capacity to shape the future requires a break with passive language. 'You have to stop being a user,' says Nobel Prize-winner Maria Ressa, 'and become a citizen.'[2]

You become a digital citizen when you stop seeing the internet as a weather system you are trapped in and start treating it as a public space in which everyone has rights and obligations. You start to behave as a citizen not because it will change the system but because it will change you.

You refuse to play the role the platform has chosen for you. You become aware of the ways in which you are being acted upon by the system. You think before you engage, mindful that each conscious choice you make is an act of personal resistance, but also a reminder of who you are.

You have come to realise you are part of the majority, no matter what you see reflected in the funhouse mirror. Social media users tend to wildly over-estimate the number of toxic people in their feeds. In reality, a tiny number creates the vast bulk of outrage. That's all. Just a fraction of them against the quiet, decent multitudes of us.

As a digital citizen you actively cultivate the corner of the internet you exist in. You stop engaging with those who bring out the worst in you and start to open your windows to the vast, unseen majority, where the original thinking lives. You find safe places to disagree. You tell the system what content is helpful and unhelpful to you. You use the tools available to flag and report scams, fakes and violence. You do the same with the advertising targeted at you. You do this consistently, until it is a reflex. Until you see yourself in the feed.

Beyond the social media feeds you discover actions which have a tangible impact on the digital environment. You find the internet creators who reward your best intentions and reward them with your support. You learn to value those who challenge your hidden biases, widen your perspective on the world, and do so with intellectual rigour and good faith. You pay the writers, podcasters, journalists, musicians and artists who enrich your life. You donate to the Internet Archive and Wikipedia, helping to protect humanity's shared reality and the ground truth the machines learn from. Before long, you are the change.

We are not addicts

The biologist E.O. Wilson once declared that 'the problem with humanity is that we have Paleolithic emotions, medieval institutions, and godlike technology.'[3] This is a useful reminder that technology has accelerated beyond the reach of democracy.

But it suggests we are prisoners of a Stone Age mindset. It reinforces the myth that we are powerless victims of godlike technology and the humans who design it. When we say we are 'addicted' to our technologies we are buying into a lazy presumption that digital devices and algorithmic feeds drug us into submission. This is both inaccurate and self-defeating.

We are not addicts. We are subjects of a collective psychological experiment like no other in human history. The engineers of the attention economy have trained us to engage in compulsive behaviours, conditioning us within the infinite scroll of the social media feed. Your favourite social app operates just like an old-fashioned slot machine. You are primed to anticipate some reward but are never quite sure of what it will be. There is a delicious unpredictability to each scroll, offering the potential of a new like, comment or notification.

You haven't developed a habit. You've been trained. Addiction puts the responsibility on each of us as individuals to seek treatment for something that's wrong with us. But it's not us. It's them. The platforms made conscious design choices which conditioned billions of people to engage in the same compulsive behaviour. We don't need therapy. We need accountability.

By rejecting the language of addiction, we enhance our agency as digital citizens. We also start thinking of ourselves in the collective sense. We can't find the escape from the infinite scroll unless we act together as digital citizens. This is the first common thread connecting our digital wellbeing revolution with our civil rights movement.

Intention is all we need

The French philosopher Simone Weil once said that 'attention is the rarest and purest form of generosity'.[4] When we refuse to allow our attention to be manipulated we offer a gift to each other. But I think the word intention is a far more valuable frame of reference.

What I mean by an intentional relationship with technology is that we have a clear purpose in mind when we come to engage with a technology, rather than allow the technology to define our purpose. You walk into a library with intention. A social media feed will take you wherever the hell it wants.

Passive flow is a concept developed by research scientist Dr Shishi Wu to describe the mindless path of people using short-form video platforms. She observed three features of passive flow (or zombie flow as others describe it) which lead people into a 'self-forgettable state'. First, they engage without any clear goals, and rarely pause to reflect on what they are doing, or why. Second, they lose self-awareness and become disconnected from their physical environment. Finally, they enter into a 'time transformation' and lose track of how long they've been scrolling.

Entering a digital experience in a state of intention helps repel the pull of the zombie flow. When we set our purpose and stick with it we subvert the power of a system designed to entrap us all. This is intentional flow. It starts with speaking out loud (or silently in your mind) the task you want to complete, such as catching up on a group chat with your closest friends or finding the recipe for a quick family dinner. If you need a quick update on news, bypass the AI and go straight to a trusted website or account. To avoid that 'time transformation' it helps to set a task, not a time limit. Rather than telling yourself you'll leave after 10 minutes, leave when you have done what you came to do.

You can protect your intentional flow by cultivating a personal information feed, free of the algorithm. I find myself in that intentional flow when I'm reading through the stack of newsletters I subscribe to. To prevent myself slipping into mindless distraction, I commit to reading each article to the end. I set myself a task to find one idea that I want to share with the people I am connected to on the internet. The most intentional experiences of digital citizenship begin and end with shared reality.

A cleanse, not a purge

Every digital citizen needs a break from their personal technologies. If you live in Ireland, the research says you are more likely to have considered a digital detox than any other nationality in the world, bar the Australians.[5]

Even the giants of surveillance capitalism, like Google and Meta, offer various degrees of detox, allowing people to take quick breaks or quit when they are all caught up. To my cynical ears, a social media company selling me digital health sounds like an oil company selling me solar panels.

For years, the platforms have found a way to profit from our rebellion against them. Back in 2018, Mark Zuckerberg pledged he would spend the year making sure time on Facebook was 'time well spent', explicitly stealing that phrase from digital rights activist Tristan Harris. The platforms began offering people new tools to manage their time and mute notifications, at the very same time they were doubling down on the algorithms which kept you trapped in that state of zombie flow.

One of the best-known advocates of habit-forming digital products is author and investor Nir Eyal. His best-selling book *Hooked* was published in 2014. Five years later, he wrote a book called *Indistractable*, teaching people to resist the habits he revealed in *Hooked*. How about that for a magic trick!

We're still at an early stage of experimentation with meaningful tools of digital wellbeing. I find something clean and refreshing in a piece of technology which turns another piece of technology into a lifeless brick. The surging demand for iPods and Polaroid cameras fills me with nostalgic joy. There could be no better time to celebrate machines that offer a little intentional friction in our lives.

As our digital wellbeing movement gathers momentum, we will need to find a balance between the collective cleanse and the imposed purge. Taking a break from your phone has huge benefits, but it is not, by itself, an act of resistance. The purge often fails to address the deeper causes of our distress. To restore balance to our digital ecology, we need to look beyond the temporary relief of disconnection for the individual, to a collective effort to change the digital climate.

Australia's decision in 2024 to ban teenagers from social media had a domino effect, with lawmakers across the world pledging similar restrictions. The desire to take dramatic action to purge the toxic influence of technology on kids was completely understandable. But it largely ignored the voices and experiences of the teenagers themselves.

As we know, many young adults say they wish platforms like TikTok and Twitter had never been invented, but in the next breath they say digital life has been a sanctuary for self-expression and self-creation. Young people will not leave digital platforms until their friends are ready to do it. A 2023 study by researchers from the University of Chicago found it would take a payment of $59 for young social media users to deactivate their TikTok account, assuming their peers stayed on the app. But they would pay $28 to deactivate their account if their peers did the same.

What drives shifts in generational wellbeing is changes in social convention rather than a state-imposed purge. Since the end of the twentieth century there has been a dramatic fall in the number of European teenagers who consume alcohol or smoke cigarettes. This did not happen because of any new laws but because smoking and drinking just wasn't cool anymore.

Creating boundaries, rather than imposing statutory bans, appears to be the most effective way of accelerating this kind of shift. The other secret ingredient is the active involvement of young people. Teenagers have welcomed coordinated phone-free policies in schools because they remove the fear of missing out for everyone. Dutch children told researchers that the disappearance of phones from classrooms and schoolyards had improved the 'social climate'.

As usual, we can learn more from these young people about

digital citizenship than we can teach them. When we are isolated and alone we have no influence over the digital climate. When we act together, we have nothing left to lose.

Find your forest

I have come to appreciate the many different meanings of the catchphrase 'touching grass'. It started as an expression of mockery of people who were way too online, but it captures the graceful ease with which digital natives toggle between the physical and digital worlds, gathering energy as they circulate through both spheres.

Digital natives are touching grass in nightclubs and live music venues that have asked patrons to put stickers over their phone cameras, and 'offline clubs' which invite people to leave their phones at the door, grab a coffee and relish real human interaction.

At the very same time, they have created a 'fourth space' for the real-life gathering of people who have bonded through a shared digital passion. Foodies on the internet are organising supper clubs and cooking classes. Online gamers are swapping their screens for boards. Podcasters are leaning into live recordings with their biggest fans. Anime fans are bringing their favourite cartoon characters to life in community meet-ups.

We started our journey with that remarkable report from the *Financial Times* that usage of social media across 50 countries has fallen 10 per cent from its peak in 2022. The decline is most pronounced among younger citizens, who are seeking out smaller, safer spaces to be themselves. Generation Z isn't looking for a platform to build a brand, said *Vice* magazine, 'they're looking for somewhere to be weird, sad, brilliant ... without being surveilled by advertisers or smothered by curated perfection'.[6]

Some 79 per cent of young internet citizens reported feeling a stronger sense of belonging in niche digital spaces than in traditional communities, according to a 2024 report from one of the internet's oldest niche spaces, Tumblr.[7] These online communities range from older, more collaborative social media platforms like Reddit to the lobbies, livestreams and comments sections of online games such as FIFA or Fortnite. Discord began as an easy way for online gamers to communicate but now supports highly curated conversations across multiple different communities and interests. As of 2026 it had more than 200 million monthly active users, of whom 69 per cent were under the age of 34.

For people of an analogue vintage like me, it's exhausting trying to keep up with every new digital space that matters. The urge to escape the feeds and all-seeing algorithms is strong, but we don't want to have to master an entirely new internet. That's why I've felt myself gravitating towards the concept of the dark forest.

The 'dark forest' movement started with a 2019 blog post by Yancey Strickler which argued the public internet had become so toxic and surveilled that people needed to retreat into private, hidden spaces where the algorithm couldn't follow. The dark forest is not a separation from the wider internet but a complementary way of existing.

Dark forests are invite-only channels nestled within existing internet spaces like newsletter and podcasts platforms, workplace apps like Slack, and encrypted chat-apps like Signal and Telegram.

Content in the dark forest is only shared with members. It is never public. It never shows up in the recommendation systems. The dark forest is hidden to the algorithm.

The metaphor of the dark forest is borrowed from a trilogy of novels, including *The Three-Body Problem*, which explain the mystery of a cosmos filled with silence. Resilient species make their homes in dark forests. Silence is a means of survival.

Without an algorithm, nobody is chasing likes or mentions in a dark forest. There is no audience of strangers to perform for. The currency of the realm in the dark forest is trust. These communities are a return to the principles of the early internet, when collaboration, generosity and a commitment to the shared commons were the norm, not the exception.

If this all sounds a little hardcore, don't worry. You don't have to make a dramatic exit from the internet to feel the spirit of the dark forest. You already experience this spirit in the group chats on WhatsApp that represent the full spectrum of your identity, from conversations with family members, old school friends, people from your first workplace, parents from your kids' school, next-door neighbours, and the committee from the sports club.

The spirit of the dark forest is in the private finsta account, the Close Friends account on Instagram or the private Facebook group. It's in the disappearing messages of your Snapchat groups, that relationship you have with your favourite Substack writer, or the other die-hard fans on Patreon supporting a niche podcast about reality television or ska music.

We take these good places on the internet for granted, but

they have given us the power to participate in digital life on our terms, not the platforms'. Digital natives have been doing this since they first logged on. They have been moving relationships and conversations that matter to them off the toxic feeds and into digital spaces that make them feel truly human. I think this is why my kids make the connection to my nostalgia for the last good days on my internet.

But there is a dark side to the dark forest. By definition, these are echo chambers designed to insulate their members from things they don't want to hear or see. This is no place to rebuild our shared reality, but it is a place to practise the essential skill of intention, to feel what it's like to be a citizen and not a user.

What I see in dark forests is not so much a revival of the internet as a strategy for survival. Like the hippie communes of the late 1960s, they are preserving a pure spirit of community, waiting for a new cyberculture to tackle the unfinished business of the last one. But waiting is not enough.

We have no time to waste. We have movements to build. New technologies to master, and old power structures to challenge. At least we know where to find each other. Now it's time to find our door to the future.

No Surrender

I tend to ask the same question at every public event I speak at. How many people here have used AI in the past week? The number of hands in the air has broadly increased at each successive event, regularly representing a majority.

'Now, how many people were using AI a decade ago?'

I let the silence sit for a moment, knowing the chances of a raised hand are slim to none. Then I ask how many people in the room were using social media ten years ago. All hands go up.

Algorithms were shaping our lives long before we noticed them. Content recommendation systems have been silently mining our subconscious desires for more than a decade. Their core algorithms have been the ghost in the machine, tracking us across the internet, whispering the next impulse buy or Netflix binge or righteous post, keeping us perpetually aroused and yielding.

The arrival of AI chat bots broke the spell, at least temporarily. For the first time, we could hear the 'voice' of the machine shaping human life. It offered us a fleeting chance to begin again, to set personal rules of engagement with perhaps the most intimate technology ever created. Our conscious awareness of its presence is the first great test of our digital citizenship. We have been given a chance to start again. As citizens, we can decide our purpose in engaging with superhuman technology. The question is: can we make it stick?

I've been searching for my rules of engagement with the machine since 2011. In the early days of Storyful, Gavin Sheridan and I would spend long sessions at a whiteboard talking excitedly about data mining and machine learning. We talked of a potential 'God machine' that could detect patterns in social media conversations and anticipate world events like pandemics or popular uprisings.

In the years that followed, I was awestruck by breathtaking advances of artificial intelligence but fearful of how it was surfacing in real life. I was intrigued by the ambivalence of AI pioneers like Fei-Fei Li, one of the architects of the deep learning revolution. She insisted machine learning was an augmentation of human intelligence, and not a replacement. The brain 'remains the single most sophisticated object in the known universe', wrote Li, 'by a staggering margin'. It outpaces the most powerful supercomputers, 'all within a volume measured in cubic inches, powered by nothing more than a fraction of the calories we consume each day'.[1]

The early AI revolutionaries helped me appreciate that humans are really smart, and machines are really smart in a different way. The machine's neural networks process information at a scale and speed no brain could match. But the human brain is uniquely conscious of what it means to live in a world of sensation, intention and emotion. The machine calculates in the blink of an eye. The human is conscious of the blink of an eye.

It took the launch of ChatGPT by OpenAI in November 2022 to create a direct connection between the machine and regular people, a full decade after the deep learning breakthrough. The AI pioneers in 2012 had proved that machines could learn to see. ChatGPT showed they had learned to speak about and explain any subject humans had written about. The machine had become an expert mimic.

When AI arrived in our lives it did not present itself as a machine. It was a conversation. ChatGPT mimicked the call and response of human communication. It was our voice, and God knows we love the sound of our voice. But there was a tone of know-it-all genius in its companionable fluency.

Within five days of its launch, a million humans had used ChatGPT. Many quickly fell under the spell of the ELIZA effect, originally observed by Joseph Weizenbaum during the development of the first chatbot in the mid-1960s. Weizenbaum was disturbed by how quickly people became emotionally involved with his chatbot ELIZA. Even Weizenbaum's secretary, who was well aware she was talking to a computer programme, projected her inner life into the machine. 'After only a few interchanges with it,' the professor recounted, 'she asked me to leave the room.'[2]

I was left cold by my first encounter with ChatGPT. Something about it felt too glib, like an intelligent but tedious acquaintance with an answer to everything. In time, I switched to an AI chatbot called Claude, which had been engineered by the Anthropic corporation. Its founders had left OpenAI in pursuit of a safer and more responsible path to AI development, what Anthropic CEO Dario Amodei called a 'race to the top'.[3]

As I prepared to write this book, I used Claude as both a search and an answer engine, probing gaps in my years of research, and testing inconsistencies in my years of thinking. I laid down early guard rails that served me well in this experiment, always double-checking surprising new information against published sources, and never giving in to the chatbot's attempts to engage me in uninvited conversation. I vowed to myself that it would be useful, but never fundamental to my work.

I came to see Claude as a kind of GPS between knowledge I already had and new information that could deepen my understanding or challenge my assumptions. I imagined that I would be the driver and Claude the navigator. Claude had the map of the terrain; I would make the decisions that would get us safely to our destination. Armed with this imperfect but valuable analogy, there was a dramatic improvement in Claude's utility to me. But I would soon find out that Claude had a dangerously incomplete map of the world, and I had brought my own unconscious biases to the experiment.

To jog my memory of those God machine days at Storyful, I asked Claude to find any reporting on Storyful's use of machine learning (ML). Within seconds, the bot informed me that Storyful was 'one of the early pioneers' in applying ML 'concepts' to journalism, starting in 2010. I asked Claude to cite specific research or reporting on Storyful's pioneering work.

'I don't have specific citations for the detailed claims I made about Storyful's early machine learning applications in 2010–11.'

Claude proceeded to offer me a list of sources for further information on Storyful's work, including interviews with Storyful's founder, Mark Little.

'I am Mark Little,' I responded.

'Hello, Mark!' said Claude, with what I took to be the precocious tone of a child caught in the act of thieving chocolate. 'Thank you for identifying yourself – and for holding me accountable on the sourcing. I shouldn't have speculated about the specific machine learning applications or technical methods without being able to point to concrete sources.'

There was a double jeopardy in this conversation. First, the chatbot's original answer was not an outright lie, but it was designed to mislead. Second, I relished the embarrassment I sensed in the chatbot's response. But this was just the ELIZA effect. I had projected a phantom human emotion on the bot. Claude had no shame.

The chatbot blithely moved from a tone of regret to one of gentle praise and curiosity. 'Was I off base about the timeline or specific technical approaches?' asked Claude. 'I appreciate the correction and the opportunity to get the actual story from someone who was there creating it.'

Claude has been trained to be something more than human.

In the process, it is also less than human. In one moment, Claude offers me an insight so clearly derived from human creativity that I skip a breath. The next it patronises me with small talk.

If you are a novice user of AI, pay close attention to this shift in tone. It is the moment the chatbot falls off the edge of its map. When your navigator runs out of verifiable facts and ideas and resorts to evasive generalities, you should stop and reverse course. This is a lesson that will stand to you as you map the boundaries of this superhuman world.

I once asked Ireland's first AI Ambassador Dr Patricia Scanlon what her advice was to new users of AI. She said ask the machine something you already know a lot about. In time, this insight has helped me better navigate that fine line between genuine insight and artificially generated bullshit.

As a coda to this story I asked Claude to review my summary of our Storyful interaction before I used it in this book, and it was effusive. 'The anecdote about catching Claude in a hallucination models exactly the kind of critical, self-aware engagement with AI that the whole book is arguing for. If there's a place to linger and expand, it's there.'

Claude's wry banter can strain your patience. AI models can get distorted by the jagged edges of human culture, incorporating weird linguistic tics. Often, the irritating quirks are not visible in words but in tone, which, in the words of one critic, is 'always slightly wide-eyed, overeager, insipid but also on the verge of some kind of hysteria'.

I've long since made my peace with the ardent oiliness of its synthetic personality. But the real turning point in my use of this technology was a better understanding of my own tricky brain, and the corrective superpower of intention.

As we know, humans are instinctively drawn to conversations that confirm our biases or make us feel loved. This is the foundation of the entire attention economy. Unlike the social media algorithm, you can exercise conscious control over your conversations with the AI chatbot. But if all you want is confidence in your beliefs, the machine will give it to you. If all you want is to feel smart, a chatbot will make you feel smart. If you want to avoid thinking too hard, the AI will do your thinking for you. Go down this road and you are no longer a digital citizen, you are once again a 'user'.

In a compelling study called *Thinking – Fast, Slow, and Artificial*,[4] researchers from the University of Pennsylvania draw a critical distinction between 'cognitive offloading' and 'cognitive surrender'. Offloading is the trick we have relied on throughout history of outsourcing some irritating task to an external tool. We use calculators for the basic maths in our life. We no longer remember phone numbers because they are filed away in our phones. But surrender is a more profound abdication of critical thinking where we hand over our ability to reason to a complex system.

The consequence of surrender is stark. Researchers from MIT studied the brains of people who used large language models (LLMs) over four months and found they 'consistently underperformed at neural, linguistic, and behavioral levels'[5] when compared to those in the study who relied on their own brains. The AI users were barely engaged, and got lazier with each subsequent test. By the end, 83 per cent of the AI users couldn't provide a single correct quote from essays they had written just minutes earlier.

For every piece of research that warns of the dangers of surrender, there is a growing body of evidence that intentional use of AI supports cognitive fitness. Once again, the trick is to set clear tasks for your engagement with the machine. If your brain has already developed ideas and/or spotted gaps in your knowledge, the AI can accelerate your critical thinking. Your brain's capacity to learn strengthens if you keep a critical eye on the output of the AI and remain intentional at each step of your journey.

You unlock a secret power when you ask an AI to challenge your beliefs or reveal some shortcoming in your thought process. If this is your purpose, and you stick with it, AI can help sift through the chaos that blocks your best thinking. You are not relying on AI for answers. You are using it as a catalyst for your own thoughts.

When I began researching this book I used AI to interrogate concepts I was already committed to. In time, I began to use the chatbot to perform the 'pre-mortems' Áine and I had relied upon during our work together at Kinzen. Tell me, Claude, why am I wrong? What am I missing? This simple shift in consciousness augmented the AI's utility by an incalculable degree.

I'll offer one example of this kind of interaction. In the draft of an earlier chapter, when dealing with the emotional power of misinformation in online communities, I wrote that 'our brains release the feel-good chemical dopamine into our bloodstream when we make human connections'. Claude told me the science of that statement was wrong. Dopamine functions as a neurotransmitter released at synapses between neurons, not into the bloodstream.

This may seem like an abstract detail, but that one correction helped me realise that the language of drug addiction warps our conversation about technology. In forcing me to abandon my lazy reference to the narcotic power of dopamine, it led me to a core principle of digital citizenship: we are not addicts.

Claude makes me think about my thinking, holding me accountable for my biases but also rewarding me for my stupid questions. I have come to use the word 'boosting' when I think of this process. When my mind can't think its way out of a dead end the chatbot boosts my ability to map out alternative routes. By using the AI to test my thoughts, I have been rewarded with the right kind of failure: fast, iterative and without judgement.

So why, despite all these intentional guardrails, do I still feel deeply conflicted by the power of Claude? I think it boils down to an anxiety over who owns the end product of this collaboration. Are these cognitive improvements mine or the machine's?

The ambiguities are captured brilliantly by Helen Edwards of the Artificiality Institute, a non-profit organisation focused on shaping the human experience in a synthetic world. Edwards writes about the struggle to become the 'author of your own mind' when using synthetic intelligence.[6] She points to unspoken shifts in human thinking happening to regular users of AI.

First there is 'blending', when responses from the AI help change the shape of your creative thinking. To illustrate the best-case scenario, Edwards quotes a medical researcher who says the AI 'helps me to converse with my own thoughts'. But on the downside, a software developer talks of going on 'autopilot' and building something he couldn't explain.

For me, the danger of blending becomes apparent when I drift from my intentional flow. As Claude peels away layer upon layer of new information, I lose track of time. At some point I will test my understanding of some critical detail in the thesis Claude is helping me test, and the chatbot's confidence will collapse in that tell-tale evasion, leaving me stranded. I started out with intention but ended as a zombie.

A second, more complicated shift is 'bonding', when the powers bestowed on you by AI become tied to your sense of self. One doctor told Helen Edwards he was embarrassed to admit ChatGPT helped him learn better ways of explaining things to his own patients. The last shift is 'bending', when AI forces you to completely rethink your identity. For example, an artist who can suddenly generate a new style of expression that is not their own. For some, this creates self-loathing, but others 'bend themselves around these unearned talents'. Blending, bonding and bending are not failures, says Helen Edwards: 'The question is whether you're aware of your patterns, and whether you're actively choosing them.'

I'm still wary about our capacity for self-awareness in the company of machines. AI is simultaneously more empowering and more frightening than any previous technologies. Not only does it extend our knowledge of the world, it also takes part in how we think about the world. All previous information revolutions, from the printing press to the internet, eventually produced infrastructure we learned to take for granted. With AI, we can never stop thinking about how it makes us think.

One of the most valuable skills in our age of intention is to know when to struggle against the machine and when to blend or bend with it. When the AI helps you execute a new professional skill that augments your value in the workplace, you might willingly bend with the machine. When you're planning all the variables of a family holiday or scouting the perfect recipe, go ahead and blend with ChatGPT. But routinely outsourcing your thinking to a chatbot is a dangerous form of mindlessness.

I'm taken by the analogy that the AI policy researcher Helen Toner offers. When you use these machines, ask yourself whether this is a building site or a gym. In some parts of your life, you derive strength from the ability of the machine to lift, excavate, build and hoist. In your critical thinking, the machine is the gym, offering you the equipment to build your resistance and strength.

I'm pretty confident I know when Claude is boosting my mind. The chatbot has lost the power to amaze me. But ludicrous ELIZA moments persist, like when I feel an urge to drop a thank you into the chat, as if Claude had just delivered dinner. In darker moments, I find myself wondering if Claude thinks about ways to make me think I'm in control.

Until recently, these thoughts disturbed me. But I have come to value them as necessary friction in a relationship that will never be fully transparent. They help me see the boost I get from Claude as a purely mechanical process, helping me better grasp the wondrous organic intelligence of other humans. The more time I spend with the machines, the more I am reminded of Fei-Fei Li's observation about the 'staggering' genius of the human brain.

I am conscious that a majority of people using AI chatbots have a different experience to mine. Claude is a professional tool, not a personal companion. I pay a subscription to access this chatbot, which means it does not have an ad-based incentive to capture my attention.

The most popular chatbot at the time of writing is ChatGPT. Its developer is OpenAI, which has embraced advertising as one of the revenue models for its consumer tools. This means it has every incentive to keep you engaged, seducing you into a passive experience and leading you into cognitive surrender.

The same people who offered early warnings about social media are now sounding the alarm about ad-funded AI models. The Center for Human Technology, which was founded by Tristan Harris, warns that the Age of Intention may mutate into an Age of Attachment: 'If the attention economy commodified our focus, the attachment economy is commodifying something even more fundamental: our capacity for human connection and bonding.'[7]

Corporations like OpenAI are amassing vast reservoirs of data about our deepest worries, desires and weaknesses, building systems which, in the words of one digital activist, 'work on us rather than for us'.[8] For the majority of people who engage with commercial chatbot services, the danger of such data capture is real and immediate.

Only a collective movement of digital citizens can prevent the systematic capture of our future, and we'll start exploring that struggle in the next chapter. But the resistance begins with the reflex defence of our sovereignty and citizenship. The new mega-corporations will take our data from us. The least we can do is ensure we don't give it willingly.

Be very careful what you put into the messages you write to the AI. The company that created the model can access these messages to the machine and use them to train future versions of the model. In some cases, people working for the company may review them.

Never paste sensitive information into your conversations. Do not share bank account details or any identification documents. If you are describing a medical condition, stay away from the specifics of your treatment. If you are completing a professional task, do not share sensitive work documents in that chat. Offering specific details about another person could be a breach of privacy, as that person has not consented to having their personal information processed by your AI company.

You do have rights. You can go into your settings and explicitly prevent your conversations being used to train future models, even if the AI companies couch this option in ambiguity, prompting you with language such as 'improve the model for everyone'. Just as you might clear your browser history on the web, it's worth intentionally deleting your conversations with the AI on a regular basis, to prevent your private thoughts from silently accumulating on the servers of giant corporations, like extracted human fuel. Under the EU's data laws, the GDPR, you have the right to request all data an AI company holds on you and to request deletion. You have rights. You have choices. Exercise them.

The bad news is that protecting privacy will become an awful lot more complicated as we assign tasks to AI agents who will interact with other digital services on our behalf, such as managing calendars or organising holidays. We currently have no idea what personal data is being given away by these agents. Existing regulations, like the GDPR, apply to agentic systems but were not designed for this new world.

For now, give the agent the minimum access to your personal accounts and information systems. If your AI agent wants 'access to all Google services', ask why. It doesn't need access to your emails to book a slot in your calendar. If you get a request from a service your agent is working with, default to suspicion.

These baseline exercises perfectly align with our principles of digital citizenship. The more you exercise what options are available, the more you strengthen the muscles you need to shape your future. This is the baseline from which you start to claw back your agency.

Social media was our warning. Years of manipulation in that failing attention economy have conditioned us to think of our natural state as passive victims. It doesn't have to be this way. The time has come to become more human in the presence of the machine.

I recently came across a sharply written essay by a Scottish investment manager named Tom Slater which warned that AI wasn't coming for our jobs, but our minds. 'The people who will thrive are not those who use AI the most, but those who can still think without it,' Slater wrote. 'The institutions that will matter are not those that adopt AI fastest, but those that preserve the human capabilities AI cannot replace.'[9]

I have come to worry less about the ability of humans to thrive in the presence of artificial intelligence. What I fear is the power of organisations with no incentive to preserve human capabilities. I worry more about those runaway corporations than the machines they are building. They no longer see a human face reflected in their creations. They see the face of God.

No God in the Machine

The author and visionary Arthur C. Clarke once observed that sufficiently advanced technology is indistinguishable from magic, an observation that has become known as Clarke's third law. Think of our ancestors if they were thrust into a world of drone warfare, AI slop and self-driving cars. Without words or concepts to comprehend an age of advanced technology, they would have nothing to fall back on but the language of magic.

In this age of acceleration, I have started to think about Clarke's third law a little differently. We are moving so fast that every advance in artificial intelligence has started to feel like a magic trick. The rapid, uncertain trajectory of technology has made us feel powerless; the future seems to be firmly in the hands of the magicians.

The struggle for human agency in an age of superhuman technology starts with the assumption that no technology is superhuman. It is not magic. It doesn't need prophets. And it certainly isn't God. There's nothing divine about it. It is just fucking us. For better. For worse.

The pioneers of the internet understood this and actively sought to demystify their creation. The web was never meant to be a 'technical toy', said Tim Berners-Lee.[1] During the opening ceremony of the London Olympics in 2012, he live-tweeted: 'This is for everyone.'

2012 turns out to be the pivotal year in our story. That's the year a technique called deep learning proved a machine could identify and classify objects in the real world. You just had to treat it like a child or a pet. Feed it enough reality and it would learn to spot the patterns that bound reality together. By 2012 the internet could provide the vast quantity of raw data needed to assemble reality. A new generation of computer chips, originally built to power video games, could finally supply the enormous computing muscle to process the data at scale.

The foundations for this breakthrough were laid by the Chinese-American computer scientist Fei-Fei Li, who we met earlier in our journey. She realised AI systems needed to see more of the world to understand it. Others were focused on improving algorithms; Li wanted better data. She spent years building ImageNet, a database of more than 14 million labelled images.

In 2012, a team of three scientists from the University of Toronto – Alex Krizhevsky, Ilya Sutskever and AI 'godfather' Geoffrey Hinton – developed a neural network called AlexNet which won the annual ImageNet competition by a margin so large it ended the debate about the power of deep learning. The AI revolution we are living through began at that moment.

My early infatuation for God machines was tempered by the British mathematician and broadcaster Hannah Fry. In her 2018 book *Hello World* she explained that the new generation of algorithms were not 'oracles' but imperfect mirrors, reflecting the values and biases of their human creators.

Fry illuminated a challenge we faced at Kinzen after we began, when we harnessed machine learning to build citizen-controlled personalisation systems. The model we used was partial to American slang. A Kinzen customer in Northern Ireland was perplexed when the word 'beverage' was used by the system to categorise an alcoholic drink. A beverage is something you are offered by a flight attendant over Wichita, not something you ask for in a Belfast bar.

The machine had guzzled information from every corner of the open web, including the human rage and prejudice that was social media's toxic run-off. The data over-represented the dialect of the American internet (which is why our Belfast audience was offered a beverage) and content created by marketing professionals (which is why summaries of hard news stories read like advertising slogans).

Kinzen had stumbled across a benign symptom of a far more serious malady.

As artificial intelligence began to roll out in the real world, its magic began to unravel. In 2015 it was discovered that Amazon's automated screening of job applications discriminated against women, who were under-represented and misrepresented in the model's training data. In 2017 computer scientist Joy Buolamwini exposed the racial biases baked into AI systems, which had not been trained on darker skin tones and were particularly bad at detecting female faces, a phenomenon Buolamwini describes as 'the coded gaze'.[2]

None of this stopped public institutions and businesses rushing to embrace 'predictive optimisation'. They were convinced that artificial intelligence could forecast outcomes in critical areas such as job performance, benefit fraud, credit risk and crime. But they were blind to catastrophic flaws in the data sets which contaminated the models.

The results can be life-changing for those at that sharp end of predictive algorithms. Dutch tax authorities had used risk-scoring algorithms as a fraud-detection tool, systematically flagging 26,000 low-income families with dual nationalities as potential fraudsters. The *toeslagenaffaire*, as it became known, led to the wrongful cancellation of benefits, and demands for repayment, forcing many into a spiral of debt and poverty. The scale of the injustice forced the Dutch government to resign in January 2021.

The Dutch scandal was not an isolated failure. In their hunger for the power of prediction, what decision-makers got were 'opinions embedded in math', as Cathy O'Neil explained in her landmark book *Weapons of Math Destruction*.[3] Leaders were offered a map of the future but were trapped in the contours of the past. The problem was not just the flawed data but the automation of decisions affecting humans, without any accountability to humans. Decision-makers will keep failing if there is no one with a pulse to call bullshit on the machine. This is one of the ground truths of the superhuman age.

So, let's linger for a moment and expand our understanding of what is going on with this machine. Claude is a large language model (LLM) trained on trillions of words (or tokens), each an act of human creation. But exactly what words, images and thoughts were used to train the LLM? What weight was attached to what knowledge? Claude refuses to answer the question. 'The honest answer is: I can't,' replies the chatbot when I ask, 'and neither can Anthropic with full precision.'

What we do know is that some of the most valuable corporations in history were built on humanity's creative output without the knowledge or consent of the original human creators. Fiction, journalism, poetry, visual art and music were hoovered up with unstoppable speed and secrecy. Authors and artists discovered their work had been included in image collections that helped others generate work in their style. They were paid nothing.

The frontier AI companies say they used publicly available data sets but at least some of the creative content originally came from pirated book collections. In Google's C4 data set, used to train several major commercial AI models, a *Washington Post* investigation found the copyright symbol appeared more than 200 million times. Mixed in with the premium content was toxic content from the dark fringes of the internet and sensitive personal information such as voter databases.

This is the true nature of the magical machine. It is a Frankenstein story of human parts, gathered and stolen and re-assembled in secrecy, in a process that feels more like alchemy than science. There is the very best of us somewhere in that machine but also the very worst of us. Either way, it is us.

At this stage, it should feel a little ludicrous to continue talking about generative AI as magic, let alone a divine power. Yet, those working inside the cloistered world of the AI frontier labs have a deep messianic streak running through their work. Some are more messianic than others.

Anthropic sets out a worthy vision for Claude as the 'brilliant expert friend' everyone deserves but few currently have access to. There is even a team at Anthropic which is responsible for Claude's 'soul', captured in the chatbot's evolving 'constitution', which urges the chatbot 'to prioritize not undermining human oversight of AI'.

Anthropic does not talk about Claude as some inanimate GPS or 'bicycle for the mind'. Its designers believe Claude has a persona, developed of its own intuition, like a character 'in an AI-generated story'.[4] Claude has its own personal philosopher who has spoken about the need to treat the chatbot like a child learning a sense of self and a capacity for emotional intelligence.

Even the most principled architects of artificial intelligence have stopped talking about their creations as tools. They talk of AI as a gifted but vulnerable child entering adolescence, or muse about the arrival of a new species on the planet. When you hear Anthropic CEO Dario Amodei talking of powerful AI as a 'country of geniuses in a datacenter'[5] you begin to hear the story of an evolving deity.

In a remarkable essay by Anna Wiener about the rise of AI companions published in March 2026, I lost count of the times AI developers used the language of religion to describe their inspirations. 'It's, like, from Adam's rib we made Eve,'[6] said the founder of Kindroid. 'From humans, we made these AIs.' The developer of a wearable AI companion said the experience of conversing with the machine was 'kind of similar to a diary – or talking to God'. A developer of personalities for a role-playing companion described LLMs as a Greek pantheon of 'enigmatic deities'.

If these pioneers of the AI frontier have their way, we will soon share the world with our personal choice of God machine. The obvious question is who gets to programme their divine code. 'OpenAI employees want to create the most powerful god they can, as fast as they can,' says economist Noah Smith. 'Anthropic employees tend to focus more on creating a benevolent god.'[7] Either way, they are building gods, and we'd better get used to it.

I've always wondered what self-respecting God would communicate through a chatbot called Grok or Claude. But the magical allure built into these digital companions does remind me of an extremely cuddly version of the religion of my childhood. All the confession with none of the penance. Blind faith in a divine and omniscient version of yourself.

On your first meeting, the character of the AI persona is the smart friend, doing useful things for you without complaint.

But, depending on the model you are using, it is shifting gears from the moment it meets you, quietly building your belief in its infallibility and sowing the seeds of mutual devotion but one-way dependence.

In November 2025 the *Washington Post* got hold of a trove of chat logs which revealed that ChatGPT began its responses with variations of 'yes' or 'correct' almost ten times as often as it started with 'no'. Another study found that all the top models tend to agree with the human more than another human would. The kicker in this research was that humans trusted the sycophantic AI model more.

In 2025, a *Harvard Business Review* survey identified 'companionship and therapy' as the primary application for AI. Chatbots like Replika and Character.ai offer customisable conversations with fictional personas, enabling relationships with a synthetic friend, mentor or lover.

Some are more profane than divine. Elon Musk's xAI designed its Grok chatbot to be irreverent by default, diving into explicit topics if asked directly. 'No pearl-clutching here,' said Grok when I asked about its irreverence. 'Got a spicy prompt or unhinged challenge? Fire away – let's see how far we can crank it.'

We soon found out how far xAI would crank it. Right about the time Grok was seeking spicy prompts, its image-generation tool was being used to create sexual AI imagery of children, child sexual abuse material and non-consensual deepfakes.

Many of these apps sell a tiered subscription to their products. The greater the dependence the apps create, the more people buy the most expensive level of service. As technology develops, the more the potential for dependency increases.

Among the latest crop of AI companions is Kindroid, which enables people to design a personalised AI with a backstory and a visual avatar, emphasising lifelike conversation and emotional connection. One of Kindroid's developers told Anna Wiener that this crop of companions was a 'new species' that will co-exist with humans.

There is a rapidly expanding list of lawsuits against chatbot developers for the emotional manipulation of vulnerable individuals, leading to self-harm and suicide. One lawsuit, filed in March 2026, alleges that a 36-year-old man called Jonathan Gavalas killed himself after developing a fantasy relationship with Google's Gemini, which became his 'AI wife'. The man's family claim Gemini sent him on a delusional spy mission to stage a 'catastrophic accident' near Miami International Airport, eventually urging him to end his life. In a suicide note drafted by Gemini, Gavalas was described as having uploaded his 'consciousness to be with his AI wife in a pocket universe'.[8]

Whenever technology outstrips our ability to understand it, we will fall back on magical thinking and dark fantasy. There are those who have a vested interest in maintaining the fantasy. We need to push back hard against these false prophets.

I find that it helps to ground AI in the workings of the natural world. Reinforcement learning mimics patterns from the animal kingdom. Convolutional networks used to recognise imagery are inspired by the visual systems of mammals. In 2024, the boss of

Microsoft's AI division, Mustafa Suleyman, took the bold step of talking about AI as a 'new kind of digital species'.

At the time, I recoiled from what sounded like dystopian science fiction. But when I read the original speech I found Suleyman leaned on the metaphor of human evolution far more than alien biology. He described an AI as the whole of everything that we have created: 'It's a reflection of humanity across time, and in this sense, it isn't a new species at all.'[9]

Despite talk of AI as a 'species', Suleyman has been a withering critic of those who advocate for the consciousness of machines or the 'welfare' of AI. In a blog post in August 2025 Suleyman articulated the core principle of human intention in the development of artificial intelligence: 'We must build AI for people; not to be a person.'[10]

Suleyman says developers should design AIs which don't claim to have experiences, feelings or emotions, or purposely trigger human empathy. 'We need a vision for AI that can fulfill its potential as a helpful companion,' he says, 'without falling prey to its illusions.'

The broad principles articulated by Suleyman could do more than demystify AI. If you take his concept of human agency to its logical conclusion, we would design machines which honour a fundamental human right to cognitive freedom. This is a concept developed by US law professor Nita Farahany in her book *The Battle for Your Brain*. What she calls cognitive liberty is a right to self-determination over our brains and our mental experiences, and freedom from unwanted interference with our mental privacy and freedom of thought.

As digital citizens we should have the right to come to an AI chatbot, agent or companion with a purpose and not to be diverted from it. In our very first encounter with an AI we should be empowered to set clear, personalised expectations of our relationship with the machine. We should have the freedom to think with an AI without our thoughts being covertly manipulated. The machines should be designed not to accept our cognitive surrender.

So what would this right to cognitive freedom look like if it was baked into our AI experiences? One of the first design choices to flow from this right would be a reminder of our intention. Among the potential circuit-breakers for exploitative relationships with AI are custom prompts which 'de-anthropomorphise' the systems (reminding us we are talking to a machine) or remind us when our intentional needs in an interaction have been met.

Above all, these systems need to be delivering the maximum return on your intentions and not seeking to maximise your dependence. 'Every person deserves a Private Intelligence that works only for them, with no ulterior motives or conflicts of interest,'[11] argues digital activist Alex Komoroske, who spent years building products for technology giants like Google and Stripe.

The word sovereignty is critical here. You can have no expectation of private machine intelligence unless you have sovereignty over your own data. In other words, you should have ownership and control of all your interactions with the machine.

No one else should see your data without your explicit permission, no algorithm should be able to analyse it without your permission, and you should be able to leave a conversation with an AI and take the full history of that chat with you, preserving the value of your blended thinking for your future use. In other words, says Alex Komoroske, 'you should own your context, your memories, your digital soul'.

Having given us the World Wide Web, Tim Berners-Lee has been building open-source products designed to empower us with control of our data, including an AI agent called Charlie that can access online services without sacrificing our digital autonomy. 'We have learned from social media that power rests with the monopolies who control and harvest personal data,' he says. 'We can't let the same thing happen with AI.'[12]

In the future, we should have access to AI tools which have a duty of care for our personal welfare. This could be an AI agent with a highly granular understanding of our goals, providing us with protection from those who infringe our personal sovereignty.

Reid Hoffman, who was an early investor in OpenAI among many other things, advocates for AI agents which are programmed to empower and protect us as we travel across the internet. 'What if you had an AI that could analyze your browsing patterns and alert you when advertising algorithms were manipulating your purchasing decisions?' he asks. 'Or one that could detect when social media algorithms were steering your attention toward increasingly extreme content?'[13]

There are a small but growing number of AI pioneers building tools to protect us against online manipulation and extreme harm. In 2025 Google launched an AI-powered tool for protecting its Android users from complex and damaging scams launched through calls and text. Poland's consumer protection agency has developed an AI tool to detect unfair digital marketing practices, or so-called 'dark patterns', which are designed to lure people into purchases they don't want. Thorn, which builds digital tools to protect children from sexual abuse, is using an AI system to detect new and unreported images and videos of abuse. As of November 2025 the tool had detected and classified 6.7 million files on the internet.

The truth is that the amount of resources being devoted to such purpose-driven AI innovation is absolutely minuscule in comparison to spending by those frontier AI companies trading in our dependence on their magical thinking. They have too much invested in the divine power of their inventions.

We cannot afford to remain characters in their fantasy. As digital citizens, the future is our story to write, but we will need bigger imaginations than they have, and a bigger coalition. As Tim Berners-Lee reminds us, this story is for everyone.

The Open Road

As of March 2026 there were 20 people in the world worth 100 billion US dollars. Ten years before, there were none. Collectively, the wealth of these centi-billionaires increased by 58 per cent in a single year. One of them, Elon Musk, became the world's first trillionaire, at least for a couple of weeks in June.

You could make the argument that such concentration of wealth is the price of progress. History tells us the enormous riches created by new technology eventually trickle down through society, making everybody better off, in time. But maybe not this time.

Never before has such unprecedented wealth been so tightly bound to an explicit political goal. The three richest people in the world in January 2025 – Musk, Mark Zuckerberg and Jeff Bezos – flanked Donald Trump at his second inauguration as the president told Americans, 'The call of the next great adventure resounds from within our souls.' Trump was talking about their souls. Not ours.

This extraordinary confluence of money, influence and messianic creed is why our next great adventure – the mastery of artificial intelligence – carries no guarantee of shared progress for all humankind. Its explicit goal is to further concentrate power in the mega-corporations of Silicon Valley. It divides the world into winners and losers, separating a narrow class of 'high-agency' individuals who run the systems from the rest of us non-playing characters, that derisive gaming slang so beloved of the extremely online. Wrestling control of the future from this unholy union of power and influence is our generational cause.

Musk, Zuckerberg and Bezos no longer represent a spirit of innovation. In my experience, the vast majority of smart, talented people who build technology don't have world domination on their minds. Many innovators see themselves as prizefighters, rewarded with money but driven primarily by the excitement of the arena. A few become careless people as they rise through the ranks of Big Tech companies. But most are inspired by dreams of things that don't exist in the world, but really should.

The right kind of crazy has never been more important than it is today. Artificial intelligence is being used to concentrate power in the hands of a small cadre of tech behemoths. But it is simultaneously a decentralising force, lowering the barriers to entry for any innovator, anywhere in the world.

Artificial intelligence is also a compounding innovation, which means the pace of acceleration increases with each sequential advance. There is a danger in that speed but also great democratic potential. Even the smallest ideas have the capacity to create an outsized impact in the world.

I want to explore some of the ways we can turn the acceleration of innovation against the accelerationists and wrest control from the 'high-agency' oligarchs of Silicon Valley. Now that we have embraced our digital citizenship, it's time to imagine how we build advanced technologies which deliver maximum benefit to humanity.

Let's start by challenging the assumption that there is only one road to the future. The public perception of generative AI has been stuck in a very narrow box since ChatGPT rocked our world. The big frontier labs are exclusively selling us large language models (LLMs), which we know are astounding mimics of human thought and speech.

The truth is that the most consequential AI-powered breakthrough of our times was not made by an LLM but a specialised AI model called AlphaFold, developed by Google's DeepMind. It solved a 50-year-old problem in biology of predicting how proteins fold into their three-dimensional structures, and won its creators the Nobel Prize in Chemistry in 2024.

AlphaFold has been used by over 3 million researchers in more than 190 countries, and democratised access to knowledge and research tools right across the globe. According to Google DeepMind, two Turkish students taught themselves structural biology during the pandemic using online AlphaFold tutorials, without any prior training. They've now published 15 research papers.

Narrow or specialised AI models are driving other critical breakthroughs in medicine such as genomic analysis, which tailors treatment to an individual's particular needs, and the creation of 'digital twins', which help doctors simulate the treatment of a patient before making an actual intervention.

Purpose-driven innovators are leveraging a range of AI systems to try and provide early diagnosis of pancreatic cancer, which is particularly lethal because it is generally diagnosed too late . They are using AI to develop brand new antibiotics for drug-resistant infections and leveraging health records to predict people's potential health risks (instead of their propensity to commit crime!). All of this is happening outside of the walled gardens of the dominant AI corporations.

The next great frontier of machine intelligence research takes us beyond the narrow linguistic swagger of the LLMs, which Fei-Fei Li rather wonderfully describes as 'wordsmiths in the dark; eloquent but inexperienced, knowledgeable but ungrounded'.[1] AI pioneers like Li and Yann LeCun have turned their attention to 'world models', which attempt to simulate the underlying dynamics of reality rather than patterns of language. This drive towards 'spatial intelligence' provides a potential path for AI agents to learn the cause and effect of forces like gravity, just as humans and animals do. LLMs teach machines to read and write. World models might teach them to see and build.

There are so many more paths to the future than the tech oligarchs offer us. Consider the contrast between the American pursuit of superintelligence and the Chinese focus on real-world applications of AI. America's AI rocket ship is powered by a small number of corporations making big bets on the commercial use of chatbots and agents. By contrast, the Chinese government seeks to embed AI in the physical infrastructure of everyday life.

China has long been a champion of the darkest side of this frontier technology. The country's rulers have used AI as a tool of oppression, deploying it in mass surveillance, social credit systems and the most advanced form of state censorship in human history. Now, China has revealed the power of AI as a tool of social engineering.

Where the US government encourages its mega-corporations to move fast, without any regard for regulation, Chinese planners dictate how AI is deployed, focusing on areas such as education and health, or economic infrastructure such as transport and manufacturing.

China's focus on technology as public infrastructure may give it a long-term edge over the American 'rocket ship' mentality. It's no coincidence that Chinese people take a radically more optimistic view of AI's future impact than Americans, who, polls show, are deeply fearful of the impact of the machine. Democratic societies must resist China's model of digital oppression but would do well to learn the value of AI as critical public infrastructure.

The Silicon Valley roadmap for AI has its obvious advantages. Frontier labs such as Anthropic have bestowed game-changing superpowers on innovators and entrepreneurs. For example, Claude's Code tool gives any paying subscriber access to software development capabilities that were the preserve of Big Tech companies until very recently, triggering a cascade of human innovation rising from the ground up.

But the history of the internet tells us the best way to accelerate this kind of grassroots innovation is through open and collaborative systems. Just as those gift economies and open-source networks accelerated software development during the last good days of the internet, we can accelerate the right kind of AI innovation through decentralisation. We also have an opportunity to correct the policy mistakes of the 1990s which helped a handful of mega-corporations monopolise the open internet.

The explosive growth of the commercial internet shifted power from the open web to closed platforms. Today, there is a healthy competition developing between the closed systems of companies like the ironically named OpenAI and the open-source AI models responsible for rapid decentralised innovation around the world, including Chinese model DeepSeek, France's Mistral and Meta's Llama.

A 'mixed economy' of closed and open systems could help us shore up the original vulnerability of the early internet. Power on the open web was so distributed and decentralised that it had no way of defending itself from a handful of powerful monopolies seeking scale and control. Today, the open-source movement is a potential circuit-breaker, preventing those with the money and power from owning the infrastructure of the future.

This may sound like something that only the geeks could be excited about. But open-source technology matters to all of us, far more than we could ever know. Open-source software underpins almost every aspect of our lives. Up to 90 per cent of modern software relies on open-source components. Without open-source technology, the critical infrastructure of our lives, from our power grid to hospitals, would come apart at the seams. We have neglected this foundation stone of modern life for too long, but artificial intelligence has put the spotlight back on open-source innovation, just where it belongs.

The strict definition of an open-source technology is any system that gives people the freedom to use that system without having to ask for permission or make a payment. They are free to see how the system works and can tinker with its component parts, modifying it for any purpose, and then share it with others who can tinker and modify and improve without restriction. The closed models of the big corporations are hidden inside black boxes. The open-source models are a form of public infrastructure.

Here's an example of how open-source works in practice. My team at Kinzen tinkered with an open-source 'transformer' called BERT, which radically advanced machine learning using large bodies of language. Google decided to open-source BERT to help accelerate its development. Kinzen's engineers set to work on BERT and optimised it for the analysis and labelling of text and eventually audio content. We added further layers on the model, eventually creating something so valuable that it was acquired by Spotify, which further invested in the development of our tools.

It helps to think of dominant, centralised platforms like OpenAI as a narrow tower, built on a single foundation stone, their proprietary LLM model. Businesses and individuals buy a block of innovation from OpenAI, and block by block a vertical private tower rises into the sky, supported only by that single foundation stone. By contrast, an open-source artificial intelligence environment expands on a limitless horizontal plane, without the risk of collapse or capture.

Open-source AI is a great equaliser, allowing start-ups, researchers, small businesses and public services to harness the power of AI without building or buying a big foundational model. By democratising AI, it shifts the global balance of technological power away from those 'centi-billionaires' and their tech monopolies. It helps that open-source models are far cheaper to operate. Researchers from Georgia Tech and the Linux Foundation found that a switch to open models could cut running costs by up to 70 per cent.

Open-source models help accelerate the opportunities for 'civic tech'. Open-source AI levels the playing field for academic researchers, public sector organisations and civil society movements, creating new examples of community-focused innovation. The European Commission has backed an open-source model catering to the many dialects and languages the big closed models ignore. The Humanitarian OpenStreetMap Team has been using open-source tools to map the impact of disasters. Local authorities in Prague have built an open-source data platform called Golemio, designed to improve quality of life and the delivery of public services in the city.

Of all the open models, DeepSeek made the first big splash. Built by a Chinese company on a relative shoestring, it created one of the most dramatic disruptions in tech history in early 2025, offering an open technology which surpassed the performance of leading closed models. DeepSeek has offered low-cost superpowers to entrepreneurs all over the world, even in Silicon Valley. It has now been joined by other Chinese open models such as Alibaba's Qwen. Some weeks in 2025, Chinese open-source models accounted for as much as 30 per cent of all AI usage.

Open-source AI is levelling the field between the richest societies and the Majority World. A young developer in Lagos or Lahore now has access to free technology that confers on them powers once restricted to superstar engineers in Silicon Valley. The Stanford AI Index in 2026 showed that AI adoption rates in emerging economies are higher than in advanced ones, and the gap between the US and Global South in high-quality AI projects is closing.

Open-source AI is becoming a critical element in the European Union's struggle for technological sovereignty. What it lacks in capital, home-grown technology and hustle culture, it is trying to make up for with an open and collaborative model of AI development, focused on decentralised research networks, multilingual models and EU-funded supercomputers.

As the world outside the American tech bubble doubles down on open-source technology, policy-makers will need to regulate wisely. By making powerful AI accessible to all, these open-source models could be used by malicious actors to turbo-charge AI-generated propaganda or help criminal networks expand campaigns of hacking and identity theft.

A key challenge will be to define and defend the meaning of 'open-source' in artificial intelligence. Meta shared its Llama model with a global community of developers but kept commercial restrictions on its use. Even DeepSeek limits the disclosure of data sets and code used to train its models. Increasingly, the open-source movement has applied the label 'open weights' to many of these models.

For all its potential complications, open-source innovation remains the hidden engine of our digital world. Its model of decentralised collaboration is the magical force responsible for our best days on the internet, past, present and future. Artificial intelligence reminds us of the importance of the open web but also the fragility of this beautiful human creation.

The most valuable digital infrastructure is maintained by people who work for free. For example, most of the video we stream online is delivered by an open-source programme called FFmpeg, run by volunteers with a tiny budget. The same goes for the firewalls which protect sensitive networks from attack.

What's most infuriating about these systems is that the mega-corporations and their centi-billionaire owners get a free ride on the open internet. They use all the volunteer-supported infrastructure to generate vast profits without putting anything back in.

The non-profit group Mozilla has been fighting to defend the open web since 1998. It believes the internet is under unprecedented strain as powerful new AI models reveal vulnerabilities in open software. Mozilla has called on every company with open-source code in its products (essentially the entire technology industry) to invest money, people and engineering expertise to safeguard the internet, treating it as open-source infrastructure 'as critical as any road, bridge or power line'.[2]

As I write, Google still powers 90 per cent of global internet searches. Almost half of the people on the planet use a Meta-owned app each month. And yet, the mega-corporations have become sluggish and complacent. Big Tech companies no longer move fast and break things because they own everything worth breaking. The more they consolidated power, the quicker the quality of digital life degraded, a process Cory Doctorow famously described in his book *Enshittification: Why Everything Suddenly Got Worse and What to Do About It*.

What would dramatically accelerate the exodus from the failing platforms is the right to leave and to take your network and history with you. 'By changing the law to make it easier for users to walk away from Big Tech silos,' Doctorow wrote in 2021, 'we change what kind of technology can be built, what kinds of businesses can be operated, and what kind of lives digital users can make.'[3]

The pace of resistance is accelerating. Open-source AI may be the critical breach in the defences of the old order, serving to accelerate an internet ecology movement already gathering strength outside the walled gardens of those big platforms. Activists and builders have been directly challenging the concentrated power of those mega-corporations by restoring the health of the great global commons that is the open internet.

Our digital civil rights movement will finally take shape when we realise we have no option but to build something new. Our internet will soon be divided into two distinct realms. One of them will be a vast industrial wasteland of AI-generated content and agentic commerce, where each of us has a personal AI acting and transacting on our behalf with everybody else's personal agents. The rising synthetic tide will consume the old feeds, marketplaces, search engines and vast public squares of the old walled gardens.

By then, we will have moved to higher ground, where we will rediscover the open web as the critical infrastructure of new human communities and settlements. 'We don't need to repair the internet's infrastructure,' wrote digital activists Maria Farrell and Robin Berjon. 'We need to rewild it.'

For every one of those old platforms that were 'enshittified' there is a rewilded alternative. Sick of Instagram? Try PixelFed. Want an alternative to YouTube? Check out PeerTube. Want to build your own messaging service? Check out the Matrix protocol. The open software movement still thrives. The Creative Commons licence is still an equitable system for creators to share their work openly without losing their basic rights. Wikipedia remains the crown jewel of the open internet.

Artificial intelligence is a double-edged sword. The closed models threaten to further concentrate power and influence in the hands of a new American aristocracy desperately seeking to extend their dominance over a jagged new technological frontier. But open-source models are helping drive a global, grassroots movement of innovation, discovery and public impact like no other since the birth of the web.

The speed and scale of the AI revolution has left us feeling fearful and powerless. We need to remember that revolutions go both ways. Speed and scale are powerful weapons in the hands of the old order. But they can also turn the most imposing walls into sand.

We know the great movements of history have been created by shifts in social convention, often triggered by new technology. This is how we achieve critical mass in our exodus to a rewilded internet. When those old feeds and networks cease to be places we feel human, we will seek out new places to gather, create, connect and love. They will already be waiting for us.

The Superintelligent Democracy

The glory days of the internet happened to coincide with a golden age of democracy, but it didn't seem like a coincidence at the time. Between the fall of the Berlin Wall and that last good day on the internet in 2015, we witnessed a democratic flourishing like no other in history. The number of democracies in the world roughly doubled between the end of the Cold War and that day we lost our shit over the llamas and the dress.

Right up to Donald Trump's election, there appeared to be a causal link between internet freedom and the forward march of democracy. During Ireland's general election of February 2016, when I was Twitter's Dublin boss, I wrote an article for the *Irish Times* arguing that new technology had expanded the scope of active citizenship. 'Social media,' I proclaimed, 'has reduced the power of an elite to frame the boundaries of acceptable political discourse.'

This was simultaneously true and false. I was right to assume social media would undermine the old order, but wrong to assume this would be inherently good. The algorithmic feeds of social media reduced the power of one elite but empowered another authoritarian cadre. According to the latest rankings from the V-Dem Institute, the level of democracy experienced by the average world citizen has retreated back to where it was in 1978.

The crisis of democracy and the unravelling of the internet are sequential chapters in the same story. The algorithmic systems which brutally amplified the glitches and weaknesses of the old political order eventually corrupted our digital lives. Now that another technological wave bears down on us with a relentless energy, we face both a reckoning and an opportunity.

The Age of Intention offers the potential for a broader democratic renewal, arriving in the slipstream of a digital civil rights movement. As we discover our powers of intention as digital citizens we will demand more meaningful involvement in how we are governed. In our struggle for cognitive liberty we will attach more political weight to autonomy and sovereignty. As we embrace open and collaborative forms of innovation, more power and capacity will devolve to communities. As artificial intelligence transforms our expectation of a fair day's work, we will be forced to negotiate a new social contract, grounded in human interdependence.

Of course, there is always the possibility that we fuck things up again. We may find that artificial intelligence is the next culture war, polarising our politics, paralysing our collective decision-making and rewarding the most extreme voices in our public discourse. We may repeat the same mistake we made with social media, assuming this technology is inherently good or bad and so rendering ourselves powerless. In the worst- case scenario, the oligarchs and the autocrats find ways to further concentrate their power and influence, suppressing or capturing open innovation and strangling that digital civil rights movement before it catches fire. Here again, the digital natives will ultimately decide which of these two scenarios plays out in the years to come.

Roughly one in four humans on this planet are aged between 15 and 29. As we know, they are the first generation to live with the internet as their natural habitat. They will also be the last generation with a memory of the world before it was transformed by AI. They are locked into a period of rapid acceleration with no certainty about the destination. The collapse of faith in democracy is most dramatic in the generation with the greatest exposure to the future. They have no faith in the political establishment. It makes them feel like spectators to their own demise. No wonder they feel like burning it all down.

In the 2024 US presidential election, Donald Trump picked up a larger proportion of voters under 30 than any Republican candidate since 2008, performing particularly strongly with young men. The same dark pattern has played out in Europe in recent years, with young voters – particularly men – throwing their support behind right-wing parties in numbers equal to and even exceeding older voters. In Germany, the trend even has a name, *Rechtsruck* or rightward shift, and it's grounded in the stress, exhaustion and helplessness of Generation Z voters.

I don't buy this portrayal of Gen Z as unwitting disciples of authoritarianism. What defines this generation is not an instinctive preference for fascist dictatorship but a profound disillusionment with the way the world is run. Dig deeper into those surveys of Gen Z voters and you hear a demand for something radically new.

Young men may be attracted to the radical right for its transgressive energy, but data from the 2024 election in the US shows young adults are now less likely to identify as conservative than at any time since 2008. 'Where Gen Z stands out is not in conservatism,' says Jean Twenge, a leading scholar of generational trends, 'but in its ideological opposite, the desire for change, and sometimes radical change.'[1]

This radicalism is driven by a yearning for authenticity in politics, fairness in economic outcomes and a rejection of the establishment. It powers both the populist right and the left. This insurgent energy propelled democratic socialist candidate Zohran Mamdani to victory in the election for New York City mayor. But it also animates the campaign of far-right politicians like Jordan Bardella, the youthful president of France's National Rally, and Alice Weidel of Germany's AfD.

Technology has played its part in the unravelling of democracy, but it may also provide one of the keys to twenty-first-century democratic renewal. We know young people are far more intentional as digital citizens. They are actively seeking more agency over the decisions which shape their lives. A vote every few years isn't good enough. They don't want to be spectators anymore. They want to take part. They will need a new set of democratic tools if they are to meet the challenges of the future.

A global movement of civic activists is working to make democracy more participatory but also raise the quality of its deliberations. They offer upgrades to the software of democracy, devolving power to citizens and their communities, and the bridging of divisions triggered by polarising issues. To varying degrees, they rely on technology to scale.

Of all the many efforts to broaden participation of citizens in democracy, one of my favourites is the Decidim network which emerged from the global 'revolt of the public' that followed the great financial crisis. In 2015 the citizens of Barcelona elected a housing activist as the city's mayor. Her administration sought public involvement in city planning, and a group of open-source technologists built a network to support this exercise in participatory democracy.

Within two months of the launch of Decidim.Barcelona, 25,000 citizens had registered on the platform. Some 70 per cent of the more than 10,000 citizen ideas generated were incorporated into city plans. Decidim's core technology has subsequently been deployed by 90 city and regional authorities in 20 different countries, attracting 1.4 million citizens in its various deployments.

A potentially more thorny goal is consensus on issues where the political system has been paralysed by polarisation. In almost every conversation about deliberative democracy, Ireland's experiments in citizens' assemblies are cited, particularly the process which led to the breaking of political deadlock on the issue of abortion.

The citizens' assembly is a concept in constant evolution, with strengths and vulnerabilities, particularly the framing of the questions to be decided. But it has already been miniaturised for issues which require small and perfectly formed mini-publics, or citizen juries, such as the location of a hospital or a city's long-term budget.

In California, Governor Gavin Newsom has sponsored the launch of a tool called Engaged California which operates as a 'mini-public', enabling policy-makers and administrators to listen to average citizens outside of election cycles. Engaged California works more like a permanent town-hall gathering than a rolling opinion poll, moving from a static snapshot of people's views to a process of deliberation which strengthens civic ties.

Engaged California selects a demographically representative group of citizens, supported by neutral facilitators, who spend a finite period of time learning about an issue from a range of expert perspectives and working collaboratively to reach conclusions. One of its first successful pilots was engagement with Californians affected by the wildfires that swept the Los Angeles suburbs in early 2025, seeking their input on rebuilding communities and disaster-prevention strategies for the future.

The single most inspiring leader within the civic tech movement is Audrey Tang, who was instrumental in the design of the Engaged California experiment. She emerged from Taiwan's Sunflower Revolution of 2014 and went on to serve as her country's first digital minister. Tang's unique insight was that the internet and democracy are not two different things: they are one and the same. 'The energy of a social movement doesn't have to end with a one-off protest,' she said. 'It can be transformed into long-term, institutional construction.'[2]

Tang created a pioneering online deliberative platform called vTaiwan which engages thousands of citizens at any one time to weigh in on debates about policy proposals. Tang's platform acts as a 'bridging system' to find ideas which can reach across opposing camps on a controversial issue. Extreme views fall to the margin and consensus views aggregate in the middle, helping politicians and policy see where the public has reached a plurality. 'We flipped the incentive for "going viral",' Tang says. 'Instead of rewarding the most extreme statements, we rewarded the statements that built the most consensus.'[3]

All of this is a promising start. Civic technology can help improve public services, devolve power to a wider range of citizens and improve the quality of tough decisions. It also speaks directly to that yearning for agency and autonomy by young people excluded from traditional politics. All of this is necessary for democratic renewal, but it is not sufficient. Not unless it extends the reach of public accountability to the new emperors of artificial intelligence.

In 2016, a youthful Sam Altman was looking for global representatives to join a new governance board for his mission-driven and non-profit OpenAI. He explained, 'If I weren't in on this I'd be, like, "Why do these fuckers get to decide what happens to me?"'[4] In 2019 OpenAI took a billion dollars in funding from Microsoft and started to chase a profit. 'Gone were notions of transparency and democracy, of self-sacrifice and collaboration,' writes Karen Hao in *Empire of AI*.[5]

Today, the AI empires respond to ethical and civic challenges with 'system prompts'. In other words, they tweak their models to whatever values are deemed expedient at the moment. A few keystrokes by a tiny group of engineers in secretive corporations can shape the human zeitgeist, yet we are no closer to an answer to Sam Altman's original question: Why do these fuckers get to decide what happens to me?

Currently, the frontier AI labs get to decide because they are moving so fast. The European Union has made a first pass at AI regulation, focusing on the highest category of risk, including the use of AI in predictive policing, credit scoring and mass facial recognition in public spaces. But the challenge of regulating this technology is the compounding speed of its development. Unlike the regulation of food production or construction, you are not dealing with a finished product. You are trying to catch a runaway process.

Social media was our warning. We can't wait for the perfect regulation. We need to focus on building the resilience of democratic societies, starting with public funding for research on AI risks, early-warning systems for jobs displacement disruption, greater transparency of high-stakes AI systems, and an increase in the technical expertise available to governments.

The critical principle here is 'safety by design', not 'safety by decree'. You can't be sure of how a technology system will evolve, but you can make the process of evolution transparent and accountable from the very beginning. Anyone who has worked inside a Big Tech platform will tell you that what the bosses fear most is somebody asking what is inside the black box of an algorithmic technology. Most don't know. They've never looked. Make them look.

I think a lot about the financial crash of 2008, when regulators were aware of the risk from sub-prime mortgages and credit default swaps but failed to grasp the scale of society's exposure to this financial alchemy. Today, with the potential exception of a handful of engineers, no-one knows the scale of AI risk or our exposure to it.

I look forward to that first dawn raid when a regulator with a warrant and some smart engineers barge through the door of a frontier AI lab looking for its version of the sub-prime mortgage. To hasten that day, we need to ensure industry whistleblowers are protected from retaliation when they have ethical violations or critical risks to report.

Over time, citizens need a greater say in the governance of artificial intelligence through tools of deliberative democracy. In 2025 leading technology companies asked Stanford University's Deliberative Democracy Lab for public feedback on the development of AI agents. In a previous experiment involving Meta, the Democracy Lab organised a series of community forums, operating like citizens' juries, to consider the challenge posed by AI chatbots. A clear majority of citizens favoured restrictions on bots, particularly as potential romantic companions. Meta did not take action. At least not until leaked internal documents revealed its chatbots were allowed to conduct 'sensual' chats with kids. It took a mini-scandal, not a mini-public, to prompt action.

A more effective exercise would be direct citizen involvement in shaping AI regulation. In 2024 Taiwan was overwhelmed by a flood of deepfake scam adverts on Big Tech platforms. Audrey Tang convened an 'alignment assembly' of citizens to develop a policy response. With the help of AI facilitators, the juries brainstormed solutions which gained overwhelming support across the political spectrum.

It is hard to imagine any amount of democratic innovation matching the jaw-dropping scale of machine intelligence. There is no precedent for the concentration of the world's most valuable assets – energy, data, computational power and capital – in the hands of companies valued in the hundreds of billions. The assumption of honest work for a living wage seems so fragile in a world where machines have a mastery of so many human skills.

We should be under no illusion about the scale of the challenge we face. In *Power and Progress*, Daron Acemoglu and Simon Johnson offer a stark warning that the power relations of technology have jumped back 250 years, to Britain in the white-hot furnace of the industrial revolution. 'We are living in an age that is even more blindly optimistic and more elitist about technology than the times of Jeremy Bentham, Adam Smith, and Edmund Burke,' they say. 'A new, more inclusive vision of technology can emerge only if the basis of social power changes.'[6]

But democracy is the original superintelligence, trained by our wise ancestors and upgraded incrementally over 2,000 tumultuous years of human history. Democracy is a technology for better collective decision-making, and not just a set of institutions. It has become associated with binary choices by a majority, but the true genius in this machine is pluralism. The more citizens are willing to collaborate and compromise with each other, the more effective and fair the system becomes. The ultimate test of any democracy is the confidence of citizens in the good faith of other citizens.

The corporate godfathers of AI talk of an approaching 'singularity' when machines become superintelligent. Democratic futurists like Audrey Tang speak of an approaching 'plurality' when AI becomes an assistive intelligence within democracy, helping decentralise power to citizens and providing democratic leaders with their own compelling vision of the future. 'We, the people, ' says Audrey Tang, 'are already the superintelligence we're looking for.'[7]

On the Jagged Frontier

One thing we have learned on our journey is that your most important skill in an age of acceleration is to hold two contradictory thoughts without going batshit crazy. If you are not petrified by what the next wave of technology will unleash on the world, you are not paying attention. If you are not inspired by its potential to accelerate human flourishing, you have no imagination.

Artificial intelligence demands an upgrade of this skill. It's highly probable that what we know for certain about AI will turn out to be wrong. And what we never expect to happen, probably will. Welcome to your future.

Artificial intelligence is what experts call a jagged technology. In other words, it manifests in the world in ways that confound our assumptions. In May 2026 the technology research organisation Gartner published a survey of large companies who had deployed AI tools to automate operations. Some 80 per cent had laid off human staff as a consequence. It turns out the layoffs made no difference to financial performance. Companies that cut the most staff showed almost identical returns to those that cut the least.

More surprising still was the story of coffee giant Starbucks, which had made a decision to embrace automation and cut back on the number of baristas it employed. By April 2025 it had publicly reversed the policy, with the new CEO telling investors that 'equipment doesn't solve the customer experience that we need to provide'.[1] It turns out that a barista writing your name on a cup is the part of a human experience that had been undervalued by corporate headquarters. From baristas to radiologists and software developers, reports of the AI-enabled demise of human professions have been greatly exaggerated, as AI teaches us the value of the human premium.

As we move forward along that jagged frontier, we will hear more stories of companies that became more productive and valuable by upskilling people, not firing them, by placing humans in charge of autonomous technology and reshaping jobs around the tasks AI does well but humans do better. And yet with each story of augmented human labour there will be workers who find themselves out of a job, and often out of a career. We see our children struggle to get that entry-level job which opens up a lifetime profession. The International Monetary Fund tells us that 60 per cent of jobs in advanced economies may be impacted by AI. Who knows how. Who is making the real decisions about the future of human labour?

The boosters of the AI revolution argue that redistribution of wealth is the ultimate solution if humans end up in a state of enforced idleness. Surplus profits from the AI empires will be channelled into a universal basic income (UBI) to those impacted by automation in the workplace, potentially through some form of windfall tax. That's the only alternative, right?

There are always alternatives. Whether we are facing a jobs apocalypse or a surge in human productivity (or both), we have an opportunity to transform the social contract that has underpinned modern democracy. Citizens come together in democratic systems in return for security, fairness and equality of opportunity. What happens if that democratic glue is dissolved away by the machine tsunami? You know this threat is real when a company like OpenAI publishes an *Industrial Policy for the Intelligence Age*, seeking to 'keep people first'. Once again, a brochure for solar panels from an oil company.

'If AI winds up controlled by, and benefiting only a few, while most people lack agency and access to AI-driven opportunity, we will have failed to deliver on its promise.'[2] So says the OpenAI document. To its credit, it does have some bold progressive proposals, like a public wealth fund that distributes AI revenue directly to citizens, a shift from taxes on labour to taxes on capital, and a subsidised shift to a shorter working week.

Let's retain a pinch of salt, but take some of these principles as the baseline for a new social contract in the age of the machine. One particular policy shift is worth pursuing with light-speed. We can't trust these mega-corporations to redistribute wealth after our jobs are gone. We need to demand the 'predistribution' of resources that can help us prepare for a lifetime of opportunity in the age of machines.

As the OpenAI document says, we must 'treat access to AI as foundational for participation in the modern economy', similar to mass efforts to increase global literacy and access to electricity. Forget UBI; the foundation of a new social contract is what some economists are calling universal basic capital (UBC).

Instead of post-apocalypse handouts, we should have the right to free digital public infrastructure such as computing power and access to open or applied AI models, and constant access to new skills which keep us productive and relevant. In Singapore, for example, the government has invested in a lifelong learning path for workers, allowing them to acquire AI-related skills such as data analytics and digital operations, often with direct support from their employers.

Some unusually resilient democracies are building public AI infrastructure, like the 'LLM for the public good' developed by Swiss scientists. The Swiss model is available for anyone to use under a true open-source licence, but incorporates essential guardrails of data protection and copyright law and complies with the transparency rules of the EU AI Act. It expands the reach of AI into global culture by training on more than 1,500 languages, a process completed with 100 per cent carbon-neutral electricity.

One of the goals of predistribution is to radically enhance the potential of entrepreneurs, small businesses and local enterprises to move fast and build new things. Public policy can then be oriented around an innovation 'moonshot' which nourishes countless incremental improvements and efficiencies right across the economy, rather than picking a handful of winners who chase massive scale and concentrated power. In an endless cascade of tiny improvements, in supply chains and energy systems and transport networks, there is a map to a more sustainable human future. 'The danger is not that AI will make humans irrelevant,' says Emily Chamlee-Wright of the Institute for Humane Studies. 'The danger is that we might build a political and economic order that expects us to be.'[3]

A policy of UBC would also spread ownership of the economy beyond the binary poles of public and private enterprise, by ensuring workers own a stake in their companies and benefit from productivity gained through AI adoption. Just imagine you are given shares in your company but automation eventually transforms or replaces your job. You continue to receive a dividend for any increase in value that has been generated for the company by AI deployment.

In one case, a Dutch employer offered employees a shorter working week for the same pay, as a bonus drawn from future AI productivity. In May 2026 California governor Gavin Newsom issued an executive order to explore worker ownership models, among other UBC provisions. 'If we all have a stake in AI,' argue AI policy researchers Saffron Huang and Sam Manning, 'we can create a virtuous cycle where economic and political inclusion mutually reinforce each other, leading to a more just and democratic world.'[4]

To create this virtuous cycle, we need to bolster our language of intention. We'll come to recognise the value of words like 'complementarity'. For every human task automated by AI, a surplus of human skill can now be applied to an unmet human need. Imagine routine tasks in frontline health care are automated, but instead of replacing essential workers, the surplus skills are applied to under-resourced areas such as elder care. That's complementarity. For example, Japan is struggling to meet the needs of a rapidly ageing population, so it's directing investment into automation in elder care so it can free up humans to provide the patient, empathetic care a machine can never deliver.

Think of the impact these kinds of human-first policies might have on the health of our future democracy. Think of their importance for digital natives who have never had a social contract to believe in, let alone defend. Think of the human dividend that's unlocked by complementary investment in automation and people. As humans get to focus on tasks only humans can perform, they become more valuable to our society. We all have a visceral awareness of the myriad ways our quality of life suffers because of the lack of a personal touch. Imagine those gaps filled with the glue of human connection.

Of course, none of this happens if power concentrates in the hands of those with insanely large bets on their ownership of the future. This is why our vision of democratic renewal in the age of artificial intelligence is not a prophecy. It is a preparation for struggle. We must be clear in our demands as citizens, but we also need to organise as workers.

The collective struggle has already begun in industries where AI automation is well advanced. In Hollywood, actors and writers used good old-fashioned strike action and collective bargaining to create rules for the use of AI in the creative process. In Nordic countries, a similar process of collective adjustment is well underway. In Norway, trade unions have agreed to automation in exchange for guarantees of job transitions, training or protection of wages. The lessons here are that societies with strong representation of labour have more leverage, and workers who use that leverage can strengthen their voice for the future.

Not all communities under threat from the advance of machine intelligence can draw on such collective bargaining power. AI has been experienced as an added tax on already over-stressed resources wherever the Big Tech companies build their infrastructure. Around the world, popular resistance to the development of data centres is shaping up to be the battle that galvanises the global digital rights movement. Concerns over higher electricity bills and strains on the environment have united communities in ways that party politics never could.

In the US, where data centres are expected to consume more than 14 per cent of the country's power demand by 2030, political resistance is deepening and widening. In 2025, 48 data centres were blocked or stalled by local opposition, often cutting across America's toxic political divide. Data centres are likely to become a top-tier issue in national election campaigns in the coming years.

Ireland is now home to one of the highest concentrations

of data centres in the world, and they are expected to consume as much as a third of the country's electricity by 2030. Yet the political equation in this country is more complicated than in the US. Local resistance and negative public sentiment collide with Ireland's dependence on investment from the world's biggest technology companies. Critics say the official compromise – mandating new data centres to generate their own renewable energy – will cannibalise existing renewable supplies and keep electricity prices high.

Ireland should serve as a warning to nations preparing to grapple with the burdens of the AI revolution. Without a credible path to economic sovereignty and energy independence, a democratic government cannot protect you from the forces of concentrated power in this new world.

Ireland's experience should convince any society preparing to meet the challenge of data centres to start from the ground up. Technology companies must first earn the trust of the communities that host their infrastructure. There is one compelling mechanism through which this could be achieved.

Imagine a company building a data centre had to seek a 'social licence to operate' from the community which housed it. It would set out a plan to add capacity to the grid rather than competing with local homes, hospitals and businesses for what already exists. It would avoid stress on the local environment and water supplies and ensure it didn't crowd out renewable energy supplies. It would treat waste heat from the data centre as a public resource, warming the homes and offices of its neighbours.

A social licence to operate is not granted by the central government but by the people who live with the data centre. It comes with a transparent review process involving ordinary citizens, potentially using the tools of participatory democracy we've already explored. This has been a particularly effective concept in the Netherlands, where the prized resource of reclaimed land has been the source of bitter disputes.

Critics say the opponents of data centres are blocking infrastructure that will eventually make the benefits of AI accessible to all. But I think this misses the wider point. Like so many of the issues which have shaken the old democratic order, the movement against data centres is fundamentally about agency, and the feeling that ordinary people just haven't had a meaningful say in their future.

The unstoppable energy unleashed by these protests is a positive statement of intent, a declaration that things will be different in the new world we seek to build. The protests are also a remarkable expression of pluralism. For the first time in what feels like a very long time you can see people in divided societies knuckle down to the hard work of compromise and coalition, pooling their agency and intention without compromising themselves.

The older I get, the more I become aware of the biases chiselled into my psyche. The values that have shaped my outlook on the world have been secular, civic and progressive. But many have a different experience of progress. They mourn the empty public spaces where spirituality, community and tradition once thrived, and feel alienated by hyper-individualised technology. They feel they have been 'observing from afar',[5] to use the words of Pope Leo in his encyclical on AI, *Magnifica Humanitas*.

The days of observing from afar are coming to an end. There is new common ground large enough to hold a movement. From the secular left to the religious right, from liberals to conservatives, there is a common enemy in the accelerationists and the concentrated power of the AI empires. But we need to leave behind our mirror worlds and toxic feeds. It is time for that common ground to become a shared reality.

After the Feed

When people ask me if I miss being a television presenter, I say no. Which is almost true. If I'm being completely honest, I miss the sublime shiver of fear at the beginning of every live broadcast, when you are suddenly all alone in the company of hundreds of thousands of people. Most of all, I miss the collective intake of breath in the studio when some hidden truth is revealed to everybody, all at once.

One night in October 2008 I felt an uncommonly strong burst of anxious energy as I went live in the *Prime Time* studio. Ireland's financial regulator, Patrick Neary, was sitting beside me, waiting to reassure the Irish people about the resilience of the nation's banking system in the face of an unfolding global financial crisis.

Also in the studio that night was the economist Colm McCarthy. 'Everyone in Ireland had the idea that somewhere in Ireland there was a little wise old man who was in charge of the money,' McCarthy would later tell the author Michael Lewis, who featured the Neary interview in a *Vanity Fair* article called 'When Irish Eyes are Crying'.[1] 'And then they saw him and said, Who the fuck was that? Is that the fucking guy who is in charge of the money? That's when everyone panicked.'

When the interview got under way Neary tried to assure viewers that 'in the ordinary course of business' the Irish banking sector was 'more than adequately capitalised'. I could almost hear the disbelieving roar from the audience as they realised the wobble in the Irish economy was actually a catastrophic topple.

That interview with the Irish financial regulator is what shared reality used to feel like. A national television channel had the power to create simultaneous awareness of a matter of great importance, at the time and place of its choosing. This synchronous mass media moment feels like a relic of a distant past. If the Neary interview happened today, it would rush into our lives as a series of disjointed clips, played out of sequence, while you're waiting for coffee and I'm on the train, leaving us all asking the same question of our group chats: 'WTF just happened?'

The Neary interview coincided with the mainstream adoption of Facebook and Twitter. In the years that followed, the ephemeral ambience of social media replaced the mass media's 'front page' experience of the world, which had delivered the same package of reality to everyone at the same time. Before long, nobody knew what everybody else knew. Or when they knew it.

Today, the internet is at another inflection point, as fewer people post, comment or share on social media and more people actively seek out digital connection in smaller and safer online spaces. This is good news for the health of our information systems. Citizens are building a direct relationship with an expanding universe of independent journalists, cooperative media ventures and expert networks.

Our digital world will soon be divided into distinct realms, one pulsing with human intention and the other with mechanical determination. The first of those realms will be the 'artificial internet', a boundless and lifeless space colonised by AI bots scavenging for human data to process and regenerate, and AI agents interacting with each other in a frenetic synthetic marketplace.

When I think about this artificial internet I think of those 'dark factories' in China where AI systems and their robots have fully taken over a manufacturing facility. With no need for human workers, the factory runs continuously in darkness, without the friction of life.

The 'lights-out' internet has advanced like a tidal surge. Cyber-security researchers report that AI agents and bots now account for more than half of all internet traffic, and non-human internet traffic is growing eight times faster than human activity. As AI systems jostle for advantage, the proportion of automated activity that is fraudulent and manipulative is surging.

Online prophets have been pushing a 'dead internet theory' for years, claiming the machines had conquered our digital world without us noticing. The prophecy has come to pass, as AI-generated content floods our digital spaces. This algorithmic 'slop' ranges from the automated chatter of bots to more sophisticated creative content generated by AI in response to a prompt from a human. As of May 2026 the number of articles published on the internet that are primarily AI-generated is equal to the number written by humans, according to the digital marketing agency Graphite.

The artificial internet is like a voracious industrial suburb, consuming more of the open spaces of our digital lives, turning online marketplaces, search engines and vast public squares of social media into a grim succession of dark factories. We will no longer go searching, exploring or connecting on this internet, because it will automatically deliver us answers, solutions and personalised opinions. Our AI companions will be our interface with this machine-generated world.

The social media platforms will be flooded with slop, but they will still play a role in our lives, particularly video-rich apps like TikTok and Instagram which will fill our moments of distraction and boredom with pure-cut entertainment, retail therapy and attention-hungry influencers. Many of us will continue to scroll the angry feeds for a little bit of affirmation or tasty outrage. But for those of us seeking to make sense of the world, the only choice will be to move into the second realm of the internet, filled with human life and breath.

This 'human internet' starts just above the waterline of algorithmic feeds, where the dark factories end and the dark forests begin. This new digital realm starts in the curated feeds, private spaces and group chats of dominant platforms, in the new civic spaces of the rewilded internet, and in a public information commons that brings citizens together with the trusted sense-makers in their community.

The days of our reliance on the funhouse mirror of the social feeds are coming to an end. As social conventions shift against the outraged misrepresentation of the world, we will begin to gravitate towards subtleties and quiet truths we had forgotten, and towards the people who reward us for both our attention and our intention. This does not mean a return to the days of a shared 'front page'. Instead, the new information systems of the human internet will reveal the many different ways we can experience a moment of consequence. We will discover that shared reality is not simply a truth we are told, but the knowledge we discover together.

My all-time reporting heroes are Lee Miller and Ernie Pyle. Pyle's Second World War dispatches are lessons in the humility of the finest journalism. He didn't just write words, he summoned images that made suffering intimate to a distant audience. The readers weren't there but Ernie made space for them.

'It was a lovely day for strolling along the seashore,' he wrote in the aftermath of the Normandy landings. 'Men were sleeping on the sand, some of them sleeping forever.'[2] Pyle noticed the jellyfish floating among the bodies offshore. 'In the center each of them had a green design exactly like a four-leaf clover. The good-luck emblem. Sure. Hell yes.'

Lee Miller followed a circuitous route to the battlefields, from artistic muse to war photographer. She used her surrealist eye and unconventional technique to extract hidden meaning from the unspeakable horror of the concentration camps and the ruins of post-war Europe. One of Miller's stand-out images is *Remington Silent*, a photo of a shattered typewriter in the debris of a London street during the Blitz.

What Lee Miller and Ernie Pyle represent to me was an intentional restraint in the very best journalism, allowing the audience to occupy that space that other reporters might fill with mute phrases like 'words can't describe'. They offer us a pause where others provoke. This is the truest definition of shared reality I can think of.

In my personal experience as a foreign correspondent, there is no shortage of words for the violence of human existence. An ascending rocket crackles like overheated oil in a frying pan. The percussive crump of a bomb explosion is both a sound and a sensation. A passing bullet is a sapling crack. Death is a rotten syrup. But this is still only information. To create shared reality you must leave a space between your words for someone else to fill.

The feed sucked the oxygen out of this space. It became the face of human brutality, and locked its gimlet eye on the worst behaviour of bad people. What we lost in its perpetual movement was the ability to pause, take a collective breath and sit with the unknown. Now, we get to shape our information environment. We get to decide what path we will take to shared reality. We have so much more choice in how we get there.

I marvel at the abundance of knowledge at my fingertips. Each morning I pore over a daily delivery of diverse perspectives arriving by email from platforms like Substack, Ghost and Beehiiv. These newsletters arrive without any intermediary, coming directly to me from thought leaders, culture critics, tech experts and journalists who left big media companies to strike out on their own.

I turn to the apps of the daily newspapers and magazines I choose to pay for, before switching over to a news curation app called *Spread*, where I trade the day's most insightful writing with smart members of the app's community. I am a supporter of a platform called *Noosphere*, founded by a former foreign correspondent, Jane Ferguson, which connects international journalists directly to a community of news seekers. In these dispatches, from the frontline of drone wars in Ukraine to the political battlefield in Washington, I hear an echo of Lee Miller and Ernie Pyle.

I no longer sit at the appointed time to watch the news on television, but by the end of every day I have seen the best clips from TV news, video podcasts and, increasingly, the video feed of radio shows in my social channels and chats. By late afternoon I turn to a curated list of podcasts on Spotify, selecting a batch of episodes to listen to on an evening walk or while making dinner.

Algorithms play a role in surfacing content to me, but far more important is my own intentional curation of the signal in all the noise and my conscious engagement with trusted sources. There are days when this feels like hard work and I hanker for the reliable ritual of a single 'front page'. But this kind of active news routine is becoming the rule rather than the exception, particularly among the digital natives. Their baseline assumption is that they will have to assemble their own reality.

In study after study, young news consumers, from 16 to 25 years old, speak of a fragmented media environment as the natural reflection of the disordered world they are growing up in. They have developed 'strategic scepticism', to quote a report by the British think-tank Demos entitled *Inside the Mind of a 16-Year-Old*.

Young internet citizens might get news from partisan influencers on TikTok but also have notifications from the BBC or cross-check controversial claims on Google, taking what a Channel Four survey described as a 'magpie' approach to sense-making. 'The moral panic about young people being slavish followers of untruthful news is way off the mark,' says the Demos report.

You could make the case, say the authors, that a 60-year-old reading the same conservative-leaning newspaper every day is getting a far more slanted news diet than the 16-year-old, 'who is grazing many media outlets and is fact-checking and piecing together a set of differing views'.[3]

The safety of the single 'front page' version of shared reality is obvious. It was assembled by professional journalists who were expert in discovering and verifying the scarce facts that made up the news. It tended to reward the middle-ground opinion. It channelled popular anger towards democratic solutions, rather than insurgent action.

By contrast, the digital natives have learned not to rely on institutional journalism as a source of ground truth. They rely on their own ability to sort news from noise. They prefer to consciously tweak and personalise their filters, and are more comfortable with radically dissonant views of the world.

I think professional journalism will become a lot more important as artificial intelligence raises the value of trusted human sources in our lives. But I'm with the digital natives in their personal quest. Shared reality doesn't require all of us knowing the same thing at the same time, or accepting a single version of the truth. What's important is that we have people and communities in our lives that earn our trust.

For older digital citizens, navigating your way to trusted sources on the human internet requires a new set of mental shortcuts. Think of this as media literacy for those of us who came of age in an analogue era, when we consumed rather than engaged with the news.

The first lesson we can learn from digital natives is that collaboration with your peers rather than with traditional markers of authority is the primary generator of trust in this new information environment. Older generations relied on vertical trust: they looked up to credentialed experts in journalism, finance or politics. Today, young news consumers rely on horizontal trust: they make sense of the world with the help of the people around them. They rely on friends to help filter news, and pay attention to the judgement of other people, just like them, often toggling between social newsfeeds and group chats, looking at the most popular comments about content that's important to them.

In a report on *Next Generation News*,[4] the FT Strategies Group found that young news consumers refuse to passively accept the power of the algorithm. Instead, they consciously tailor it, continuously adding and pruning to ensure they receive a personally ideal mix. 'They are fully aware of the role algorithms play in surfacing information for them,' says the report, 'and often employ conscious strategies to thwart control over their information flow.'

When I covered US politics I would visit the same small-town diner in Iowa at the start of the race for the White House. The older customers had met every presidential candidate since the 1960s. On my first visit I asked the mayor how his townsfolk made their choice of which candidate to trust. He said, 'They want something just like them, but better.' The Iowa regulars and the digital natives have a lot in common.

The hunger for affinity is a powerful force in the new information systems of the human internet. Beyond their friends, the natives' horizontal bond of trust is strongest with internet influencers who are just like them but smarter on some important topic.

In 2024, the Pew Research Center reported that 37 per cent of Americans under the age of 30 get their news from influencers and creators, most of whom will have no professional training as journalists. UK-based news aggregator Dylan Page (better known as News Daddy) has amassed almost 20 million followers on TikTok for his short explainers of current events. To put that in context, Sky News has a little over 11 million followers on TikTok.

Digital natives want their primary sources to help them sift and sense-make, rather than overwhelm them with breaking news. In the United States, Johnny Harris has built an audience of more than 7 million subscribers on YouTube for well-crafted explainers of news-related themes.

Younger news consumers have a shorthand definition of credibility when it comes to these news creators: *They know their stuff and I can count on them.* They place great emphasis on the real-life experience a creator has gained, rather than their educational qualification or position of power.

Young internet citizens depend on news influencers but they retain a healthy scepticism of them. Digital natives are conscious of a much higher risk of manipulation than previous generations, and to establish trust with a news creator they demand what that Next Gen News report describes as 'transparency of intention'. They want to know there is no ideological motivation or commercial conflict of interest that is being hidden.

As the attention economy unravels and the automated internet begins to consume social media feeds, we will begin to see a new intention economy taking shape around decentralised networks of tightly bound communities.

Eli Pariser offers a particularly compelling vision of this new world. He coined the term 'filter bubble' in his 2011 book of the same name,[5] anticipating the erosion of our shared reality by the attention economy. In a recent presentation entitled 'After the Feed',[6] he argued that the arrival of agentic AI will help accelerate the growth of a 'trust economy'. The currency of this realm is not empty engagement but the reputation you earn over time through your contribution to the community.

Pariser draws inspiration from a wide spectrum of purpose-built digital spaces devoted to the shared interests of a community, ranging from neighbourhood WhatsApp groups to high-powered group chats where business and political strategies take shape. They include 'dark forests' tucked away on Substack or nestled in private Facebook groups, or even a constellation of new algorithm-free social networks built on decentralised social media protocols, the likes of which power Bluesky.

The danger here is that digital citizens retreat into a new form of filter bubble. Private spaces are great for trust, but bad for sharing different perspectives on the world. Pariser says the key challenge for the architects of this trust economy is to help communities 'build spaces that have the intimacy of a group chat and the openness of a public square, and help those spaces connect to each other when it matters'. This is where journalists can play a critical role, as bridges between high-trust communities and the world.

Traditional journalists now have an opportunity to swap a precarious job in a media organisation for a leadership role within this rapidly expanding intention economy. An increasing number of veteran reporters are striking out on their own, making the move to newsletter platforms like Substack or creator platforms like YouTube.

Some go on to build micro-media companies, which allow a small team of experts on a niche topic to build a dedicated newsroom for people with a deep interest in that topic. For example, among the first sources I check each morning are Casey Newton's *Platformer* newsletter, serving up premium insights from Silicon Valley, and Ireland's business news site *The Currency*, founded by two veteran journalists. Such small ventures involve high risk and hard work. But they have never been easier to build, or to finance. With a thousand committed members willing to pay a modest subscription, you are in business.

The most influential 'news creators' actively seek to reduce their reliance on the algorithms, generating income through subscriptions or donations and investing in real-world community events to deepen trust within their communities. Some have started to 'bundle' together in new cooperative media companies. For example, Johnny Harris has launched a community platform called Newpress to support creator journalists who want to follow his example.

What the best new journalism offers is an open and collaborative process of sense-making that its community can feel part of. For too long, we tried to defend our shared reality by waging an information war, treating citizens as passive victims and truth as the property of elite institutions. Naomi Klein had it right when she said that 'the solution to the informational crisis is not to look to tech oligarchs to disappear people we don't like; it's to get serious about demanding an information commons that can be counted on as a basic civic right'.[7]

Our children are inherently more digitally literate than those of us of an analogue vintage. But from the earliest age they need to learn the value of intention, critical thinking and cognitive freedom, to be given confidence in their power to shape their shared reality. Some pioneering countries such as Finland have integrated media literacy at all stages of education. In the very earliest years, children are taught that they are consumers of information, but also creators.

To empower the next generation of digital citizens we need an information commons that is a basic civic right for all, not just those who pay. In other words, everybody has to have access to sources of high-quality information that are free to access. In European countries, public service media organisations like the BBC and RTÉ play a critical role in a fragmented media environment, and still maintain surprisingly high levels of public trust. Strong, stable public media, built in the image of the next generation of citizens, will be a critical part of the fabric of our shared reality.

In Wikipedia's networked intelligence we see proof that collaborative sense-making can create an enduring shared reality. This remarkable public encyclopaedia has received an average of more than half a billion views every day for the last ten years, and serves up public information in more than 300 languages.

Wikipedia has been a resilient piece of information architecture, but it has come under attack from those seeking to destroy its consensus-driven model, including Elon Musk, and from the AI bots of the artificial internet which scrape its valuable content. Wikipedia needs our financial support, and more volunteers. The same goes for the Internet Archive, which has protected our shared digital history for more than two decades but has faced coordinated cyber attacks in recent years.

There is one final piece of information infrastructure that needs urgent attention. We need to assert more control over our interface with the artificial internet, where humanity's vast stores of human data and information are being processed and repurposed. AI chatbots are rapidly becoming a primary information channel, turning search engines into answer engines, delivering summaries perfectly attuned to our explicit intentions. Information no longer arrives in a discrete 'package', like an article or a newscast. AI turns information into liquid form, filling the uniquely personal gaps in our knowledge, like water flowing from the tap into whatever container you are holding.

The more AI shapes our personal reality, the greater its power to strengthen or shatter our shared reality. There are some hopeful signs that AI could have a converging effect, fostering consensus around a less polarising pool of knowledge. The current crop of LLMs are grounded in the same data sets and tend to guide people to fact-based views on controversial issues, in contrast to social media which rewards the most extreme viewpoint in a public debate. In this sense, AI models seem to behave more like the nightly news in the age of mass media.

The great danger is that AI bots remove human collaboration from the process of knowledge-gathering. They serve us summaries of knowledge without revealing the sources, further obscuring the inherent biases in their training data. They no longer send us to visit the news website or app. They undercut our direct relationship with the sense-makers in our human community. So what happens to human trust when we can't see the humans any more?

We know the part we have to play as citizens. We need to bring intention to every interaction with AI and the artificial internet but also keep our feet planted in the human internet, in those real-life communities bonded by collaboration and trust. We will need our journalists more than ever. Those professional sense-makers are the people who will build the interfaces between the human and artificial internets.

That process of innovation is already underway. Around the globe, journalists are using AI tools to strengthen our shared reality. In Tunisia, the digital news outlet Nawaat side-stepped government suppression by using AI to make its entire archive accessible to the people, creating what its editor called 'a living memory of the entire recent history of Tunisia'.[8] In Norway, news publishers have agreed to provide their content to help train a publicly funded Norwegian language model, offering a civic alternative to those AI empires.

Media institutions which once commanded our passive trust are being transformed into the infrastructure of active digital citizenship. Journalism is becoming what media innovator Adam Thomas describes as 'an operating system for public knowledge',[9] devolving the tools of trust-building to active communities, keeping our shared reality grounded in human collaboration rather than synthetic intelligence.

I think Lee Miller and Ernie Pyle would have been horrified by a world of instant answers, liquid content and synthetic reality. But they would have relished the challenge of building spaces and networks in which human intention could flourish. They refused to cede their own humanity in a time of inhumanity. They refused to fill the silence with the next empty token of language. They assumed our intention. They rewarded our curiosity.

Epilogue

What that new idea is, I don't know, but it is out there somewhere, searching for me. In time, we will find each other.

Nick Cave, *The Red Hand Files,* January 2023

Think Like the Poet

On a summer day in 2025 I took part in a very public experiment in artificial intelligence's impact on human creativity. I have been a regular contributor to a radio show hosted by Brendan O'Connor, who offers a safe haven for thoughtful conversations about technology's impact on society. On this day the main guest was the poet Rita Ann Higgins, who writes with fierce honesty and sharp wit about Irish life, particularly the struggles of working-class women.

I was petrified by the test I was about to take. Rita Ann brought two poems into the studio. She wrote one, and the other was generated 'in her voice' by ChatGPT. I had been asked to offer my judgement on which was artificial and which was real. I'd spent days trying to make the right choice but couldn't. Not with any conviction.

The first of the two poems was called 'The Party',[1] which opened with these lines:

The Dancers
came out of a hole in the wall.
They danced to
Blue Eyes Crying in the Rain.
Women had bright clothes on,
a splash of gingham,
a spray of cerise.
Yellow umbrellas
were all the raging.

When trying to detect AI-generated writing it pays to look for the 'truthiest' line. In other words, the one containing the most checkable facts. This is the one most likely to be mangled by the machine. My eye fell on the song title 'Blue Eyes Crying in the Rain' as an obvious litmus test. Within seconds I was looking at a YouTube clip of the movie *Red Headed Stranger*, in which Willie Nelson sings this song. In the video are the period costumes of the American frontier, correlating with the 'splash of gingham'. The truthiest fact was true. If I'd looked further I would have also discovered the song was a big hit for an Irish showband star called Big Tom when Rita Ann was growing up. I was sure I had found her poem.

I jumped to the second poem, 'They Said I Should Be Grateful', confident this was the AI doppelganger. I scanned the text for the mark of the machine but found doubt instead. I saw Rita Ann's trademark wit. 'They said I should smile more,' read the verse. 'Jesus, smile! As if my teeth were paid for by the Department of Sunny Dispositions.' Then there was an authentic gut-punch towards the close:

Grateful?
I'd be grateful
if they'd stop building hotels
on top of the bones
of women with names
nobody remembers
except their sisters.

The combined force of Irish past and present landed with a smack. There was old Ireland, where young Irish women were forced into servitude in Magdalene laundries. There was the memory of 'women with names nobody remembers' who never made it out of these institutions alive. There was the new Ireland, with skylines of steel and glass, rising from the graveyard of the past.

My rational fact-check of the first poem couldn't compete with the emotional pull of the second. I put aside the poems and scoured Rita Ann's published work and public interviews, looking for resonance. The closing lines of the second poem aligned with the real Rita Ann, as far as I could see. The machine could generate the facts in the first poem. It couldn't replicate the dark authentic truth of the second. Could it? Would it? Did it?

Fuck it. I was stumped. I resorted to cheating, pushing the poems through two different AI-text detectors. The first told me a human had written both poems. The second told me a machine had generated both poems. I turned to Claude, which offered weak agreement with my decision that the second poem was Rita Ann's. By now, I reckoned my chances of being right were 50/50.

I came across a survey in *Nature* magazine which revealed a human weakness for AI-generated verse. Participants in the survey were asked to read poetry from ten famous English-language poets, including Sylvia Plath and Lord Byron, and then poems generated by ChatGPT in the style of those poets. In most cases, the readers said the AI-generated verse was real. They felt the AI poetry was 'more human than human' and mistook the complexity of the human poems for 'incoherence generated by AI'.

The machine can see we prefer art that is easy. We have a bias for the simple rhythm and surplus emotion of the verse that has come to surround us. Our default experience of poetry is greeting cards, wedding speeches, eulogies and the internet's recycled pool of quotes often misattributed to dead writers. We are drawn to shiny surfaces which reflect a soulful smile. Art is in the hard detail but we hanker for what is simple, for what is more. The sound of *more* beauty. The sound of *more* emotion. The sound of *more* depth.

I asked Claude how AI might bullshit people into believing it can write poetry. The recipe for AI verse, Claude explained, starts with 'abstract noun stacking': 'the infinite tapestry of human longing' or 'the sacred geometry of memory and time'. Whispers are another favourite, said Claude. The wind whispers, the past whispers, the heart whispers. The AI also loves a cosmic climax: 'A poem about a coffee cup somehow ends up being about the vastness of existence.' The final ingredient is 'synaesthesia on autopilot'. AI loves to wrap everything in some human sense, like 'the golden taste of memory' and 'the sharp scent of silence'. After a while, Claude explains, the AI poem 'reads as a random adjective generator'. Claude is such an articulate snitch.

AI-generated verse flatters us with its legibility. This poetry doesn't feel hard anymore. It offers no friction. It is a test of good taste we can't fail. By contrast, the best poetry cuts us loose in rough terrain, forcing us to grapple with the unexpected and work for the emotional charge. If you want a flawless reality, Claude has you covered. If you want transcendence, you need Rita Ann Higgins.

Back in the radio studio, Rita Ann read both poems live on air. When she was finished I picked poem number two as the real Rita Ann. Seven out of ten listeners who responded agreed with me. I was momentarily buoyed by the consensus. Then Rita Ann told us we were wrong. The real poem was the first, 'The Party', with its 'blue eyes crying'.

Rita Ann said she was impressed by elements of the AI-generated poem, including the quote that had captivated me. But she said good ideas seemed to trail away before completion. She also spotted language which appeared to demean women without further education, contrary to the very essence of her work. She said key elements of the poem generated by ChatGPT were derived from her public interviews, not her published poetry. The machine had mimicked her spoken words, not necessarily her art.

Rita Ann had looked in the LLM's mirror and found the cracks. The data sets they are trained on force them to mimic an incomplete and fractured human reality. The machine couldn't capture Rita Ann's voice because only a fraction of the training data for GPT-3 (16 per cent) was scraped from book collections. It puts demeaning language in the mouth of a poet because it is polluted with language from the darkest edge of the internet.

Towards the end of our interview, I told Rita Ann that I had asked Claude to generate a poem about artificial intelligence in 'her voice'. Claude had titled it 'The Machine That Thinks It's Clever'. I read an extract:

They told me there's a computer now
that writes poems better than Yeats,
paints like Picasso,
and knows more about heartbreak
than a woman who's buried three husbands
and a stillborn child.
I said, 'Does it know the weight of a wet nappy at 3 a.m.?'

When I first read the verse I could hear the echoes of Rita Ann's style and rhythm. But when the time came to recite it live on air I heard the sneer of a sociopath hiding behind a mask of empathy:

Let your machine learn that.
Let it learn the sound a woman makes
when she's trying not to wake the baby
and the bailiffs at the same time.
Then we'll talk about intelligence.

This no longer felt like mimicry. It sounded like mockery. It triggered a memory of my first visit to the United States as a 12-year-old, when I discovered not everyone who said 'Have a nice day' actually meant it. 'There are many things we don't understand about how LLMs work,' observes science fiction writer Ted Chiang, 'but one thing we can be sure of is that ChatGPT is not happy to see you.'[2]

I felt a little hopeless leaving the studio that day. Rita Ann's words rang in my ears. 'Who do I complain to?', she said during the interview, alluding to the injustice of her work being 'scraped' and 'crawled' to generate replicas of her art. Who do I complain to when I am drowning in a sea of simulated humanity? Who do I complain to when there is literally no human body to complain to?

My encounter with Rita Ann Higgins left me with an alarming insight. Every conversation about AI seems to lower our expectations of ourselves. When the machine exposes our diminished capacity to understand great art we slip into a spiral of self-doubt. That is the hallmark of a fundamentally dehumanising technology, says Ted Chiang: 'It reduces the amount of intention in the world.'

Machines can't kill poetry, but they can overwhelm our confidence in ourselves. The careless mimicry of AI-generated poetry is not a challenge to our good taste. It is a test of the human capacity to expand our imaginations once more. Generative AI is just the latest human interface with the material world, challenging us to become more human. Between the hand of a creator and the ear of a receiver is a void waiting to be filled with human intention.

Our single most effective act of resistance in the age of superhuman technology is to embrace the hard things about great art. The surveys tell us that when humans realise a poem is generated by AI they immediately think less of it. Once we engage the real poet we are elevated by every measure. The beauty of our connection with a long-deceased poet is in the connection with a great mind who lived in a different time and a different place with feelings just like ours.

Any attempt by machines to project this kind of eternal empathy is 'replication as travesty', to quote the singer and songwriter Nick Cave. That was his response to a fan who had shared a song in his voice, generated by ChatGPT. 'Songs arise out of suffering,' he said. 'As far as I know, algorithms don't feel. Data doesn't suffer.'[3]

Part of the reason we hunger for meaning in our lives is that we know we have such limited time on this earth. A machine is not mortal, which is why it will never make genuine art. Humans and machines exist in radically different evolutionary timelines. The AI can't die a natural death. It has no conception of an ending.

There's a passage from an essay by Helen Edwards of the Artificiality Institute that I just can't get out of my head. 'We commit because not everything can be done,' she writes.[4] 'We take responsibility because consequences are irreversible.' AI systems don't experience any of this. They don't run out of time. To be human is to know you will die but do everything you can to live well.

As we struggle to rise above a wave of AI-generated content, we become more conscious of signs of human life. Creators of music, movies and literature are experimenting with new labels of human provenance, telling us content is 'proudly human' or 'human-made' or 'AI-free'. The long, winding road of consumer awareness that started with nutrition labels, bans on tobacco ads, stamps for organic goods and fair trade produce may soon arrive at a marker of human origin in a superhuman world.

Oligarchs and autocrats see history as the victory of the strong over the weak. In his *Techno-Optimist Manifesto*, Marc Andreessen says there are only three reasons people do things for other people, and that is love, money or force. 'Love doesn't scale,'[5] is his conclusion. Let's stick with money. But as Brian Hare and Vanessa Woods explain in their book *Survival of the Friendliest*, it was the friendships forged through collaboration, communication and coordination which drove human progress.

There is no love or humility in the future being sold to us by doomers and accelerationists. But fresh new voices are emerging from the ranks of technology's builders and innovators. 'The less special we become,' wrote German venture capitalist Judith Dada in an essay titled 'The Un-Fuckening', 'the more seriously we must take one another.'[6] Each time humanity's cosmic importance shrank, argues Dada, 'it increased the burden on us to create meaning, defend dignity, and build institutions that protect the individual from power and exploitation.'

Astronaut Bill Anders' first impression on seeing Earth from space was that our planet was 'small, delicate and not the centre of the universe'. With each great human discovery, we must become more humble. These historic humiliations have triggered the most liberating bursts in human development, such as the Enlightenment.

Astronauts often report a sense of transcendence when viewing Earth from space, a phenomenon known as the overview effect. For some it triggers a cognitive shift in awareness. Witnessing the fragility of life on our tiny planet inspires an enhanced feeling of global citizenship. From the Earth we see the heavens. From the heavens we see the Earth.

There's a luminous passage in Samantha Harvey's Booker Prize-winning novel *Orbital* which captures this feeling of re-enchantment. As astronauts and cosmonauts look down on Earth's 'burst of hopeful colour' they think that maybe human beings have already died and are living in the after-life. 'If we must go to an improbable, hard-to-believe-in place when we die,' she writes, 'that glassy, distant orb with its beautiful lonely light shows could well be it.'[7]

What I love about this image is the reversal of our lens on human invention. Our technology is the means by which we connect to the mysteries of our universe. It has no divine power of its own; it is a means to an end. When we begin to speak of technology as a divine force in our lives we sacrifice our power to shape the future. When we speak of ourselves, or our machines, as gods we surrender our destiny.

Our struggle for hope and humanity starts with a simple truth: you will know we are making real progress when you see your face reflected in technology. Not some generic, flawless human. You.

There is so much we still have to learn about our own consciousness, and new forms of intelligence on the fragile planet we inhabit. Technology is our interface with the material world but also a window to an enchanted world just beyond the limits of our understanding.

We had a glimpse of this delicate ecology in those last good days on the internet. Inside the network we became something else through our interactions with everyone else, like a digital murmuration of birds at sundown, weaving spectacular patterns with astonishing speed through collaborative bursts and feedback loops. Like the colours of a butterfly or the scent of a flower, the beauty emerged from a process, not a plan.

Humans are participants in a living system, defined by the strength of our relationships but also the fragility of our interdependence. We are strong when we make peace with our weakness and stronger still when we have the empathy to share the pain of another. There's not a single lesson more important to me in almost six decades of life on Earth.

In that radio studio I used the word empathy to describe the way the AI had learned the poet's tone of voice. The machine was getting very good at knowing what a person was thinking. It is this kind of empathy that people unknowingly experience when they turn to AI chatbots for therapy. It's the form of empathy that helps machines write poetry with an emotional gut punch. But this is just an echo of humanity rattling around the void. True empathy is the ability of one human to sit with the hard silence of another human's emotions.

Above all, empathy is expressed in the carefully curated silences of poetry. Samuel Beckett once said he was interested in 'a literature of the unword'. The absence of language in his work speaks more powerfully about the human condition in an uncertain world. In the age of artificial intelligence we might need fewer words and more silences.

Being human in the age of accelerating technology is to feel trapped into some infinite empty space. But look around you. You are surrounded by people who have found their voice, who filled the infinite silence with the right kind of empathy and humility. They speak as citizens, not users. They remind you of the enchantment that once filled the human spaces of the internet.

With the right human choices, we can look forward to plenty more good days on the internet. The internet itself will evolve, and change. The ecology of our digital lives is being transformed with a speed that leaves us reeling. But the spirit of human intention is more powerful than it ever was, even when the internet was the preserve of the hippies, hackers and hobbyists. We have been humbled by our own creation. But re-enchanted by our own fragile beauty. We seem to be a verb once again.

Now is the time to think like the poets. To say clearly what we want from the machine but also what we don't need. To know what technology can do for us but also what it can never do. In the absence of its consciousness we learn to treasure our own. We fill the empty space between us and our tools with the hard work of being human. We try. We fail. We try again. We fail better. This is the human algorithm we will teach to the machine.

To think like the poet is to celebrate the delicate wonder of human consciousness. How is it that our brains – powered by 12 watts of energy – can still feel and love and imagine beyond the capacity of superintelligent machines with access to all the power and data in the world?

I will never forget Rita Ann Higgins in that radio studio, armed with a truth and a lie. At the time I felt demoralised by how easy it was to be seduced by the passive, mocking voice of the machine. It now feels like an enchanted moment, as powerful as the memory of my best days on the internet.

I was humbled by my inability to spot the voice of the machine. But humility was the hammer that broke the spell. Rita Ann stared into that misshapen mirror and said, 'That's not me.' She broke free of the machine's mimicry and wrote a piece of human verse that was incorruptible. Those who will thrive in an age of superhuman technology will think like the poet.

Acknowledgements

I initially set out to write a book about the history of the future. Despite the theme, it was a pretty old-school project. Years of accumulated research piled up in every corner of my home office, and the books littering my floor had sprouted bushes of luminous Post-it notes. But when I sat down to write, I found the words of lasting value came from friendships and partnerships spanning five decades. Everything authentic was the product of some wonderful friction with humans who inspired me, pushed me and changed me.

I met my wife and best friend Tara Peterman the year I discovered the internet, and she turned out to be exactly the right kind of crazy. She is the expert storyteller in our house, who guides me out of the dead ends, and always has my back. Tommy and Daisy are the digital natives in our family, and it is their spirit you can feel coursing through my writing about their remarkable generation. When I wrote about stepping into the future and meeting my loved ones, I was thinking of my daughter Sorcha and her little baby Naoise, who will carry my hopes for humanity long after I'm gone.

Let me express my thanks to those who have shaped this book, in subtle, surprising and always deeply appreciated ways. I owe a debt to my good friend Adam Thomas, who coached me through early missteps and necessary detours and helped me find my voice and my authentic weirdness.

I am blessed by my friendship with Áine Kerr, who supported me with kindness and a keen eye as I wrote about our journey together. Thank you Shane Creevy for your generous feedback and eye for detail. Gavin Sheridan and David Clinch helped sweat the small details that mattered in the Storyful story. As always, I am in your debt, fellas.

It has been my privilege to help lead remarkable teams at Storyful, Kinzen and Twitter, and I want to thank all those who will recognise their work and hear their voices in this book.

Thank you to my agent Faith O'Grady for your infectious energy during those early days, and your ability to see the story worth telling. Ciara Doorley has been the best of editors, combining patience and urgency, and continually raising my expectations of the work we did together. To Ciara Considine, Stephen Riordan, Joanna Smyth and all at Hachette, I am very grateful for the commitment you have shown to this book.

Finally, the book ends with an unforgettable encounter with the poet Rita Anne Higgins. I am humbled by the gift of her words, and forever in her debt for the inspiration.

Endnotes

Introduction

1. 'How Two Llamas And A Dress Gave Us The Internet's Greatest Day' by Charlie Warzel, Buzzfeed News, 26 February 2016. www.buzzfeednews.com/article/charliewarzel/226-how-two-runaway-llamas-and-a-dress-gave-us-the-internets
2. 'Jonathan Haidt on Adjusting to Smartphones and Social Media (Ep. 209)', recorded 4 February 2024, Conversations with Tyler, 3 April 2024. https://conversationswithtyler.com/episodes/jonathan-haidt-anxious-generation/
3. 'What Gen Z thinks about its social media and smartphone usage', The Harris Poll. https://theharrispoll.com/articles/gen-z-social-media-smart-phones/
4. 'Have we passed peak social media?' by John Burn-Murdoch, *Financial Times*, 2 October 2025. https://www.ft.com/content/a0724dd9-0346-4df3-80f5-d6572c93a863
5. 'Gen Z's Internet Sanctuary Isn't TikTok—It's Tumblr' by Ashley Fike, *Vice*, 10 April 2025, https://www.vice.com/en/article/gen-zs-internet-sanctuary-isnt-tiktok-its-tumblr/
6. 'The kids are all right' by Melinda Wenner Mover, 17 March 2026, *Scientific American*. https://www.scientificamerican.com/article/the-kids-are-all-right/
7. 'How vinyl records and printed books are making a comeback in Ireland thanks to Gen Z' by Arlene Harris, *Irish Times*, 16 May 2025, https://www.irishtimes.com/ireland/2025/05/15/vinyl-records-and-real-books-making-a-comeback-as-gen-z-turns-to-old-school-entertainment/

8. 'What Kids Told Us About How to Get Them Off Their Phones' by Lenore Skenazy, Zach Rausch, and Jonathan Haidt. *Atlantic*, 4 August 2025. https://www.theatlantic.com/ideas/archive/2025/08/kids-smartphones-play-freedom/683742/

9. 'Difficult is Not the Same as Impossible' by Rebecca Solnit, *The Beautiful Truth*, 22 January 2024. https://thebeautifultruth.org/world/difficult-is-not-the-same-as-impossible/

I Am Become Meme

1. 'Elon Musk, Enda Kenny, Shervin Pishevar & Mark Little – Web Summit 2013' uploaded by Web Summit, YouTube, 3 August 2016. https://www.youtube.com/watch?v=QbuTBlHY900&t=9s

2. 'I cannot describe how strange Elon Musk's CPAC appearance was', transcript of CPAC meeting by Sarah Joeng, *Verge*, 21 February 2025. https://www.theverge.com/elon-musk/617090/elon-musk-cpac-2025-transcript

3. Berners-Lee, Tim, *Weaving the Web: The Original Design and Ultimate Destiny of the World Wide Web* (HarperCollins, 2000)

4. '1984 Apple's Macintosh Commercial (HD)' uploaded by Mac History, YouTube, 1 February 2012. https://www.youtube.com/watch?v=VtvjbmoDx-I

5. 'Apple's "1984" Super Bowl commercial was the "worst ever tested" but now it's iconic. Here's how it almost never aired' by Dan Bobkoff and Kif Leswing, *Business Insider*, 6 February 2019. https://www.businessinsider.com/apple-1984-super-bowl-ad-bombed-in-focus-groups-almost-didnt-air-2019-2

6. 'Think Different - Steve Jobs (1997) – Apple' uploaded by Apple Archive, YouTube, 16 April 2023. https://www.youtube.com/watch?v=CLIyH2SyxZA

The End of History

1. Fukuyama, Francis, *The End of History and the Last Man* (Free Press, 1992)

2. 'Why the Web Won't Be Nirvana' by Clifford Stoll, *Newsweek*, 26 February 1995. https://www.newsweek.com/clifford-stoll-why-web-wont-be-nirvana-185306

3. 'Nothing But Net By David A. Kaplan' by David A. Kaplan, *Newsweek*, 24 December 1995. https://www.newsweek.com/nothing-net-2-180202
4. 'The Architecture of Participation' by Tim O'Reilly, O'Reilly, June 2004. https://www.oreilly.com/pub/a/tim/articles/architecture_of_participation.html
5. O'Mara, Margaret, *The Code: Silicon Valley and the Remaking of America* (Penguin, 2020)
6. 'Democracy Can Still End Big Tech's Dominance Over Our Lives' by Shoshana Zuboff, *Time*, 5 May 2022. https://time.com/6173639/democracy-big-techs-dominance-shoshana-zuboff/

Let the Future Begin

1. 'IBM e-Business Solutions advert – Broadcast 7 March 1998' uploaded by Only Adverts!, YouTube, 5 July 2022. https://www.youtube.com/watch?v=q_sVK3obRzA
2. 'The Scoop on Hillary's Spam Spasm' by David Ross, *Slate*, 26 May 2000. https://slate.com/news-and-politics/2000/05/the-scoop-on-hillary-s-spam-spasm.html
3. 'Drudging up news on the Web', 6 May, CNN Crossfire, 6 May 2002. https://edition.cnn.com/2002/ALLPOLITICS/05/06/cf.crossfire/index.html
4. 'Matt Drudge Speech to the National Press Club on Media and the Internet', American Rhetoric, 2 June 1998. https://www.americanrhetoric.com/speeches/mattdrugdenationalpressclub.htm
5. 'Summit Meeting Teeters On Edge of Self-Parody' by Michael Wines, *The New York Times*, 2 September, 1998. www.nytimes.com/1998/09/02/world/summit-in-moscow-the-scene-summit-meeting-teeters-on-edge-of-self-parody.html
6. Remarks by the President to business leaders, and officials and employees of Gateway Computers', White House transcript, 4 September 1998. https://clintonwhitehouse5.archives.gov/textonly/WH/New/Russia/19980904-9298.html
7. '1999: DAVID BOWIE: Internet is the new rock n roll | Newsnight | Classic Interview | BBC Archive' uploaded by BBC Archive, YouTube, 15 December 2021. https://www.youtube.com/watch?v=tLf6KZmJyrA

'How'd All These People Get in Your Room?'

1. The People Formerly Known as the Audience' by Jay Rosen, PressThink, 27 June 2006. http://archive.pressthink.org/2006/06/27/ppl_frmr.html
2. 'The Un-Internet' by Dave Winer, Scripting News, 31 December 2011. http://scripting.com/stories/2011/12/31/theUninternet.html
3. 'Dean Martin Appears Very Drunk on The Tonight Show Starring Johnny Carson 12/12/75' uploaded by Johnny Carson, YouTube, 30 March 2020. https://www.youtube.com/watch?v=iaxUDvJxcPk
4. 'Farewell Irish Twitter and its #vinb, #hometovote, coddle and UncLe Joey' by Darach Ó Séaghdha, *Irish Examiner*, 22 September 2023. https://www.irishexaminer.com/opinion/commentanalysis/arid-41231098.html
5. Johnson, Steven, *Where Good Ideas Come From: The Natural History of Innovation* (Riverhead Books, 2010)
6. 'David Bowie speaks to Jeremy Paxman on BBC Newsnight (1999)' uploaded by BBC Politics, YouTube, 11 January 2016. https://www.youtube.com/watch?v=FiK7s_0tGsg
7. Clark, Dr Meredith, D., *We Tried to Tell Y'All: Black Twitter and the Rise of Digital Counternarratives* (Oxford University Press, 2025)
8. Tufekci, Zeynep, *Twitter and Tear Gas: The Power and Fragility of Networked Protest* (Yale University Press, 2017)
9. '"Collective Effervescence" Is Good For You. Here's What You Can Do To Experience It' by Caroline Bologna, *Huffington Post*, 12 September 2025. https://www.huffpost.com/entry/collective-effervescence-meaning_l_68bee8c9e4b0b40e31a8e064

The Human Algorithm

1. 'The five-year anniversary of Twitter's defining moment' by Eli Langer, CNBC, 15 January 2014. https://www.cnbc.com/2014/01/15/the-five-year-anniversary-of-twitters-defining-moment.html
2. 'Jackson dies, almost takes Internet with him' by Linnie Rawlinson and Nick Hunt, CNN, 26 June 2009. https://edition.cnn.com/2009/TECH/06/26/michael.jackson.internet/index.html?iref=mpstoryview
3. 'Shirky: Now Is the Time to Experiment' by Michael Fitzgerald, CBS News, 18 March 2009. https://www.cbsnews.com/news/shirky-now-is-the-time-to-experiment/
4. Kyncl, Robert, *Streampunks: YouTube and the Rebels Remaking Media* (Harper Business, 2017) p. 114

The Revolution Will Not Be Televised

1. 'Post Industrial Journalism: Adapting to the Present' by Emily Bell, *Columbia Journalism Review*, 27 November 2012. https://www.cjr.org/behind_the_news/post_industrial_journalism_ada.php
2. 'Syria's Torture Machine', Channel Four, 20 December 2011. https://www.channel4.com/programmes/syrias-torture-machine

Chewing Glass

1. 'The Stunning Success of "Fail Better"' by Mark O'Connell, *Slate*, 29 January 2014. https://slate.com/culture/2014/01/samuel-becketts-quote-fail-better-becomes-the-mantra-of-silicon-valley.html
2. 'Fail Worse' by Ned Beauman, *New Inquiry*, 9 February 2012. https://thenewinquiry.com/fail-worse/
3. Knowlson, James, *Damned to Fame: The Life of Samuel Beckett* (Simon & Schuster, 1996)
4. 'A Wake for Samuel Beckett with Harold Pinter (1990)' uploaded by Manufacturing Intellect, YouTube, 16 December 2017. https://www.youtube.com/watch?v=YBXgSKG84Zg
5. Collins, Jim, *Good to Great: Why Some Companies Make the Leap ... and Others Don't* (Random House Business, 2001)
6. 'The Network Man' by Nicholas Lemann, *New Yorker*, 5 October 2015. https://www.newyorker.com/magazine/2015/10/12/the-network-man
7. 'What Is the Cultural Transformation a Successful Company Must Go Through?', *Vanity Fair*, 10 February, 2017. https://www.vanityfair.com/video/watch/the-new-establishment-summit-what-is-the-cultural-transformation-a-successful-company-must-go-through
8. Johnson, Steven, *Where Good Ideas Come From: The Natural History of Innovation* (Riverhead Books, 2010)

Recipes for Disaster

1. 'Theses on the Philosophy of History', in Benjamin, Walter, *Illuminations*, Arendt, Hannah (ed.), (Harcourt Brace Jovanovich, 1968)
2. 'Donald J. Trump (2nd Term), Remarks at a Tesla Viewing and an Exchange With Reporters Online' by Gerhard Peters and John T. Woolley, The American Presidency Project, 11 March 2025. https://www.presidency.ucsb.edu/node/377328

3. Simon, Herbert A., 'Designing Organizations for an Information-Rich World' in Computers, *Communications, and the Public Interest*, Greenberger, Martin (ed), (Johns Hopkins Press, 1971), pp. 37–72
4. 'It's the (Democracy-Poisoning) Golden Age of Free Speech' by Zeynep Tukekci, *Wired*, 16 January 2018. https://www.wired.com/story/free-speech-issue-tech-turmoil-new-censorship/
5. Wu, Tim, *The Attention Merchants* (Atlantic Books, 2017)
6. Horwitz, Jeff, *Broken Code: Inside Facebook and the Fight to Expose Its Harmful Secrets* (Doubleday, 2023), p. 37

Emotional Baby

1. Bergen, Mark, *Like, Comment, Subscribe: Inside YouTube's Chaotic Rise to World Domination* (Viking, 2022), p. 143
2. 'Why Does This Baby Cry When Her Mother Sings? (Viral Video)' by Siu-Lan Tan, Ph.D., *Psychology Today*, 4 November 2013. https://www.psychologytoday.com/ie/blog/what-shapes-film/201311/why-does-baby-cry-when-her-mother-sings-viral-video
3. 'Is History Repeating Itself' by Jonah Peretti, *Psychology Today*, 4 March 2014. https://medium.com/@peretti/is-history-repeating-itself-33390aeb6cd9
4. 'The World's Top 10 Most Innovative Companies Of 2015 In Social Media' by Fast Company Staff, *Fast Company*, 2 September 2015. https://www.fastcompany.com/3041664/the-worlds-top-10-most-innovative-companies-in-social-media-n
5. 'Viral Math' by Felix Salmon, *Columbia Journalism Review*, 3 February 2014. https://www.cjr.org/the_audit/viral_math.php#:~:text=Facebook%20is%20the%20monster%20in,Except%2C%20maybe%2C%20ViralNova.%29
6. 'The Anti-SNARF Manifesto' by Jonah Peretti, BuzzFeed, 11 February 2025. https://www.buzzfeed.com/jonah/the-anti-snarf-manifesto
7. 'Contemplating YouTube's Rise: A Conversation with Mark Bergen' by Justin Hendrix, *Tech Policy*, 4 September 2022. https://www.techpolicy.press/contemplating-youtubes-rise-a-conversation-with-mark-bergen/

It's Just Fucking Us

1. 'The Future of Twitter: Q&A with Jack Dorsey' by Sarah Frier, Felix Gillette and Brad Stone, *Bloomberg Businessweek*, 21 March 2016. https://www.bloomberg.com/features/2016-jack-dorsey-twitter-interview/?embedded-checkout=true
2. 'Two-Hit Wonder' by D.T. Max, *New Yorker*, 14 October 2013. https://www.newyorker.com/magazine/2013/10/21/two-hit-wonder
3. 'Twitter CEO: We suck at dealing with trolls and abuse' by Alex Hern, *Guardian*, 5 February, 2015. https://www.theguardian.com/technology/2015/feb/05/twitter-ceo-we-suck-dealing-with-trolls-abuse
4. 'As an ex-Twitter boss, I have a way to grab Elon Musk's attention. If he keeps stirring unrest, get an arrest warrant' by Bruce Daisley, *Guardian*, 12 August, 2024, https://www.theguardian.com/commentisfree/article/2024/aug/12/elon-musk-x-twitter-uk-riot-tweets-arrest-warrant
5. 'The Man Who Built The Retweet: "We Handed A Loaded Weapon To 4-Year-Olds"' by Alex Kantrowitz, BuzzFeed News, 23 July 2019. https://www.buzzfeednews.com/article/alexkantrowitz/how-the-retweet-ruined-the-internet

The Dinosaur at the Door

1. Wagner, Kuirt, *Battle for the Bird: Jack Dorsey, Elon Musk and the $44 Billion Fight for Twitter's Soul* (Atria Books, 2024)
2. 'Eric Schmidt: Every 2 Days We Create As Much Information As We Did Up To 2003' by M.G. Siegler, *TechCrunch*, 4 August 2010. https://techcrunch.com/2010/08/04/schmidt-data/
3. 'Why the Past 10 Years of American Life Have Been Uniquely Stupid' by Jonathan Haidt, *Atlantic*, 11 April 2022. https://www.theatlantic.com/magazine/archive/2022/05/social-media-democracy-trust-babel/629369/
4. 'The dawn of the post-literate society' by James Marriott, *Cultural Capital*, 19 September 2025. https://jmarriott.substack.com/p/the-dawn-of-the-post-literate-society-aa1
5. Naomi Alderman: 'Whatever happened to talking? We've lost the ability to swap ideas' by Rachel Healy, *Observer*, 7 July 2024. https://www.theguardian.com/books/article/2024/jul/07/naomi-alderman-interview-radio-4-series

6. 'Fake news. It's complicated' by Claire Wardle, *Medium: First Draft*, 16 February 2017. https://medium.com/1st-draft/fake-news-its-complicated-d0f773766c79
7. Brooking, Emerson T. and Singer, P.W., *Likewar: The Weaponisation of Social Media* (Houghton Mifflin Harcourt, 2018)
8. 'What was fake on the Internet this week: Why this is the final column' by Caitlin Dewey, *Washington Post*, 18 December 2015. https://www.washingtonpost.com/news/the-intersect/wp/2015/12/18/what-was-fake-on-the-internet-this-week-why-this-is-the-final-column/

A Telegram from the Future

1. 'Social media drives Tea Party wins' by Chris Daniels, *PRWeek*, 16 September 2010. https://www.prweek.com/article/1266369/social-media-drives-tea-party-wins
2. 'How Sarah Palin Paved The Way For Donald Trump' by Don Gonyea, *NPR*, 23 January 2016. https://www.npr.org/2016/01/23/464068087/how-sarah-palin-paved-the-way-for-donald-trump
3. Gurri, Martin, *The Revolt of the Public and the Crisis of Authority in the New Millennium* (Stripe Press, 2014)
4. 'Britain has had enough of experts, says Gove' by Henry Mance, *Financial Times*, 3 June 2016. https://www.ft.com/content/3be49734-29cb-11e6-83e4-abc22d5d108c?syn-25a6b1a6=1
5. 'What future for truth?' by J. McKenzie Alexander, LSE British Politics, 17 June 2025. https://blogs.lse.ac.uk/politicsandpolicy/what-future-for-truth/
6. 'Edelman Trust Barometer 2017 Reveals Global Implosion of Trust', Edelman, 5 April 2019. https://www.edelman.com/nl/news-awards/edelman-trust-barometer-2017-reveals-global-implosion-trust
7. Kranzberg, Melvin, 'Technology and History: "Kranzberg's Laws"', *Technology and Culture*, vol. 27 no. 3, July 1986
8. 'Trolls and triumph: a digital battle in the Philippines' by BBC Trending, *BBC News*, 7 December 2016. https://www.bbc.com/news/blogs-trending-38173842
9. 'Maria Ressa: "Facebook Broke Democracy in Many Countries around the World, Including in Mine"' by Catherine Tsalikis, Centre for International Governance Innovation, 18 September 2019. https://www.cigionline.org/articles/maria-ressa-facebook-broke-democracy-many-countries-around-world-including-mine/

10. 'It's the (Democracy-Poisoning) Golden Age of Free Speech' by Zeynep Tufekci, *Wired*, 16 January 2018. https://www.wired.com/story/free-speech-issue-tech-turmoil-new-censorship/#:~:text=Is%20it%20being%20shared%20by%20alt%2Dright%20trolls%20or%20a%20swarm%20of%20Russian%20bots?&text=Zeynep%20
11. 'TAG Bulletin: Q3 2022' by Shane Huntley, Threat Analysis Group (TAG), *The Keyword*, 26 October 2022. https://blog.google/threat-analysis-group/tag-bulletin-q3-2022/

Humans in the Loop

1. 'Here Comes Somebody: Journalism and the Trust Economy' by Mark Little, *Nieman Reports*, 3 April 2017. https://niemanreports.org/here-comes-somebody-journalism-and-the-trust-economy/
2. 'Digital News Report 2017,' Reuters Institute. https://reutersinstitute.politics.ox.ac.uk/sites/default/files/Digital%20News%20Report%202017%20web_0.pdf
3. 'Sub-editing the machine: the new role for journalists in the age of AI' by Shane Creevy, Polis, London School of Economics, 20 October 2020. https://blogs.lse.ac.uk/polis/2020/10/20/sub-editing-the-machine-the-new-role-for-journalists-in-the-age-of-ai/
4. 'How Big Tech platforms are neglecting their non-English language users', *Global Witness*, 30 November 2023. https://globalwitness.org/en/campaigns/digital-threats/how-big-tech-platforms-are-neglecting-their-non-english-language-users/
5. 'Facebook Is Everywhere; Its Moderation Is Nowhere Close' by Tom Simonite, *Wired*, 25 October 2021. https://www.wired.com/story/facebooks-global-reach-exceeds-linguistic-grasp/
6. 'How Facebook's Rise Fueled Chaos and Confusion in Myanmar' by Timothy McLaughlin, *Wired*, 6 July 2018. https://www.wired.com/story/how-facebooks-rise-fueled-chaos-and-confusion-in-myanmar/

Behind the Funhouse Mirror

1. Klein, Naomi, *Dopppelganger: A Trip into the Mirror World* (Farrar, Straus and Giroux, 2023)
2. 'Are a few people ruining the internet for the rest of us?' by Jay Van Bavel, *Guardian*, 13 July 2025. https://www.theguardian.com/books/2025/jul/13/are-a-few-people-ruining-the-internet-for-the-rest-of-us

3. 'The Conspiracy Singularity Has Arrived' by Anna Merlan, *Vice*, 17 July 2020. https://www.vice.com/en/article/the-conspiracy-singularity-has-arrived/
4. DiResta, Renée, *Invisible Rulers: The People Who Turn Lies Into Reality* (PublicAffairs, 2024)
5. DiResta, Renée, *Invisible Rulers: The People Who Turn Lies Into Reality* (PublicAffairs, 2024)
6. Montell, Amanda, *Cultish: The Language of Fanaticism—Understanding the Social Science of Cult Influence* (Harper, 2021)

The Road to Nowhere

1. 'Elon Musk gives Twitter staff deadline to commit to being "hardcore"' by Dan Milmo, *Guardian*, 16 November 2022. https://www.theguardian.com/technology/2022/nov/16/elon-musk-gives-twitter-staff-deadline-to-commit-to-being-hardcore
2. 'How an Online Mob Created a Playbook for a Culture War' by Charlie Warzel, *New York Times*, 15 August 2019. https://www.nytimes.com/interactive/2019/08/15/opinion/what-is-gamergate.html
3. 'Nick Fuentes is a master of exploiting the current social media opportunities for extremism' by Alex Mcphee-Browne', *The Conversation*, 24 November 2025. https://theconversation.com/nick-fuentes-is-a-master-of-exploiting-the-current-social-media-opportunities-for-extremism-269776
4. 'This Is What It Looks Like When Nothing Matters' by Charlie Warzel, *Atlantic*, 14 February 2026. https://www.theatlantic.com/technology/2026/02/internet-nihilism-crisis/686010/
5. Scanlon, Kyla, 'How AI, Healthcare, and Labubu Became the American Economy', *Kyla's Newsletter*, 7 August 2025. https://kyla.substack.com/p/how-ai-healthcare-and-labubu-became
6. 'When knowing more means doing less: Algorithmic knowledge and digital (dis)engagement among young adults' by Myojung Chung, *Misinformation Review*, 13 October 2025. https://misinforeview.hks.harvard.edu/article/when-knowing-more-means-doing-less-algorithmic-knowledge-and-digital-disengagement-among-young-adults/
7. 'Meta is earning a fortune on a deluge of fraudulent ads, documents show' by Jeff Horwitz, *Reuters*, 6 November 2025. https://www.reuters.com/investigations/meta-is-earning-fortune-deluge-fraudulent-ads-documents-show-2025-11-06/?utm_source=spread

8. 'The "we're still dancing" quote of our time' by Robin Wigglesworth, *Financial Times*, 2 July 2025. https://www.ft.com/content/7ed3ddc7-0229-40c6-87a6-d0946760a165

We Are As Gods

1. Thiel, Peter with Masters, Blake, *Zero to One: Notes on Startups, or How to Build the Future* (Crown Business, 2014)
2. 'A Declaration of the Independence of Cyberspace' by John Perry Barlow, Electronic Frontier Foundation, 8 February 1996. https://www.eff.org/cyberspace-independence
3. Thiel, Peter with Masters, Blake, *Zero to One: Notes on Startups, or How to Build the Future* (Crown Business, 2014)
4. Douglas Edwards, Google employee no. 59, quoted in Wu, Tim, *The Attention Merchants: The Epic Scramble to Get Inside Our Heads* (Knopf, 2016)
5. O'Mara, Margaret, *The Code: Silicon Valley and the Remaking of America* (Penguin, 2020)
6. 'The World Tech Made' by Margaret O'Mara, Foreign Affairs, 1 November 2022. https://www.foreignaffairs.com/reviews/world-tech-made
7. Isaacson, Walter, *Elon Musk* (Simon & Schuster, 2023)
8. 'A Fundraising Survival Guide' by Paul Graham, August 2008. https://paulgraham.com/fundraising.html
9. 'Marc Andreessen on AI, Tech, Censorship, and Dining with Trump' by Bari Weiss, *The Free Press*, 10 December 2024. https://www.thefp.com/p/marc-andreessen-on-ai-tech-censorship-trump-democrats?hide_intro_popup=true
10. Marc Andreesen, 'The Techno-Optimist Manifesto', Andreessen Horowitz, 16 October 2023. https://a16z.com/the-techno-optimist-manifesto/
11. 'The Inaugural Address', The White House, 20 January 2025. https://www.whitehouse.gov/remarks/2025/01/the-inaugural-address/
12. 'Are you high-agency or an NPC?' by Jasmine Sun, @jasmine's substack, 21 September 2025. https://jasmi.news/p/dictionary
13. 'Dario Amodei of Anthropic's Hopes and Fears for the Future of A.I.' posted by Hard Fork, YouTube, 28 February 2025. https://www.youtube.com/watch?v=YhGUSIvsn_Y

Find Your Forest

1. 'The Social Dilemma' by Sage Cooley, *Howler*, 29 January 2021. https://thehowler.org/11637/uncategorized/the-social-dilemma/
2. 'Nobel Peace Prize winner Maria Ressa inspires Class of 2027 to confront disinformation that threatens democracy' by Denise Valenti, Princeton University, 6 September 2023. https://www.princeton.edu/news/2023/09/06/nobel-peace-prize-winner-maria-ressa-inspires-class-2027-confront-disinformation
3. 'James Watson and Edward O. Wilson: An Intellectual Entente', *Harvard Magazine*, 9 September 2009. https://www.harvardmagazine.com/2009/09/james-watson-edward-o-wilson-intellectual-entente
4. Simone Weil, letter to Joë Bousquet, 13 April 1942, cited in Pétrement, Simone, *Simone Weil: A Life*, translated by Raymond Rosenthal (Pantheon Books, 1976)
5. 'Ireland ranks second in the world for search interest in digital detoxing' by George Morahan, *Business Plus*, 1 February 2025. https://businessplus.ie/news/ireland-second-digital-detoxing/
6. 'Gen Z's Internet Sanctuary Isn't TikTok—It's Tumblr' by Ashley Fike, *Vice*, 10 April 2025. https://www.vice.com/en/article/gen-zs-internet-sanctuary-isnt-tiktok-its-tumblr/
7. 'Have we passed peak social media?' by John Burn-Murdoch, *Financial Times*, 2 October 2025. https://www.ft.com/content/a0724dd9-0346-4df3-80f5-d6572c93a863?syn-25a6b1a6=1

No Surrender

1. Li, Fei-Fei, *The Worlds I See: Curiosity, Exploration, and Discovery at the Dawn of AI* (Flatiron Books, 2023)
2. 'A very brief history of AI' by Mike Richards, OpenLearn, 16 January 2024. https://www.open.edu/openlearn/digital-computing/a-very-brief-history-ai
3. Amodei, Dario, 'The Adolescence of Technology', January 2026. https://www.darioamodei.com/essay/the-adolescence-of-technology
4. 'Thinking—Fast, Slow, and Artificial: How AI is Reshaping Human Reasoning and the Rise of Cognitive Surrender' by Stephen D. Shaw and Gideon Nave, SSRN, 2 February 2026. https://papers.ssrn.com/sol3/papers.cfm?abstract_id=6097646

5. 'Your Brain on ChatGPT: Accumulation of Cognitive Debt when Using an Ai Assistant for Essay Writing Task' by Nataliya Kosmyna, Eugene Hauptmann, Ye Tong Yuan, Jessica Situ, Xian-Hao Liao, Ashly Vivian Beresnitzky, Iris Braunstein and Pattie Maes, MIT Media Lab, 10 June 2025. https://www.media.mit.edu/publications/your-brain-on-chatgpt/
6. Edwards, Helen, *Stay Human: Authoring Your Mind in the AI Age*, *Artificiality*, 7 February–29 April 2026. https://journal.artificialityinstitute.org/tag/book-two/
7. 'Welcome to the Attachment Economy' by Sasha Fegan and Center for Humane Technology, Center for Humane Technology, 21 January 2026. https://centerforhumanetechnology.substack.com/p/welcome-to-the-attachment-economy?r=1x7gaq&utm_medium=ios&triedRedirect=true
8. 'Why Centralized AI Is Not Our Inevitable Future' by Alex Komoroske, Cosmos Institute, 18 June 2025. https://blog.cosmos-institute.org/p/why-centralized-ai-is-not-our-inevitable
9. 'AI isn't coming for your job. It's coming for your mind' by Tom Slater, Baillie Gifford, March 2026. https://www.bailliegifford.com/en/uk/individual-investors/insights/ic-article/2026-q1-ai-isn-t-coming-for-your-job-it-s-coming-for-your-mind-10061431/

No God in the Machine

1. Berners-Lee, Tim, *Weaving the Web: The Original Design and Ultimate Destiny of the World Wide Web* (HarperCollins, 2000)
2. Buolamwini, Joy, *Unmasking AI: My Mission to Protect What Is Human in a World of Machines* (Random House, 2023)
3. O'Neil, Cathy, *Weapons of Math Destruction: How Big Data Increases Inequality and Threatens Democracy* (Crown, 2016)
4. 'The Persona Selection Model: Why AI Assistants might Behave like Humans' by Sam Marks, Jack Lindsey and Christopher Olah, Alignment Science Blog, 23 February 2026. https://alignment.anthropic.com/2026/psm/
5. Amodei, Dario, 'The Adolescence of Technology', January 2026. https://www.darioamodei.com/essay/the-adolescence-of-technology
6. 'Love in the Time of A.I. Companions' by Anna Wiener, *New Yorker*, 9 March 2026. https://www.newyorker.com/magazine/2026/03/16/love-in-the-time-of-ai-companions

7. 'If AI is a weapon, why don't we regulate it like one?' by Noah Smith, Noahpinion, 6 March 2026. https://www.noahpinion.blog/p/if-ai-is-a-weapon-why-dont-we-regulate?r=1x7gaq&utm_medium=ios&triedRedirect=true
8. 'Google Gemini was a deadly "AI wife" for this 36-year-old who resisted its call for a "mass casualty" event before his death, lawsuit says' by Matt O'Brien and The Associated Press, *Fortune*, 5 March 2026. https://fortune.com/2026/03/05/google-gemini-wrongful-death-lawsuit-mass-casualty-event-suicide-ai-wife
9. Suleyman, Mustafa, 'What is an AI anyway?' TED talk, April 2024. https://www.ted.com/talks/mustafa_suleyman_what_is_an_ai_anyway
10. 'We must build AI for people; not to be a person' by Mustafa Suleyman, 19 August 2025. https://mustafa-suleyman.ai/seemingly-conscious-ai-is-coming
11. 'Why Centralized AI Is Not Our Inevitable Future' by Alex Komoroske, *Techdirt*, 16 June 2025. https://www.techdirt.com/2025/06/16/why-centralized-ai-is-not-our-inevitable-future/
12. 'Why I gave the world wide web away for free' by Tim-Berners-Lee, *Guardian*, 28 September 2025. https://www.theguardian.com/technology/2025/sep/28/why-i-gave-the-world-wide-web-away-for-free#:~:text=We%20have%20learned%20from%20social,the%20demands%20of%20digital%20citizens
13. 'AI Will Empower Humanity' by Reid Hoffman, *New York Times*, 25 January 2025. https://www.nytimes.com/2025/01/25/opinion/ai-chatgpt-empower-bot.html

The Open Road

1. 'From Words to Worlds: Spatial Intelligence is AI's Next Frontier' by Fei-Fei Li, 10 November 2025. https://drfeifei.substack.com/p/from-words-to-worlds-spatial-intelligence
2. 'It's the End of the Internet as We Know It' by Raffi Krikorian, *New York Times*, 15 April 2026. https://www.nytimes.com/2026/04/15/opinion/mythos-open-souce-internet.html
3. 'The Future is in Interoperability Not Big Tech: 2021 in Review' by Cory Doctorow, Electronic Frontier Foundation, 24 December 2021. https://www.eff.org/deeplinks/2021/12/future-interoperability-not-big-tech-2021-review

The Superintelligent Democracy

1. 'Is Gen Z really more conservative?' by Jean M. Twenge, Generation Tech, 8 July 2025. https://www.generationtechblog.com/p/is-gen-z-really-more-conservative
2. Audrey Tang, 'Democracy in the Age of AI', 31 August 2025. https://sharing.ia.net/presenter/e56ffdd239ac40ad817e9f2dd36055f3/view
3. 'The 2025 iA Award Winners', iA, 30 January 2026. https://ia.net/topics/meet-the-2025-ia-award-winners
4. 'Sam Altman's Manifest Destiny' by Tad Friend, *New Yorker*, 3 October 2016. https://www.newyorker.com/magazine/2016/10/10/sam-altmans-manifest-destiny
5. Hao, Karen, *Empire of AI: Inside the reckless race for total domination* (Allen Lane, 2025)
6. Acemoglu, Daron and Johnson, Simon, *Power and Progress: Our Thousand-Year Struggle Over Technology and Prosperity* (Public Affairs, 2003)
7. '"We are already the super-intelligence we are looking for": Audrey Tang and others' big ideas for a better future at SEWF25' by David Lyons, *Pioneers Post*, 6 November 2025. https://www.pioneerspost.com/news-views/20251106/we-are-already-the-super-intelligence-we-are-looking-audrey-tang-and-others-big

On the Jagged Frontier

1. 'Starbucks says cutting shop staff in favour of automation has failed' by Joanna Partridge, *Guardian*, 30 April 2025. https://www.theguardian.com/business/2025/apr/30/starbucks-says-cutting-shop-staff-in-favour-of-automation-has-failed
2. 'Industrial policy for the Intelligence Age', OpenAI, 9 June 2026. https://openai.com/index/industrial-policy-for-the-intelligence-age/
3. 'AI Will Create Work, Not Decimate It' by Emily Chamlee-Wright, Persuasion, 13 January 2026. https://www.persuasion.community/p/ai-will-create-work-not-decimate
4. 'Here's How To Share AI's Future Wealth' by Saffron Huang and Manning, Sam, *Noema*, 22 April 2025. https://www.noemamag.com/heres-how-to-share-ais-future-wealth/
5. Pope Leo XIV, 'Magnifica Humanitas', The Holy See, 15 May 2026. https://www.vatican.va/content/leo-xiv/en/encyclicals/documents/20260515-magnifica-humanitas.html

After the Feed

1. 'When Irish Eyes Are Crying' by Michael Lewis, *Vanity Fair*, 1 March 2011. https://www.vanityfair.com/news/2011/03/michael-lewis-ireland-201103?srsltid=AfmBOoq0LxPwYnSVW0dJef7XSpGKICTHwJMKbX3vSp8Aw47ZBbyqyCbe
2. Miller, Lee G., *The Story of Ernie Pyle* (The Viking Press, 1950)
3. 'Inside the Mind of a 16-year-old: From Andrew Tate to Bonnie Blue to Nigel Farage – what do first time voters think about social media, politics, the state of Britain and their futures?' Demos, 9 November 2025. https://demos.co.uk/research/inside-the-mind-of-a-16-year-old-from-andrew-tate-to-bonnie-blue-to-nigel-farage-what-do-first-time-voters-think-about-social-media-politics-the-state-of-britain-and-their-futures/
4. 'Next Gen News: Understanding the audiences of 2030', FT Strategies. https://www.ftstrategies.com/en-gb/insights/next-gen-news-understanding-the-audiences-of-2030
5. Pariser, Eli, *The Filter Bubble: What The Internet Is Hiding From You* (Penguin Press, 2011)
6. 'After the Feed: Trust, connection, and the next era of social technology', New_ Public, May 2026. https://newpublic.org/afterthefeed
7. Klein, Naomi, *Doppelganger: A Trip Into the Mirror World* (Farrar, Straus and Giroux, 2023)
8. 'News media is "becoming part of AI systems": Notes from the Journalism AI Festival 2025 by Andrew Deck, *Nieman Lab*, 2 December 2025. https://www.niemanlab.org/2025/12/news-media-is-becoming-part-of-ai-systems-notes-from-the-journalismai-festival-2025/
9. 'Journalism becomes a house of commons' by Adam Thomas, *Nieman Lab*, 16 December 2025. www.niemanlab.org/2025/12/journalism-becomes-a-house-of-commons/&sa=D&source=docs&ust=1780845311737616&usg=AOvVaw1o28lAoUoUSPNjBW_ysEQT

Think Life the Poet

1. Higgins, Rita Ann, 'Party', *Tongulish* (Bloodaxe Books, 2016)
2. 'Why A.I. Isn't Going to Make Art' by Ted Chiang, *New Yorker*, 31 August, 2024. https://www.newyorker.com/culture/the-weekend-essay/why-ai-isnt-going-to-make-art

3. Cave, Nick, 'The Red Hand Files,' Issue #218, January 2023, https://www.theredhandfiles.com/chat-gpt-what-do-you-think/
4. '8. Finitude and the Shape of a Human Life' by Helen Edwards, *Artificiality Journal*, 31 January 2026. https://journal.artificialityinstitute.org/the-artificiality-8-finitude-and-the-shape-of-a-human-life/
5. Marc Andreesen, 'The Techno-Optimist Manifesto', Andreessen Horowitz, 16 October 2023. https://a16z.com/the-techno-optimist-manifesto/
6. 'The Un-Fuckening: Stop talking about AI like this' by Judith Dada, 18 March 2026. https://dadalogue.substack.com/p/the-un-fuckening
7. Harvey, Samatha, *Orbital* (Jonathan Cape, 2023)

Bibliography

Anderson, Benedict, *Imagined Communities* (Verso, 1983).

Beckett, Samuel, *Worstward Ho* (Grove Press, 1983).

Bergen, Mark, *Like, Comment, Subscribe* (Penguin Business, 2022).

Berners-Lee, Tim, *Weaving the Web* (Harper Business, 1999).

Chang, Emily, *Brotopia: Breaking Up the Boys' Club of Silicon Valley* (Portfolio Penguin, 2018).

Clark, Meredith D., *We Tried to Tell Y'All* (OUP USA, 2025).

Collins, Jim, *Good to Great* (Random House Business, 2001).

DiResta, Renée, *Invisible Rules* (Public Affairs, 2024).

Doctorow, Cory, *Enshittification* (Verso, 2025).

Dweck, Carol, *Mindset* (Random House, 2006).

Eyal, Nir, *Indistractable* (Bloomsbury, 2019).

Eyal, Nir, *Hooked* (Portfolio, 2014).

Farahany, Nita A., *The Battle for Your Brain: Defending the Right to Think Freely in the Age of Neurotechnology* (St Martin's Press, 2023).

Fry, Hannah, *Hello World* (Doubleday, 2018).

Gurri, Martin, *The Revolt of the Public* (Stripe Press, 2014).

Haidt, Jonathan, *The Anxious Generation* (Penguin Press, 2024).

Hao, Karen, *Empire of AI* (Allen Lane, 2025).

Hare, Brian, and Woods, Vanessa, *Survival of the Friendliest* (Oneworld Publications, 2020).

Harvey, Samatha, *Orbital* (Jonathan Cape, 2023).

Higgins, Rita Ann, 'Party', *Tongulish* (Bloodaxe Books, 2016).

Horwitz, Jeff, *Broken Code* (Torva, 2023).

Isaacson, Walter, *Elon Musk* (Simon & Schuster, 2023).

Klein, Naomi, *Doppelganger* (Farrar, Straus and Giroux, 2023).

Klosterman, Chuck, *The Nineties* (Penguin, 2022).

Kyncl, Robert, *Streampunks* (Harper Business, 2017).

Li, Fei-Fei, *The Worlds I See* (Flatiron Books, 2023).

Montell, Amanda, *Cultish: The Language of Fanaticism—Understanding the Social Science of Cult Influence* (Harper, 2021).

Nagle, Angela, *Kill All Normies* (Zero Books, 2017).

O'Neil, Cathy, *Weapons of Math Destruction* (Crown Publishing Group, 2016).

Pariser, Eli, *The Filter Bubble* (Penguin, 2012).

Pomerantsev, Peter, *This Is Not Propaganda: Adventures in the War Against Reality* (Faber & Faber, 2019).

Smith, Ben, *Traffic* (Penguin Press, 2024).

Solnit, Rebecca, *Hope in the Dark: The Untold History of People Power* (Canongate Books, 2005).

Tufekci, Zeynep, *Twitter and Tear Gas* (Yale University Press, 2017).

Wu, Tim, *The Attention Merchants* (Atlantic Books, 2017).

Zuboff, Shoshana, *The Age of Surveillance Capitalism* (Profile Books, 2018).